CONTENTS

———◆———

Contents

THE JEW'S BODY

I̅H̅S

Auxilium meum â Domino. *Psalm. 120.*
Ni Deus adfuerit, Viresq̃ infuderit herbis
Nil tibi Dictamnus, nil panacæa iuvat.

IESU. IEHOVA IUVA

Erranti, pereunti, ægro, via, vita, Salusq̃
Christe, tuum rege, duc, et benedic Medicum.
Auxilioq̃ tuo pereat Medicaster Apella,
unica cui, Christi, est cura, necar genus.

The contrast between the "Christian" body, that of Christ as the healer, with the body of the Jewish quack, taken from a 1698 tractate against Jewish physicians. All of the Jew's physical attributes point toward his dishonesty. From Christian Trewmundt, *Gewissenloser Juden-Doctor In Welchem Erstlich Das wahre Conterfeit eines Christlichen Medici, und dessen nothwendige Wissenschafften / wie auch gewissenhaffte Praxis, zweytens Die hingegen Abscheuliche Gestalt dess Juden-Doctors Wie auch dessen Unfehigkeit zur Lehr und Doctors-Würde / und die schad-volle Bedienung der Krancken Aus geist- und weltlichen Rechten / mit unumstösslichen Gründen vorgestellt wird* (Freyburg: n. p., 1698) (Source: National Library of Medicine, Bethesda, MD).

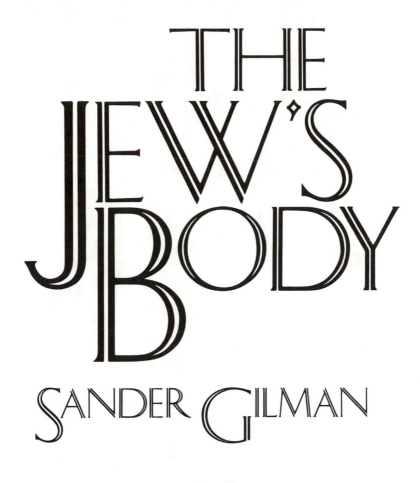

THE JEW'S BODY

SANDER GILMAN

ROUTLEDGE • NEW YORK & LONDON

Published in 1991 by

Routledge
An imprint of Routledge, Chapman and Hall, Inc.
29 West 35 Street
New York, NY 10001

Published in Great Britain by

Routledge
11 New Fetter Lane
London EC4P 4EE

Library of Congress Cataloging in Publication Data

Gilman, Sander L.
  The Jew's body / Sander Gilman.
    p.   cm.
  Includes bibliographical references and index.
  ISBN 0-415-90458-7 (hb).—ISBN 0-415-90459-5 (pb)
    1. Antisemitism—Psychological aspects. 2. Freud, Sigmund,
  1856–1939—Views on Jews. 3. Psychoanalysis. 4. Jews—Public
  opinion. 5. Self-perception. 6. Stereotype (Psychology)
  I. Title.
  DS145.G43   1991
  305.8'924—dc20   91-16485

British Library Cataloguing in publication data also available

This Volume is Dedicated to My Friends
George L. Mosse
and
Elaine Showalter

Contents

◆

All he needed was a foreskin,
otherwise he felt all right.
He lived it up like a Duke on his castle,
with pheasant shooting and old paintings,
all he needed was a little foreskin,
otherwise he was all right.

He lived it up like the Roi de Soleil
on Trianon, they feed him oysters with a spoon,
all he needed was a bit of skin,
otherwise he was all right.

He lived it up like Zeus in the Parthenon,
makes it only with Goddesses,
all he needs is a bit more skin
and everything will be fine.

Jakov Lind, *Counting My Steps:*
An Autobiography
(London: Macmillan, 1969), pp. 135–36.

PREFACE

The Fall of the Wall

———————◆———————

This collection of essays reflects on the complexity of being understood or seen as different and creating out of this sense of imposed
difference a meaningful sense of one's own identity. The center of
these essays is Sigmund Freud and these essays reflect on my own
sense of Freud's meaning at the close of another century. To begin
a volume with an essay on the differences of the voice of the Jew
and close it with an essay on the image of the Jew in the (now-
antiquarian) West German literature on AIDS in 1989, means moving from the internalization of the sense of being different among
Jews to a sense of the difference attributed to Jews. But this is all
part of the same loop. For we understand ourselves in psychological
terms as a product of our world. There is a creative tension resulting
from the attribution of difference. This tension can serve as the
model for other primary group identities in cultures such as those
of Europe and the United States in which difference is a complex,
often stigmatizing factor.

Thus I am not speaking here about "realities" but about their
representations and the reflection of these representations in the
world of those who stereotype as well as those who are stereotyped.
In this volume I am not interested in determining the line between
"real" and "fabled" aspects of the Jew. This can be done only by

ignoring the fact that all aspects of the Jew, whether real or invented, are the locus of difference. My argument is not merely one of "labeling," as Edward Shorter has claimed about my work.[1] Rather, I am engrossed by the ideological implications associated with the image of the Jews (and other groups) as "different." This says nothing at all about the "realities" of the difference. Indeed, I have consistently claimed that all of the patterns I have examined are rooted in some type of observable phenomenon which is then labeled as "pathological." Some of these phenomena may well be "pathological" responses to stress, as Shorter claims. But it is not the "reality" of the phenomenon which is central to my own examination but rather its representation. This can be seen in every aspect of the Jew discussed in this study, including the "voice" of the Jew.

It is evident that some Jews do speak in a way which is different from their linguistic context. This can be a social reality, as Deborah Tannen has clearly shown.[2] There is no doubt that ethnic groups, including Jews, can speak differently. Jews can be multilingual either because of their religious practices or because of their patterns of migration. They can also "code-switch" (like everyone else in a society), speaking differently from social context to social context. And one of these contexts can be the ethnic or religious group. But it is how this difference is understood and how that understanding is integrated into an individual's self-perception which is central to my exploration. One anecdote should suffice. It is taken from an anti-Semitic study of Jews published at the beginning of the Third *Reich*, but reflecting an age-old tradition:

> The Jews *jüdeln* [Jew] in their speech even when they do not *mauschel* [speak with a Jewish accent] and this Jewing is virtually impossible for an Aryan to copy in either its intonation or in its logic. Julius Korngold, the father of the composer Erich Wolfgang Korngold, once praised the Aryan journalist Hans Liebstöckl, who could Jew extraordinarily well, by saying that one could hardly note any difference between him and a Jew. There upon Hans Liebstöckl, replied, using his Jew accent: "There is a difference: I can Jew; you've got to."[3]

This view of the "hidden language" of the Jews contains within it a set of associations about the corrupt and corrupting nature of the Jew. In myths about the "hidden language" of the Jews, even those Jews who do not speak differently, whose language is identical to that of the reference group, are "heard" as speaking differently. And that difference extends into content as well as form. To be visible or audible in this manner creates a need to respond to this type of image. Is it of little wonder that modern Hebrew developed a set of sociolinguistic practices which were the antithesis of this ancient stereotype?[4] Where the hidden language attributed to the Jew in the Diaspora was understood as devious, modern Hebrew is self-consciously straightforward; where it was elliptical, it is now direct; where it was ingratiating, it is now aggressive, if not "tough."

These essays represent my most recent work in tracking the meaning attached to the Jew and the response by individuals who identify with this constructed meaning. Thus a "Jew" would be defined as much by the social setting as internally. Indeed, my sense is that the greater the identification of the Jew with the goals and values of the broader society, the more impacted the Jew is by the power of such images. But no one who identifies, either positively or negatively, with the label "Jew" is immune from the power of such stereotypes. It reflects the relative powerlessness of the Jew in the Diaspora and the hostility which Christian society (even in its most secularized form) has against the Jews. The shifts in rhetoric which these essays reflect are but variations on age-old themes. But the variations are meaningful; they, in turn, disclose the specific contexts and locations in which the idea of the Jew and the reality of Jews come into conflict.

These essays are meant to be sketches of approaches and problems—not to be final answers. They raise the question of the study of the images of the Jew as a means of comprehending the status as well as the representation of the Jew in the Christian Diaspora. In all cases these images present the complexity of the idea of the Jew and of the Jewish response to this projection of difference. My concern is not only what the image of the Jew is but what the forces are which shape this image of difference and—perhaps most importantly—how those labeled as different respond to this construction of their identity. My assumption is that the Jew in the Western Diaspora does respond, must respond, to the image of the Jew in such cultures. This is a complicated relationship, as Richard Onians has shown.[5] For there are "realities" of the Jewish body, such as the practice of infant male circumcision, which also become part of the social construction of the Jew's body within the mytho-poesis of Western culture.

The essays range across the body of the Jew and chart the Jew's response. I begin by listening to the myths about the Jew's voice and use these myths to examine certain contemporary responses about the way Jews are supposed to speak. My eye then drops to the lowest possible point on the body, to the myths about the Jew's foot and gait and their social implications. Then to the myths about the practice and meaning of circumcision and the way they are played out in Sigmund Freud's account of a case of hysteria. The other myth of the turn of the century, that of the Jewish Jack the Ripper, is revealed to be intimately linked to the construction of myths about gender. The nature of the Jew's mind, introduced in the opening chapter, returns in a series of case studies of the Jew and the Jew's relationship to the question of creativity. Freud reappears as a Jew responding to myths about his own body in essays on the construction of the myth of creativity and Freud's reading of Heinrich Heine's work and life as central to an understanding of the relationship between race, gender, and creativity. The double question of the nature of the Jew's coloration, as a key to the myths about race in the West, and the oddly related question of the shape of the Jew's nose brought me to examine the origin of the "nose job." The response of other marginalized scientists within the world of psychoanalysis is examined in the chapter on the essence of the Jew. And finally, I come to the impossibility of expelling the stereotype of the Jew and examine the question of the meaning of "plague" in Germany in 1939 and 1989. These essays are all of a piece. They sketch how certain myths reflect basic cultural and psychological ways of dealing with the difference of the Jew, and become part of the generalized vocabulary of difference in Western culture.

The gender designation of the term "Jew" as used in these studies is masculine. While some women (and images of women) are present in the various investigations, the central figure throughout is that of the male Jew, the body with the circumcised penis—an image crucial to the very understanding of the Western image of the Jew at least since the advent of Christianity. Full-length studies of the actual roles of Jewish women in this world of representations and their own complex response are certainly needed and in fact such studies at present are in the planning or writing stages by a number of feminist critics. My own work, however, has generally focused on the nature of the male Jew and his representation in the culture of the West; it is *this* representation which I believe lies at the very heart of Western Jew-hatred.

Anti-Semitism is a real and ongoing category in Western culture which is transmuted from age to age and from location to location.[6] I believe that one can speak of the anti-Semitism of Western culture even though this term evokes a specific stage in the history of Western Jew-hatred. Coined by Wilhelm Marr as part of the scientific discourse of race in the nineteenth century, it is half of the dichotomy of "Aryan" and "Semite" which haunted the pseudoscience of ethnology during this period and beyond. Maurice Olender illustrates this extraordinarily well in a recent study.[7] It is a socially constructed category which was used in Europe and the European colonies specifically to categorize the difference between "Semites" and Others. The terms were taken from nineteenth-century linguistics. This was not an accident, for, as we shall see, language has played a vital role as a marker of Jewish difference. Thus the complaint, voiced again recently in the "letters to the editor" of the *Times Literary Supplement*, that "Arabic, like Hebrew, is a Semitic race; and in so far as it is possible to talk of an Arab race, that race is Semitic. It is therefore nonsense to talk about Muslim anti-Semitism," quite misses the point.[8] The very choice of the label "anti-Semitism" was to create the illusion of a new scientific discourse for the hatred of the Jews and to root this hatred in the inherent difference of their language. And their language was believed to reflect their essence. This canard had to do only with the social construction of ideas of race, not with any linguistic entity. It has no validity except as a marker of the discourse of Jewish

5

difference. I use this term as the blanket label for all stages of Jew-hatred as a means of emphasizing the inherent consistency of Western attitudes toward the Jews. It is not a valid category of racial identity. That Jews exist and so self-label themselves as "Jews" (with a very wide range of meanings) is without a doubt the case. The use of the term "anti-Semite" makes no reference to this act of self-labeling. Indeed, it has been widely noted in the course of the twentieth century, from fin-de-siècle Vienna to Poland in the winter of 1990, that the label "Jew" could be applied to virtually anyone one wished to stigmatize whatever their religious, ethnic, or political identity or background. Its use does not imply any transcendent value to this dichotomy, nor does it imply or deny the real existence of such groupings.

I use the self-consciously ethnological term "Aryan" as the antithesis to "Jew" rather than the more evident term "Christian" throughout most of this book. What I am stressing is the long history of the racial definition of the "Jew" which we shall discuss in the conclusion. It is clear that the terms "Jew" and "Christian" may take on racial as well as religious significance from the eighteenth through the twentieth centuries. The debate about the nature of race during this period is reflected in the very use of the terms "Aryan" and "Jew" which reflect the ideology of the science of race.

It is vital to understand that Jews (like all other groups who are labeled as different) must acknowledge the world in which they are geographically and culturally situated. This response is structured by the conception of the Jew (which may or may not be itself structured by "realities" of the self-labeling of any given Jew or Jewish community). This response may, however, take a wide range of forms. It may be internalizing and self-destructive (self-hating) or it may be projective and stereotyping; it take the form of capitulation to the power of the image or the form of resistance to the very stereotype of the Jew. But there is the need to respond, either directly or subliminally.

These essays are the measure of my own response. Perhaps the most telling of them, the last but not the most recent, was written in the summer of 1989, while I was serving as a visiting professor of modern German literature at the Free University of Berlin. I had been in Berlin as a graduate student in the early 1960s and had returned on and off over the following decades. When I was invited by my friend Ulrich Profitlich, then the Chair of the Department of German, to teach there I put this invitation off for a number of years for reasons still unclear to myself. My own relationship to Berlin had in general been a positive one. Having come, as an American Jew, from my graduate studies at the University of Munich, with its unreconstructed and quite brutal negative reaction to everything labeled as "foreign," Berlin in the early 1960s seemed to me intellectually free and open, even though politically divided and isolated. Returning to Berlin over twenty years later, then, I decided I had to write something based on my current experiences of the city, one which I had both liked and avoided. Therefore, during the summer of 1989 I began, through the good offices of the best gay bookstore in Germany, the Prinz Eisenherz Buchhandlung, to read the German-language AIDS literature. Through the suggestions of the staff, I came to read the novel discussed in the chapter on the "Jewish Disease." Berlin came to seem a potential focus of the German struggle with AIDS, not because of the gay community in Berlin, but because Berlin had become the center of IV drug use in West Germany. So I wrote, from my own, idiosyncratic "foreign," i.e. American-Jewish perspective, the essay on AIDS in German culture. The essay appeared that fall in *MLN* thanks to the efforts of its editor, Richard Macksey.

By the late fall—perhaps better stated, by the evening of *Kristallnacht*, the fortieth anniversary of which I had helped commemorate the year before by organizing a panel of my Cornell colleagues who had been children in Germany during 1938—everything which had seemed real to me in the summer of 1989 had vanished. A new Germany was in the process of being created and my own sense of where I stood was totally disrupted. The essay which had been written as a critical comment on a dystopic view of German culture, now seemed as remote as Jules Verne's trip to the moon. But there was a reverse side to my alienation from what I felt when I wrote that essay in the "island-city" of Westberlin. The irony is that the further back into history my essays went, the more "real" they seemed to me. Turn-of-the-century Vienna was a more real place in my imagination that was the present-day city of Berlin. Writing about American-Jewish anxiety over Jewish visibility as the first SCUD missiles fall on Tel Aviv and as the "island city" of Berlin is transformed into the newly reunified (old?) capital of a new (old?) Germany, is disconcerting. Fin-de-siècle Vienna, a world and a century away, seems more real, certainly more stable in my mind's eye. Much has been written about Saul Friedländer's extraordinary work about memory, especially the memory of Jews. But historical memory *is* safer—we know how and when the story ends. It ends horribly, in the ovens at Auschwitz, but that is the past, and, as such, a safe because known past. What is more frightening is the continual complexity of the present, with its last act always unseen. My own anxiety about the resurgence of right wing anti-Semitism in the wake of German reunification (which was widely stated in talks throughout 1989 and 1990) was a response to the elimination of what I had internalized as the final act of the Shoah, the division of Germany. (A revised version of that talk has appeared in a special issue on German reunification of *New German Critique* 52 [1991]: 173–91.) The fact that there are no final acts, that the anxieties of Jews present in fin-de-siècle Vienna reappear in hardly disguised form in New York and London and Bombay in the 1990s, that the fantasies about the Jews present in the sixteenth century echo in the recently liberated halls of Eastern Europe, is the lesson I continue to learn. The product of that lesson is in this volume.

The revisions of this book were written while I served as the visiting historical scholar at the National Library of Medicine, National Institutes of Health, Bethesda, MD during 1990–1991. I am grateful to Heather Munro, Chandak Seengoopta, John Davidson, and Catharine Gelbin for the work they put into the preparation of the book. In addition I want to thank the staff at Olin Library, Cornell University, and the National Library of Medicine for their help in locating materials. The visual sources are from a number of collections as noted in the captions. I wish to thank the owners for giving me the permission to reproduce them. I want to thank William Schubach of the Wellcome Institute for the History of Medicine for helping me locate one of the illustrations. I am especially grateful to my editor at Routledge William P. Germano and to Jack Zipes and Russell Berman, the readers for Routledge, who provided close and detailed critiques of the manuscript. I am also very grateful to Diane Gibbons, who turned this manuscript into readable English.

The work on this volume was furthered by grants from the National Endowment for the Humanities (Program on Humanities, Science and Technology) and the Lucius Littauer Foundation. I am grateful for the help extended by these institutions which enabled me to undertake the work on this book.

The intellectual "godparents" of this volume (and, indeed, of much of the work I have undertaken in the past decade) are George L. Mosse and Elaine Showalter. It is Mosse who risked the first assertions of the nature and impact of anti-Semitic fantasies about the Jewish body on Jews and whose detailed historical work using cultural sources has set the pattern for my work. Showalter provided one of the most compelling case studies for the reading of medical traditions through the question of gender and its meaning. Her work has helped move my own into new and more difficult paths. Their scholarship and personal friendship made the writing of this book possible.

Of the following essays, "The Jewish Murderer" has appeared in a special issue of the Chicago-based art journal Whitewalls: A Journal of Language and Art 23: Regarding An/Other (Fall 1989): 100–26; "The Jewish Reader" in the *Southern Humanities Review* 24 (1990): 201–18; "The Jewish Essence" in *Social Research* (Special Number on the History of Psychoanalysis) 57 (1990): 993–1018; "The Jewish Disease" in *MLN* (Comparative Literature Issue) 104 (1989): 1142–71. All of these essays have been revised for the present volume. I wish to thank the editors and publishers of these journals for having given me permission to republish them.

Bethesda, Maryland / March 1, 1991

1

THE JEWISH VOICE

Chicken Soup or the Penalties of Sounding Too Jewish

◆————————————◆

In his most recent novel Philip Roth again evoked the specter of what it means to sound too Jewish. Projecting his anxiety about the formation of an American-Jewish literary identity on to his image of England, Roth has his unnamed protagonist tell the following anecdote. He has seen a commercial on British television in which a "youngish middle-aged, rather upper class English actor" begins to remove his makeup having just performed Dickens's Fagin. "To relax after the performance he lights up one of these little cigarillos, contentedly he puffs away at it, talking about the flavor and the aroma and so on, and then he leans very intimately into the camera and he holds up the cigarillo and suddenly, in a thick, Faginy, Yiddish accent and with an insinuating leer on his face, he says, 'And, best of all, they're cheap.' "[1] The protagonist's immediate response is to phone an Anglo-Jewish friend to ask him about the commercial. He is admonished that he will "get used to it." "It" being British anti-Semitic representations of the Jew. But the protagonist worries about such insults, as well as being criticized for making "such a fuss about being Jewish."

It is, of course, not being Jewish which is the problem against which Roth's figure protests, but sounding Jewish. The "Faginy, Yiddish" accent marks the stage Jew as different, as not really belonging to cultivated British society with its Oxbridge accent. Roth's protagonist protests by calling his Anglo-Jewish friend and speaking with him in his American-accented English. He must sound different, but this difference is in no way represented in Philip Roth's text. Philip Roth writes a clear, mid-Atlantic literary language, undifferentiated from the language of most other contemporary American writers. Indeed if Martin Amis's most recent novel, *London Fields*, with its American-Jewish novelist-protagonist is any indication, it is the language of modern socially critical fiction, even to British ears. And yet the fear of sounding different, sounding too Jewish (which may well mean sounding too "New Jersey" in the ear of Roth's imagined British listener) haunts Philip Roth's work.

Roth's critique of the British image of the Jew mirrors the anxiety which his protagonist has about his command of his own language, not the Yiddish-accented language of the anti-Semite's image of the Jew, but the language of high culture, the literary language of the Anglophone novelist. Jews, according to Roth, compulsively tell stories: "With the nigger it's his prick and with the Jew it's his questions. You are a treacherous bastard who cannot resist a narrative . . ." (93) It is the Jewish author's command of the language of the narrative, the language in which the questions are asked, which is drawn into question.

The creation of the image of the Jew who is identifiable as different because he or she sounds "too Jewish" provides a model through which we can see the structure of the image to create an absolute boundary of the difference of the Jew even as this boundary historically shifts and slides. Jews sound different because they are represented as being different. Jewish authors have felt compelled to respond to this image of difference, and to create a counter image of the Jew who sounds Jewish, for within their creation of texts, Jewish authors are Jews who sound Jewish. Within the European tradition of seeing the Jew as different, there is a closely linked tradition of hearing the Jew's language as marked by the corruption of being a Jew. In the British fin-de-siècle journal *The Butterfly*

11

[PLATES 2–3] there are images which associate a specific Jewish physiognomy with a specific manner of speaking. Not merely a "Jewish" accent, but an entire discourse about capital and trade which was supposed to characterize the Jew. In a German postcard of the same period [PLATE 4] the rising interest in Zionism is linked to the language of the Jews. The caption reads: "And when they are all in there, then Lord, then close the gate and all Europe will have peace." The language of the Jews in the boxes next to their bowed legs has them speak nonsense (in a Yiddish-accent dialect) to match their Eastern European Jewish clothing: "Now our people are crazy" and "Let's now make a rabbi." The Jew's true nature as a usurer is revealed in the inset. All of these Jews are represented as acting Jewish but also as sounding Jewish.

What does it mean to sound too Jewish? I have argued in my study *Jewish Self-Hatred* that there is a long tradition of representing the "hidden" language of the Jew as a signifier of specific difference.[2] And that the difference represented is always an attempt to present the qualities of the Jew (usually negative, but sometimes, indeed, positive) as separate from the referent group. The image of the "Jew who sounds Jewish" is a stereotype within the Christian world which represents the Jew as possessing all languages or no language of his or her own; of having a hidden language which mirrors the perverse or peculiar nature of the Jew; of being unable to truly command the national language of the world in which he/she lives or, indeed, even of possessing a language of true revelation, such as Hebrew.

The stereotype of the Jews' language is rooted in the earliest history of the rise of Christianity (or rather in the separation of the early Church from Judaism) and is mirrored in a static manner in a series of texts—the Gospels, or, as the early Christians referred to them, "The New Testament"—which were generated dynamically over time.[3] As early as Eusebius and Athanasius (in the fourth century ACE) these texts become the central canon of Christianity as the so-called "pseudo-Gospels" (such as the Gospel of Nicodemus) are removed. In the Gospels, Christians are given a representation of the Jew who sounds too Jewish and a direct message about the inherent difference of the Jew. It is in the continuity of the Gospels at the center of Christianity—not in the theology or indeed in the practice of the Church—that the representation of the Jew who sounds too Jewish is preserved. And it is to this central stereotype that Western (that is, Christian or secularized) society turns when it needs to provide itself with a vocabulary of difference for the Jew. Thus it is quite unimportant whether the Gospels (or the "Q" document) were first drafted in Aramaic or Greek. What is central is that in the reception of the Gospels there is a contrast between the language of the Gospel narrative (whether Greek, Latin, German, or English) and Jesus' *ipsissima verba*.[4]

The creation of the image of the Jew who sounds too Jewish in the reception of the Gospels can be understood by examining/comparing four analogous passages. Let us turn to the Gospels in their canonical (i.e. received) order and read one passage, the last words of Christ in all of them. Focusing on the presentation, we see that in the first set of passages Jesus Christ speaks in Aramaic. Matthew, the first gospeler, represents a Christ whose last words are as follows: "And about the ninth hour Jesus cried with a loud voice, saying, 'Eli, Eli, Lama Sabachthani?' that is to say, My God, My God, why has thou forsaken me?" (27: 46). Mark has Christ "at the ninth hour . . . [crying] with a loud voice, saying 'Eloi, Eloi, Lama Sabachthani?' which is, being interpreted, My God, My God, why hast thou forsaken me?" (15: 34). This significance of this lies in the presentation of Christ as speaking the language of the Jews: his words need to be translated into Greek, Latin, German, or English for the self-labeled Christian reader to understand. The reader is thus made aware of the foreignness of Christ's language—he speaks the language of difference; he is a Jew who sounds Jewish. Placed in the mouth of Christ, the "hidden" language of the Jews is the magical language of difference. It generates a positive image of difference. But it still labels him as a Jew.

But in the second ("later") set of passages, Christ speaks directly to the reader. If we take the parallel passage from Luke we can trace the same course with very different results. Christ is taken to Calvary and there he is crucified. "And when Jesus had cried with a loud voice, he said, Father, into thy hands I commend my spirit: and having said thus, he gave up the ghost" (23: 46). In John, the

"Vy d'you vear all dem ringth, Ithaacth?"

"Vell, you thee, I travelth a good deal, and ven I gets into converthation with a gentleman, ten to vun I thells him a ring, don'd yer know."

"But all the sthoneth ith turned inthide."

"You thilly fool! I don'd talk like that!———

PLATE TWO

The image of the "cheap Jew" is linked with the Jew's corrupted language in a short-lived "humorous and artistic periodical" from the fin de siècle. The periodical also published a series of "Ghetto Travesties" in which the same device was used. Language and gesture were closely linked in determining the meaning of the Jew's language at the fin de siècle. Gestural language was understood by anthropologists of the day such as John Lubbock as a sign of the primitive state of a culture. The image of the "cheap Jew" is here evoked by language, gesture, and physiognomy. *The Butterfly* (May–October, 1893) (Source: Private Collection, Ithaca).

l talks like thith ! ! ! "

PLATE THREE

last of the Gospels which related the life of Jesus, Christ is taken to Golgotha and there "he said, It is finished: and he bowed his head, and gave up the ghost" (19: 30). His language needs no translation; it is transparent, familiar not foreign. The later Gospels provide a verbal sign of difference between the image of the Jews and that of the early Christians represented in the text—Jews who were at the time becoming Christians in a world in which the valorized

15

language was Greek. As Christian readers who read through the Gospels in their canonical order, we thus abandon the image of Christ as one who sounds Jewish and replace him with the image of one who sounds like ourselves (whether we speak Greek, Latin, German, or English). He becomes a Christian. Thus the existence of a "hidden" language which would mark Christ as a "real" Jew, i.e., as a non-Greek-speaking Jew and therefore of lower status, was impossible.

In Luke and John there is no need for translation or interpretation. The language of this passage is completely transparent to the Christian reader of the Gospels. The reader of the passage understands that Christ speaks the same language as the reader. This "lucanization," according to Morton Scott Enslin, "reflects a marked sameness of tone, [a] smoothness and freedom from the

PLATE FOUR

A turn-of-the-century postcard representing the German fantasy of the nature of the Jew. Rooted in the stereotype of the Eastern Jew, this image depicted all Jews in Germany. The use of "Yiddish" words which could be so recognized in this context meant evoking the hidden language of the German Jews, their fantastic inability to do anything but *Mauscheln* (Source: Private Collection, Ithaca).

16

little idiosyncrasies which stamp the man himself . . . ."[5] This movement in the Gospels from the image of Christ as a Jew who sounds too Jewish to that of the Christian whose discourse is separate and distinct from that of the Jew, becomes clearest in the writings which codified the views of the early Church. In *Acts*, Peter's first speech to his fellow Jews in Jerusalem is recounted in a manner that differentiates between Greek, the language of his readers (now feeling themselves as "Christians"), and the representation of the Jews' discourse. He writes, for example, "And it was known unto all the dwellers at Jerusalem; insomuch as that field is called in their proper tongue, Aceldama, that is to say, The field of blood" (1: 19). But the utterances of Jesus in *Acts* never needs this type of translation. His language is consistently accessible. His language is not the language of the Jews.

A similar movement of the text is to be found in the recounting of the defense of the first Christian martyr, Stephen. The movement away from the "hidden" language of the Jews reveals itself to be more than a rejection of the language of the Jews. It is also an appropriation of the discourse of the Jews which Stephen reveals to the reader as having been misused by the Jews themselves. By stripping away the polluting nature of the "hidden" language of the Jews Stephen reveals to the reader that the very discourse of the Jews was never really their own.

Stephen, a Greek-speaking Jew, had begun successfully to evangelize among the Jews. He was prosecuted by Jewish priests who brought false witnesses to accuse him of blasphemy. His defense is quite extraordinary. He begins by recounting to his Jewish accusers a synoptic history of the Jews as represented in the Torah from the appearance of God to Abraham through the building of the Temple to—the coming, death and resurrection of Christ:

> Ye stiffnecked and uncircumcised in heart and ears, ye do always resist the Holy Ghost: as your fathers did, so do ye. Which of the prophets have not your fathers persecuted? and they have slain them which showed before of the coming of the Just One; of whom ye have been now the betrayers and murderers . . . But he, being full of the Holy Ghost, looked up steadfastly into heaven, and saw

the glory of God, and Jesus standing on the right hand of God . . .
(Acts 7: 51–55)

The entire story of the Jews is reduced to a preamble to the coming of Christ. The sense of continuity between the "real" Jews of the past and the "new" Jews of the early Church, between the "true" Jewish experience actually written "on the heart" and not merely inscribed on the skin, becomes his defense. The act of circumcision, the traditional sign of the special relationship between the (male) Jew and God, becomes here a false sign, a sign written on the body of the hypocrisy of the hidden language of the Jew. The continuity between the Torah and the Gospels, the Christian demand that the Jews of the Torah prefigure (and thus are replaced by) the Christian experience removes the discourse of the Jews about their own history from their own control. As St. Augustine stated in his manual for new converts to Christianity: "the New Testament is concealed in the Old; the Old Testament is revealed in the New."[6] The Torah suddenly becomes the Old Testament. The "hidden" language of the Jews disappears from the tradition of the early Church, even though it is preserved in what now comes to be called the "New" Testament as a sign of the difference of Christ's nature from that of the Jews. The successful separation of the "Church" from the "Synagogue" is indicated in the latest of the Gospels, *Revelations*, as well as in the Pauline epistles, where the separation between the divine discourse of the Church and the corrupt discourse of the Jews is absolute.

The rhetoric of European anti-Semitism can be found within the continuity of Christianity's image of the Jew. It is Christianity which provides all of the vocabularies of difference in Western Europe and North America, whether it is in the most overt "religious" language or in the secularized language of modern science. For it is not merely that the Jew is the obvious Other for the European, whether the citizen of the Roman Empire or of the Federal Republic of Germany. Anti-Semitism is central to Western culture because the rhetoric of European culture is Christianized, even in its most secular form. This made the negative image of

18

difference of the Jew found in the Gospel into the central referent for all definitions of difference in the West.

"Racial" or "scientific" anti-Semitism of the late nineteenth century is thought to have formed a radical break with the "medieval" religious tradition of Jew-hating, due to its self-confessed atheism. But this is not true. The nature of the secularization of religious models within the biological sciences of the nineteenth century is misunderstood. The basic model of the Jew found within "religious" contexts is merely secularized in the course of the eighteenth and nineteenth centuries. In both models the special language and related discourse of the Jew reflects the continuity of the image of the Jew. This is related to the continued presence at the heart of the self-definition of the Christian world of the Gospels with their complex and shifting image of the Jew.

The early Christians found proof of the inferiority of the Jews in their refusal to accept Jesus as the Messiah and convert to Christianity. This blindness and intractability became the definition of those psychological limitations of the Jew which precluded the Jew from ever becoming a truly "cultured" member of Western society. The perversity of the Jew's nature in betraying Christ over and over again throughout history (remember the central trope of Christianity is the regular reenactment of the crucifixion) becomes the biologically determined quality of the Jew which leads to the Jew's heartless role in the rise of capitalism (or communism—take your pick). The Jew's role in literally destroying the life of Christians, whether through the ritual use of Christian blood or the mass poisoning of wells in order to cause the Black Death becomes the Jew's biological role as the transmitter of diseases such as syphilis (and, according to at least one commentator in Chicago in 1988, AIDS[7]).

The image of the Jew who sounds too Jewish is the counter-image of the hidden language of the Jew. The language used by the Jew reveals or masks the Jew's corrupt nature. But the informed listener hears the Jew hidden within no matter whether this difference is overt or disguised. The image of the "hidden" language and corrupt (and corrupting) discourse of the Jews is reflected within the tradition of Jews dealing with their internalized sense of difference. (Thus the memory of language is never neutral for Jews, especially German Jews.) The ancient Western tradition labels the language of the Jew as corrupt and corrupting, as the sign of the inherent difference of the Jew. This tradition sees the Jew as inherently unable to have command of any "Western," that is, cultural language. The Jew is not only "not of our blood," as Msgr. Joseph Frings of Cologne expressed it in 1942, but also "does not speak our language."[8] The Jews' language reflects only the corruption of the Jews and their discourse, a corruption that is made manifest in the essential Jew's language from the eighteenth century to the present, Yiddish. It is against this view that Jewish writers—Jewish because they internalize the label of "Jew"—must establish dominance over the language and discourse of their culture. The image of the language of the Jews and the idea of a "Jewish" language and discourse is central to any self-definition of the Jew in the Christian West.

We can take a specific example from the 1940s, the most recent period when the Jews were simply labeled as unable to command the language of their "host" nations. The stigma of being Jewish was central to the definition of all German "Jews," no matter what their prior religious, ethnic, or cultural self-definition. Theodor Adorno, writing in 1945, juxtaposes in two aphorisms his view that "Anti-Semitism is the rumor about the Jews" and "Foreign words are the Jews of language."[9] Jews are the product of language and language becomes like the anti-Semite's image of the wandering or cosmopolitan Jew. The language of the anti-Semite here defines the nature of the Jew and his/her discourse. Thus the Jew becomes the agent who uses corrupt language, while the corrupt discourse becomes the embodiment of the nature of the Jew. Adorno ironically sees the act of the passing of rumors as defining the reality of the Jews in Germany; but he also sees the nature of language (within the historic German demand for a "pure" language) as creating a category of exclusion and stigma. The interchangeability of these two categories reflects the interchangeability of the image of the Jew as possessing a unique, corrupting, and corrupt discourse embodied in the Jew's language—whether in the Jews' use of the language of culture or that special language of the Jews, Yiddish.

The Jewish Voice

◆

For language purists of the 1920s and 1930s the most corrupt version of German was *Mauscheln*, the language ascribed to the Eastern Jew who attempted to speak German. This visibility of the Jew's language mirrors Adorno's experience in the United States as well as in Germany. It is echoed in his interview with a telephone operator in the 1940s who claims that "You get so you always know a Jewish voice."[10] One can never, it seems, escape the sense that once one's voice is heard, one is instantly revealed as a rootless, cultureless Jew.

The Jewish survivors of the Shoah were quite aware of the barbaric result of the incarnation of this idea of the Jews' language in the fascist image of the bestial, non-human Jew. Jewish writers who were forced or felt themselves driven to write in these languages had to deal with the problem of writing in a language in which their own sense of control of that medium was undermined by the image of the languageless, base Jew. After the Shoah this image of the Jew remained quite alive in the rhetoric of the language in which the non-Jew wrote about Jews. How can one capture memory in a tongue that you are supposed not to command? Is it not unauthentic to write in the language of the murderers, at least about victims and the survivors? The Jew, and the language of the Jew, is therefore what the non-Jew says the Jew is. For the non-Jews, language is assumed to be authentic, at least when it represents the Jew.

This is the problem with Sartre's comment that: "Jewish authenticity consists in choosing oneself as Jew—that is, in realizing one's Jewish condition. The authentic Jew abandons the myth of the universal man; . . . he ceases to run away from himself and to be ashamed of his own kind . . . . He knows that he is one who stands apart, untouchable, scorned, proscribed—and it is as such that he asserts his being."[11] Such a definition of Jewish "authenticity," with all of its evocation of Christian suffering and martyrdom, may be fine for a Frenchman who does not find himself labeled as a Jew, but for the Jew who is so labeled, such a sense of the "authentic" limits the range of Jewish response to the model of sacrifice presented in the Gospels. What Sartre—hardly a Christian thinker—incorporates into the model of the Jew is the model of particularist

21

humility in the face of suffering. This is does not permit Jews much range to create a discourse appropriate for themselves.

This debate and the hidden language of the Jews has recently resurfaced in a new guise. In the Federal Republic of Germany during the 1950s and 1960s, there had been a traditional, liberal approach (e.g., in the writing of Ralf Dahrendorf) which tended to see the path of German history as having taken a special turn which led to the exploitation of anti-Semitism as a political platform and, eventually, if not inexorably, to the Shoah. The literary image of the Shoah at this time (as in the works of Alfred Andersch) was of a world of destruction in which the German served as the agent of destruction, destroying not only (not even primarily) Jews but other "good" Germans. Indeed, the Jew was quite often represented as mute or as passive in this liberal tradition. Or indeed, as in the central works of Günter Grass such as *The Tin Drum*, as possessing a "special" or "hidden" language which marked them as different.[12] The cultural difference of German Jews or perhaps better of Jews in the BRD, the difference of having to deal in 1989 with their growing invisibility as well as their past, has gone unnoticed in this cultural tradition. These German authors, as many of their contemporaries, had no problem in dealing with dead Jews, or old Jews, for as Henryk Broder has noted, there seems to be a "incurable love of German intellectuals for dead or half-dead Jews,"[13] and, one might add, to distant Jews (they all read Ephron Kishon). But the idea of a negative symbioses,[14] a need for Jews in contemporary Germany to struggle with their invisibility as living, contributing members of contemporary society is impossible for them to understand.

The recent German critical response to Günter Grass's plagiarism of a passage from Edgar Hilsenrath's autobiographical novel of the Shoah, *Night*, reflects the sense that Jewish writers in German are to be understood as little more than the post-modern source for their literary work. In his novel of 1979, *The Meeting at Telgte*, Grass mines Hilsenrath's account of the murder of Jews in the Shoah for an image of death completely separate from the experience of the immediate past.[15] Hilsenrath the novelist is made mute, his language is stolen from him, and the German critics speak of ironic incorporation! This "borrowing" was noted in 1987 by Christoph Sieger in the notes to the critical edition of the novel as well as by Andreas Graf in an essay in the *Deutsche Vierteljahrsschrift* in 1989.[16] Both of these critics seem to see in Grass's plagiarism only a post-modern playfulness with categories of "reality" and "fictionality." Unlike D. M. Thomas, whose plagiarism of Kuznetsov in *The White Hotel*, was widely discussed, Grass's literary steal has not made the front page of any newspaper in Germany.[17] And it most probably will not, for German critics have treated of Grass's appropriation as a legitimate literary undertaking. Grass's purposeful confusion of "reality" and "narrativity" is stressed by Graf, the subtitle of whose essay is "on the ironic interchange between literature and reality." Might I suggest another reading? For all of the questions raised by Thomas's use of Kuznetsov it was acknowledged that he maintained the context of Kuznetsov's description of Babi Yar. Thomas's novel is ultimately about the Shoah. Günter Grass's use of Hilsenrath is placed in quite a different context. Grass isolates this text and displaces it into the seventeenth century, with an evocation of the post-WW2 era and the *Gruppe 47*. He thus brackets the world which Hilsenrath inhabited. This violation of the Jew's authenticity, of the voice of the Jew narrating his own experience within the literary world of contemporary fiction, is marked by Grass's "borrowing." The Jew not only vanishes, his voice becomes the authentic voice of the German experience of the seventeenth century or the immediate postwar era.

Night, Hilsenrath's first novel, first appeared in a 1974 English translation, and was only afterwards published, with great difficulty in Germany. The book has been widely read in West Germany in the past few years with the appearance of a paperback edition. Grass's novel was widely advertised and widely discussed (if rarely read) when it appeared. Grass manages to incorporate and thus make invisible not only his source, but certainly as important, the context out of which this source springs, postwar German Jews' struggle to establish their own identity in German culture. Grass's visible Jews are marked by the flaw of the hidden language ascribed to the Jews; *his* hidden Jew, Edgar Hilsenrath, marks the invisibility of the Jew in the literary world of postwar Germany. As certainly as Markus and Matern represent the visible Jew with his contaminated discourse in the world of Grass's *Danzig Trilogy*, so does Edgar Hilsenrath function in Grass's work as the hidden Jew, representing the Jew within postwar "high" culture, neither seen nor heard. For even when they are seen—as in the popularity of Hilsenrath's novel *The Nazi and the Barber*—they are relegated to the world of the past, a world completed and closed. They are not acknowledged as part of the world of the present, taking their themes out of their own experience but casting them in the discourse of the high culture in which they live. Thus the *Spiegel* review of Hilsenrath's latest novel evokes "the Jew Werfel" and his novel of the Armenian massacre in other words a dead Jew is evoked to categorize a living author.

The question here is whether the Jew, so long the marker of what the German was not, any longer plays a central role in contemporary German thought, or have the Jews been replaced by other categories of difference, such as the Turk?[18] But these two images are clearly related. The public image of the "foreigner" and the image of the "Jew" are often associated by the far right. Graffiti in Turkish neighborhoods in Westberlin, such as "Zyklon B" or "off to Auschwitz" directly evoke the Shoah. Jewish inhabitants of West Berlin understand comments such as "Just wait until we've gotten rid of [Heinz] Galinski [the head of the Jewish Community in Berlin]—because then your time here has come as well" not merely as threats against the Turks but also as threats against themselves as "foreigners."[19] It is clear from contemporary neo-conservative historians that the role of the Jew has shifted. The German wishes to shed the burden of the past, in which the Jew was the central icon of difference. How does the history of anti-Semitism function in a world devoid of Jews, or at least, a world in which the Jew is no longer heard? And how does this unheard Jew respond? And this especially with the rise of a public discourse of anti-Semitism (especially in the former German Democratic Republic) in the light of the German reunification?

Deprived of the Shoah as the central marker of a self-defined "authentic" discourse about Jewish difference, the contemporary West German Jew had to seek other models. There has been a necessary shift from the earlier model, in which Jews internalized the extraordinary visibility given them within the culture of the Diaspora. The process of internalization is now linked to the marginal invisibility of the Jews. Thus the need for new German-Jewish periodicals such as *Semit* and *Babylon* which provide a "new language" for the German Jew—not the language of the official, post-Shoah discourse of the Jewish community under Heinz Galinsky but a new language, a unique language—now modeled on the language of the "new" Jewish left in the United States. This recent growth in the awareness of the need to generated a discourse which is "their own" has lead younger, liberal German-Jews to evolve their own "authentic" discourse. It is analogous to the model of American periodicals such as *Tikkun*, whose attempt to revivify the role of self-identified Jews within the left (where there had been a long tradition of repressing any Jewish identity, except as an ethnic marker) has resulted in a "new" manner for Jews to speak. While the old left borrowed its vocabulary from the old, often anti-Semitic European left, the new left in fact returns to the even older, *Bundist* model of cultural and political activism. Rejecting Zionism as an ideology, the new left includes as part of its agenda political critiques of contemporary Israeli politics. Here, too, a model for the appropriate language of the Jew responds to the idea of the special language of the Jew in a context—European Socialism—in which the "Christian" roots are difficult but not impossible to trace.

But the myth of the "hidden" language of the Jew is not a "German" or a "German-Jewish" problem. In post-Shoah America—the image of the "hidden language" of the Jew—the absence of the center in the Jew's character as reflected in his/her ability to command truly the discourse of the world in which he/she dwells—can be found in artifacts of higher culture from Geoffrey Wolff's 1979 autobiographical study of his father's life[20] to Bernard Wasserstein's 1988 biography of the Hungarian Jew Trebitsch Lincoln.[21] The image of the "talking" Jew—the post-Shoah manifestation of the internalization of the image of the hidden language of the Jew—can and does materialize in contemporary Jewish culture throughout the Diaspora. Its roots lie in a Jewish internalization of the Christian image of the innate difference of the Jew. One can turn

25

to the intense competition for acceptance between the German-Jewish and Eastern European-Jewish communities in the United States for one salient example. In 1939 Karl A. Menninger recounted his own Midwestern, Christian discomfort at hearing the editor of the *New York Times*, Arthur Sulzberger, tell "a story involving the imitation of the Jewish accent of Dr. [A.A.] Brill [the pioneer Eastern European-Jewish psychoanalyst], which I thought was in very bad taste. As a matter of fact, it was the second time he had told it in my presence, and he admitted that he had told it in his office when he made a speech to the employees a few days ago. He is such a cultivated, dignified fellow that it is amazing to hear him come out with this ridicule of the accent of other Jews . . ."[22] Menninger supplies his own reading of Sulzberger's reason for distinguishing between his discourse and that of someone whom Menninger sees as a "fellow Jew." Menninger comments that Sulzberger was "timid about being known to be a Jewish newspaper owner" (284). That is, he was anxious about his discourse, the discourse of the journalist being identified as a hidden Jewish discourse. The charge that the media was in the hands of the Jews had first been lodged in Germany in the mid-nineteenth century. The force of this charge had been exacerbated by the public response of the American media to the rise of the Nazis. Sulzberger's fear of the Jew within was articulated by him in his identification of the discourse of the Eastern Jew as aberrant, at a time in 1939 when, in Germany as well as in the United States, the anxiety of all Jews, even an extremely acculturated one such as Sulzberger, about their status as members of the dominant culture was high. This view was in no way limited to the news media. When David Swift, a long-time Walt Disney employee, accepted a job at Columbia Studios (with its Jewish owners), Disney snapped with a Jewish accent: "Okay, Davy Boy. Off you go to work with those Jews. It's where you belong, with those Jews."[23]

When we turn to the most recent past, we can find in the realm of American popular culture a real "Jew who sounds Jewish"—the comic Jackie Mason—whose discourse marks him as different surely as did that of A. A. Brill (and Arthur Sulzberger). The career of Jackie Mason, the last of the "borscht belt" comics, had an extraordinary rebirth during 1987. An act designed for the Catskills which had brought Mason to fame during the 1960s (including a much publicized spat with the TV-powerhouse Ed Sullivan) led to bankruptcy in 1983. Suddenly this same act became the vehicle which brought him stardom (again) in the late 1980s. Mason understood what had happened: "The Jewish people took me for granted, the young people saw me as an anachronism, then I went to Broadway where I never ever thought I'd succeed." And the reason for his invisibility was his *Mauscheln*: "People said I was too Jewish—and I even suffered from anti-Jewish prejudice from Jews themselves. There was a profound rejection problem: the reverse discrimination of Jews against other Jews who talk like me in show business. I think they were ashamed and embarrassed about my accent, that I was somehow symbolic of the whole fear that Jews would be discriminated against again."[24] For Jackie Mason, the move to Broadway provided a neutral space in which Mauscheln was no longer associated with a "Jewish" environment; that is, the audience (Jewish or not) no longer identified with the comic as a representative of the self.

During the fall of 1989 Jackie Mason starred in an ill-fated "sitcom" entitled *Chicken Soup* on ABC. It was canceled on November 8, 1989, even though it was the 13th highest rated network television show. *USA Today*, a good barometer of middle-class opinion, thought "Mason's ethnic shtick wouldn't play to the masses."[25] The use of the Yiddishism in this very phrase placed the discourse of this Jew who sounds Jewish beyond the pale of polite language, the language of middle class comedy. We have seen that over the past several decades, as Henry L. Gates, Jr. has recently noted, the representation of the African American on American television has moved from that of Amos and Andy to Dr. Clifford Huxtable, from African-Americans sounding too "black" to those possessing the dominant discourse of American culture.[26] For some Jews, the seeming lack of movement from the Jackie Mason of the 1960s to the Jackie Mason of the 1980s was offensive. The Jewish Defense League picketed the ABC studio in New York and "Dan Bloom, a Jewish children's book author from Alaska tried organizing a grass-roots campaign against the show . . . He didn't like the Jewish stereotypes portrayed." Bloom observed: "I . . . got the feeling he offended many Jews in America. They've heard this type of humor in their homes, but in the public living rooms of America for everybody to hear it seemed embarrassing."[27] Gates quotes W.E.B. Du Bois from 1921 that "the more highly trained we become, the less we can laugh at Negro comedy." The Jew who sounds Jewish, for some American Jews, represents the hidden Jew within, the corrupt Jew of the Gospel, the mark of difference which offends even after the Jew is integrated into the mainstream of American culture.

The question of Mason's discourse was not limited to the reception of his television program. Mason's role as a "Jew who sounds Jewish," a Jew visibly marked by his discourse, had become a source of comment during September and October of 1989. In the campaign for mayor in New York City, Mason backed the Republican candidate Rudolph W. Giuliani, who had made a special effort to attract the traditionally Democratic Jewish voters to support him rather than the African-American Democratic candidate, David N. Dinkins. Giuliani's desire for Jewish support in this contest was articulated by Mason in September 1989 when he stated in an interview in the *Village Voice* that "there is a sick Jewish problem of voting for a black man no matter how unfit he is for the job. All you have to be is black and don't curse the Jews directly and the Jew will vote for a black in a second. Jews are sick with complexes."[28] Mason's comment about the nature of African-American/Jewish relations led to a fire storm of accusations about Mason's "racism" and forced Mason to withdraw from his public role in Giuliani's campaign. What was most interesting was the subsequent revelation that Mason had earlier called Dinkins "a fancy *shvartze* with a mustache" during a late August meeting with four reporters from *Newsweek*.[29] It is this Yiddishism which generated a further debate about the visibility of the hidden language of the Jews.

The response to Mason, whether in his political role as a supporter of Giuliani or in his role as a television actor, was that his discourse was much "too Jewish." Mason was self-consciously seen as a Jew because his discourse (whether his comic or his "racist" discourse) set him apart from the accepted image of the Jew. His image violated the conventional (media) wisdom about the way that Jews were supposed to sound: they were not supposed to sound "different," they were supposed to sound "liberal." The question of a hidden language, a language which was "too Jewish" focused the image of Jackie Mason as a Jew, but in a pejorative sense. For some Americans, Mason's visibility on the political and entertainment fronts revitalized the time-old suspicion that Jews have a hidden, shared code in talking about others, including Others. Thus the *Newsweek* reporters refrained from breaking the story about the use of Mason's Yiddishism until after the story in the *Village Voice* about the "Jewish complex" broke. The *Newsweek* reporters discussed breaking the story after their meeting with Giuliani and Mason on August 31 because of "Mr. Mason's use of *'schvartzer.'*"[30] They decided not to use the material at all. One can speculate that it was the question of attributing a hidden language, a language which marked Mason as a Jew, which caused their hesitation to release the interview. Indeed, when the question of releasing this material was broached in another context, the removal of the use of the Yiddishism became central to the use of the interview. The liberal sensitivity to the claim that Jews sound different is a marker that this charge is alive and well in modern American society. In a list of "The Bad and The Beautiful," the "ins" and the "outs" for the readers of *Gentlemen's Quarterly*, Richard Merkin commented (in February 1991) that Mason is a "coarse and obvious little man . . . I think that Mason's contribution to Rudolph Giuliani's New York mayoral campaign showed his truest form. When *Chicken Soup*, his attempt at a TV sitcom bombed, Mason said something to the effect that at least now the rest of America knows what a Jew looks like. If Jackie Mason is even remotely like a typical Jew, then I'm in the market for a used foreskin in a medium—um, make that a medium large."[31] Merkin's response to Mason's voice evoked an image of his own circumcised body, which he then has to (jokingly) make more powerful. Mason's own blatant Jewishness makes some other Jews quite ill at ease about their own bodies. This image of the Jew is a far cry from the fantasy of the voice of Tevye in *Fiddler on the Roof* and the idealized shtetl which dominated American Jewish memories in the 1960s. Michael Selzer commented in the early 1970s on the glorification of the Eastern Jew as victim and its disappearance with the 1967 Arab-Israeli War in which "the nostalgia for the shtetl . . . gave way to the triumph of military conquest."[32] Jackie Mason's discourse is that of a "tough" Jew, to use Paul Brienes's phrase, not that of Tevye the Milkman.[33]

The extent of the power of the hidden language of the Jews in the 1980s may well reveal itself in a piece which appeared in *Esquire*— not the natural locus for texts dealing with this question. The novelist Daphne Merkin, an associate publisher at Harcourt Brace Jovanovich, comments on her inner life as the child of a survivor of the Shoah:

> Floating always among us was an awareness of the importance of avoiding, if one could help it, "too Jewish" an appearance, the dread stigma of "too Jewish" a voice. My sisters, accordingly, emerged with carefully modulated accents that sounded vaguely foreign, a mix of German and British. I, by some cruel twist of fate, developed an accent that sounded unmistakable, harshly "New Yawk." My mother and sisters wanted to know why I talked as if I came from Brooklyn, but somehow I must have wanted to shed all vestiges of the dominant culture and get back to the lusty Jewish core. . . . Can racial self-hatred be passed along, like a bad gene?[34]

Merkin comments on the fantasy of self-hatred, on the rejection of the Jewish core, of "the prominent nose, darker coloring, or intensity of gaze I associated with being Jewish." For Merkin, the return to the "lusty Jewish core" is the act of talking with a "Jewish" accent—here, the accent of the urban environment, of New York. This is not an accidental association. *The New Yorker* sounds "Jewish," as the quintessential Kansas City WASP Calvin Trillin observes: ". . . a Yiddish word and a New York word are the same thing. . . . The only pure New York word I can think of — cockamamie—sounds Yiddish, even though it isn't. It means ridiculous or harebrained and is commonly used in such phrases as 'another one of the mayor's cockamamie schemes.' "[35] Being a New Yorker in the 1990s means sounding Jewish — being a Jew in spite of oneself. (Certainly this association took place only after WW2.) But only if one is discomfited by the very awareness of one's difference, of one's identifiable sense of sounding too Jewish. It becomes a sign of one's difference, of the dis-ease of being Jewish. This association of space and voice is powerfully made in the Jewish-feminist comedy *Isn't it Romantic* by Wendy Wasserstein (1984). Here the accent of "New Yawk" becomes the accent of the Jew and the Jewish characters (unlike the other characters who are born and live in New York) are notable by their Yiddishisms. Indeed, what is striking is that the non-Jewish characters do not command the insider language of the city and are made to confuse "Naches" (joy) with "Nachos." But even this attribution of a special language to the Jewish characters in the drama has its limits. At the conclusion of the play the mother of the Jewish protagonist, whose discourse was marked by the Yiddishisms associated with the city, turns to her daughter and says: "Why do you speak so much Yiddish? We never spoke so much Yiddish around the house."[36] One can be "too Jewish" even in this very Jewish world, where the "real" language of the city is one with its inhabitants. Like Saul Bellow's Upper West Side in *Mr. Sammler's Planet*, this is a tortuous place for Jews whose very voice reveals them as Jews.

New York, the city which is itself a disease, becomes the locus of one's sense of alienation from the self. It is not merely that more Jews live in New York than in Jerusalem, but that there is a traditional association between the idea of the American city and that of the Jew. For the nineteenth- and early twentieth-century mind, cities are places of disease and the Jews are the quintessential city dwellers. For the turn-of-the-century Vienna psychiatrist Richard Krafft-Ebing, the Jew is the ultimate "city person" whose sensibilities are dulled.[37] And for Henry James, returning to the haunts of his childhood in 1907, this city of Jews—New York—is the deathbed of the English language, the "East side cafes" have become the "torture rooms of the living idioms."[38] After the Shoah the "hidden" language of the Jews in New York continues to be represented in the language of the immigrant-survivor (the mixed dialects of Merkin's sister as well as literary figures such as the protagonist of Saul Bellow's *Mr. Sammler's Planet*). Merkin attempts to set herself apart from this tradition by merging her language with the general culture, but the discourse of her attempt at acculturation, the language of "New Yawk" is also marked as a language of Jews, but of American Jews not of the European survivor.

The image of the city of Jews haunts Adolf Hitler's image of Vienna, the city in which he first learns to "see" the Jew and, therefore, becomes aware of the "hidden" difference in this language of the Jew—even when he or she is speaking "good" German. Merkin attempts to make the acculturation of her Jewish discourse into a positive marker; one can, however, note that the "Jewish American Princess" speaks a similar "jargon." Debbie Lukatsky and Sandy Barnett Toback in their *Jewish American Princess Handbook* (1982) append a glossary of "Jewish Jargon" to the volume.[39] "Jewish" terms such as "Chuppa" ("Marriage canopy. More decorative than symbolic") and "shagits" ("blond haired, blue eyed forbidden fruit who ends up marrying a shiksa") compete with terms such as "Guilt" ("Jewish hereditary disease. Symptoms including a churning stomach and feelings of deep-seated anxiety. Highly contagious, especially when the Princess spends too much time in the company of her mother") and "money" ("the ultimate aphrodisiac [Credit cards acceptable]"). Such lists were standard in all of the anti-Semitic literature of the late nineteenth and early twentieth centuries, when West European Jews were no longer marked by a "special" accent, as they came to speak German, French, or English. The lists pointed to the inherent hidden language of the Jew, his or her cultural difference and corruption. This legend of the Jew who sounds Jewish now takes on new meaning for Jews in the 1980s.

Merkin brings her piece to a close with the realization that "there is no sign that the world has grown more fond of the Jews, so there is no sign I will ever be free of a certain fascination with the darker impulses at work in myself and others. . . . There is some kind of relief in being able to recognize the aggressor, even identify with him for a while, and then walk on. Like tipping one's hat at one's enemy, it may not be a grandstanding gesture, but it's definitely a civilized one" (85). The true civilized gesture in Merkin's piece, however, lies not in its message, but in its medium. Her essay on the seduction of the Other who is one's self was written in a completely acculturated style and appeared in *Esquire*, a popular "men's" magazine with intellectual pretensions. Merkin's act of writing frees her from her sense of self-hatred in proving that she really is a member of the cultural elite of "New Yawk."

The discourse concerning the internalization of difference appears throughout contemporary Jewish writing. Daniel Landes, director of the National Education Project of the Simon Wiesenthal Center in Los Angeles, wrote in a controversial issue of *Tikkun* that the very abuse of the metaphor of the Shoah by Jews and Christians alike reflects the essence of the "self-hating" Jew:

> There really are Jews who have internalized the anti-Semitism of the societies in which they live, and who feel angry at the parts of themselves that are distinguishably Jewish. The self-hating Jews have a quandary. On some level they identify as Jews, but they simultaneously deny an essential part of that definition; either peoplehood, religious culture, or the Jews' historical relationship to the land of Israel. The Israel/Nazi analogy relieves the self-hating Jews of this tension: they can be good prophetic Jews by opposing exclusivistic Jews, fanatical Judaism, and the "Fascist" Jewish state.[40]

The discourse of the "self-hating Jew" becomes the marker of the "corrupt" (and "corrupting") locus of where the "real" Jew, the evil Jew lurks. Landes's need to "define" the Jew in a narrow manner which includes himself (evidently not a "self-hating Jew") but excludes others is striking. The pure internalization of a negative image—as in the case of those Italian "Jews" who literally discovered their "Jewishness" with the promulgation of the fascist racial laws in 1938—is not a possibility for Landes. It is the rejection of some intrinsic quality of "Jewishness"—which would include a contemporary political definition which puts their discourse, their generation of a corrupting metaphor "beyond the Pale."

Phillip Lopate, one of the literary editors of *Tikkun*, presented a similar argument—but in a very different context.[41] He is—if the subsequent exchange with Jehuda Bauer in *Tikkun* is any indicator—precisely the sort of "self-hating Jew" whom Landes condemns. In a long piece on "Resistance to the Holocaust" Lopate critiques the "kitsch" aspects of the Shoah, seeing it as an event among others in world history and bemoans the special, indeed central, status given to it by many contemporary Jews in the United States and Israel. He notes that his first exposure to this "Shoah-ization" (my word—not his) of the discourse of modern Jewry came in a "large communal seder in Houston, about 1982": " . . . the introduction of references to the Holocaust in every second or third prayer seemed to have a different function. For many of the people at that seder in Texas, the Shoah was the heart of their faith; it was what touched them most deeply about being Jewish. The religion itself—the prayers, the commentaries, the rituals, the centuries of accumulated wisdom and tradition—had shriveled to a sort of marginally necessary preamble for this negative miracle." This is the negative, corrupt discourse of the Jew—the replacement of a "true" language of difference (in the prayers, commentaries, etc.) with a false center—the metaphor of the Shoah. But what is the "real" reason for this substitution, indeed what is the "real" hidden language which marks the "true Jew" according to Lopate? He writes that: "The importance of the Shoah for such assimilated Jews must be considered within the broader framework of the erosion of Jewish group memory in the modern period. By group or "collective" memory, I mean simply all the customs, rituals, ceremonies, folkways, Yiddishkeit, cuisine, historical events, and so on that used to be the common inheritance of every Jew." This is an extraordinary leap—one which must be contrasted with that of Merkin and Landes.

The real Jew is the Eastern Jew—whose "Yiddishkeit" (and Lopate stresses the authenticity of this experience by employing the "real" language of the Jews—Yiddish) is the mark of the "hidden" language of the Jew. This is the "New Yawk" of Merkin, the goal which she, as the child of Shoah survivors seeks—the authenticity of a never-never world of the shtetl transported into Sholom Aleichem's "New Yawk." (It is also the counter-image of Philip Roth's "Faginy, Yiddish" image of the Jew employed by the British anti-Semite.) It is an intact world, a world with shared experiences—which excludes the "acculturated" survivors of the Shoah. For here Lopate reveals his hidden agenda. These Jews gathered

34

around the seder table in Houston may be many things, but they are not assimilated—they have not disappeared into the mass culture of the American experience. They may well be acculturated, like many of the Western and some of the Eastern European Jews who died in the Shoah, but their participation in a seder indicates their self-identification as part of a cultural sub-group. Lopate's definition of the Jew—like that of Landes—postulates a "good" Jew who sounds Jewish (Lopate, Landes) and a "bad" Jew who sounds Jewish (the object of their investigation). Their act of writing "proves" to the reader their command of the "good" discourse of the Jew.

Let us conclude this survey of the post-Shoah continuation of the myth of the "hidden" language of the Jews with a comment from the Indian poet Nissim Ezekiel. Ezekiel is an Anglophone Jewish poet who abandoned his mother tongue of Marathi to write poetry and drama in the dominant literary language of the commonwealth, English. This in a culture where "English" is a co-terminus concept with "Christian." In an interview he was asked whether having "been a Jew in India, sent first to a Catholic school and then a Presbyterian, and conscious of a sense of physical frailness" posed an identity problem for him?[42] He answered:

> Yes, it did create a problem. I did have a feeling of things loaded against myself, with no prospect of getting strength and confidence. My background did make me an outsider; but its too easy to talk of being an outsider. I don't want to remain negative: I feel I have to connect, and turn the situation to the positive.

But he noted that "the notion of being a world poet" makes him "feel a little empty, rootless. One needs some sense of belonging. But there is a trap in identifying one's audience in terms of specific geographic location. I write my poems for anyone who is likely to enjoy them in any part of the world, in any time." This view of literature as a "safe space" in which even the language of the Jew can be heard is echoed in his "Minority Poem" from the early 1980s:

> In my room, I talk
> to my invisible guests:
> they do not argue but wait

Till I am exhausted
then they slip away
with inscrutable faces.

I lack the means to change
their amiable ways,
although I love their gods.

It's the language really
separates, whatever else
is shared. . . . [43]

Nissim Ezekiel's attempt to bridge this perceived gap between his Jewish culture and the cultures among which he lives is to be found in his "Latter-Day Psalms," his rewriting of a series of biblical texts into the language of modern Anglo-Indian poetry. His deeply felt attempts to capture the world of Bene-Israel life in poems such as his "Jewish Wedding in Bombay" still places the voice of the Anglophone-Jewish writer in the position of the poet *per se*. There is nothing "Jewish" about his language, even though his themes may evoke the difference and separateness of the Jew. For Nissim Ezekiel's language, in marked contrast to the parodied language of his "Very Indian Poems in Indian English," are written in the language of Anglophone high culture. It is in the international world of letters, of Anglophone ("Christian") high culture that the Jew—whether in Houston, "New Yawk," or Bombay, can find a space which is seemingly neutral. But it is of course only seemingly so. For the trap is that high culture in Germany and in the United States provides a medium for Jews to "escape" the label of being unable to control the language in which they write and think, but it also lends it credibility. For "high" culture is indeed on one level the secularized fetishism of the text as practiced by Christianity.

The roots of our contemporary sense of the centrality of books is rooted in the centrality of the Book (taken over and refashioned from Judaism) which dominates the so-called Judeo-Christian world. The discourse of Western culture never completely lacks the claim that Jews cannot be part of "true" culture. One can think about Gore Vidal's attack on Norman Podhoretz in 1986 when he charged that certain American Jews were more concerned with their "Jewish" identities (i.e., Israeli politics) than their "American" cultural identities.[44] "High" culture does not provide the bulwark against the charge of being different; indeed it provides, as Sacvan Bercovitch has so cogently argued, a set of definitions for difference which seem to be more and more and concrete.[45] These ideological limits are present within the image of the Jew in Western high culture from the very beginnings of Christianity through to the present day. They are present in an infinite series of variations and permutations, but they exist within all of Western culture.

2

THE JEWISH FOOT

A Foot-Note to the Jewish Body

◆

The construction of the Jewish body in the nineteenth and early twentieth centuries is linked to the underlying ideology of anti-Semitism, to the view that the Jew is inherently different. But different from what? We must fill in the blank. The difference of the Jewish body is absolute within the Western tradition; its counter-image (from the comments of Paul, Eusebius, and Origen on the "meaning" of circumcision) is the "Christian" body which eventually becomes secularized into the "German" or "English" body with the rise of the modern body politic. Thus it is of little surprise that the image of the Jewish body shifts from the rhetoric of religious anti-Judaism to the rhetoric of the pseudoscience of anti-Semitism. By the nineteenth century, with the establishment of the hegemony of "science" within European (and colonial) culture, there is no space more highly impacted with the sense of difference about the body of the Jew than the public sphere of "medicine." No aspect of the representation of the Jewish body in that sphere, whether fabled or real, is free from the taint of the claim of the special nature of the Jewish body as a sign of the inherent difference of the Jew. As Bernhard Berliner has noted: "The total appearance of the Jew, physical and spiritual, inspires the Gentile with a secret fear which is in tune with his own fear of the father of his childhood."[1]

The Jewish Foot

The very analysis of the nature of the Jewish body, in the broader culture or within the culture of medicine, has always been linked to establishing the difference (and dangerousness) of the Jew. This scientific vision of parallel and unequal "races" is part of the polygenetic argument about the definition of "race" within the scientific culture of the eighteenth century. In the nineteenth century it is more strongly linked to the idea that some "races" are inherently weaker, "degenerate," more at risk for certain types of disease than others. In the world of nineteenth-century medicine, this difference becomes labeled as the "pathological" or "pathogenic" qualities of the Jewish body. What this chapter will examine is a "footnote" to the general representation of the pathophysiology of the Jew: the meaning attributed to the Jewish foot in the general and medical culture of the late nineteenth century.

The idea that the Jew's foot is unique has analogies with the hidden sign of difference attributed to the cloven-footed devil of the middle ages. That the shape of the foot, hidden within the shoe (a sign of the primitive and corrupt masked by the cloak of civilization and higher culture) could reveal the difference of the devil, was assumed in early modern European culture.[2] But the association between the sign of the devil and the sign of disease was well established in the early modern era. The view which associates the faulty gait of the Jew with disease caused by demonic influence is at least as old as Robert Burton's *Anatomy of Melancholy*, where Burton writes of the "pace" of the Jews, as well as "their voice, . . . gesture, [and] looks," as a sign of "their conditions and infirmities."[3] Johann Jakob Schudt, the seventeenth-century Orientalist, commented on the "crooked feet" of the Jews among other signs of their physical inferiority.[4] By the nineteenth century the relationship between the image of the Jew and that of the hidden devil is to be found not in a religious but in a secularized scientific context. It still revolves in part around the particular nature of the Jew's foot—no longer the foot of the devil but now the pathognomonic foot of the "bad" citizen of the new national state. The political significance of the Jew's foot within the world of nineteenth-century European medicine is thus closely related to the idea of the "foot"-soldier, of the popular militia, which was the

hallmark of all of the liberal movements of the mid-century. The
Jew's foot marked him (and the Jew in this discussion is almost
always the male) as congenitally unable and, therefore, unworthy
of being completely integrated into the social fabric of the modern
state. This was echoed, for example, in Johann David Michaelis's
answer in 1783 to Christian Wilhelm Dohm's call for the civil emancipation of the Jews. Michaelis argued that Jews could not become
true citizens because they were worthless as soldiers due to their
physical stature.[5] (That the Jewish woman had a special place in
the debate about the nature of the Jewish body is without a doubt
true, but it was not in regard to her role as a member of the body
politic. In the context of nineteenth-century science it was assumed
that she could not function in this manner.[6])

As early as 1804, in Joseph Rohrer's study of the Jews in the
Austrian monarchy, the weak constitution of the Jew and its public
sign, "weak feet," were cited as "the reason that the majority of Jews
called into military service were released, because the majority of
Jewish soldiers spent more time in the military hospitals than in
military service."[7] This link of the weak feet of the Jews and their
inability to be full citizens (at a time when citizenship was being
extended piecemeal to the Jews) was for Rohrer merely one further
sign of the inherent, intrinsic difference of the Jews. What is of
interest is how this theme of the weakness of the Jews' feet (in the
form of flat feet or impaired gait) becomes part of the necessary
discourse about Jewish difference in the latter half of the nineteenth
century [PLATE 5].[8]

There is an ongoing debate throughout the late nineteenth century and well into the twentieth century which continues the basic
theme which Rohrer raised in 1804. The liberal novelist and journalist, Theodor Fontane felt constrained to comment in 1870 on the
false accusation that Jews were "unfitted" for war in his observa-
tions about the role which Jewish soldiers played in the Seven
Weeks War of 1866 (which led to the creation of the dual monarchy
and the liberal Austrian constitution). His example is telling to
measure the power of the legend of the Jewish foot: "Three Jews
had been drafted as part of the reserves into the first battalion of
the Prince's Own Regiment. One, no longer young and corpulent,

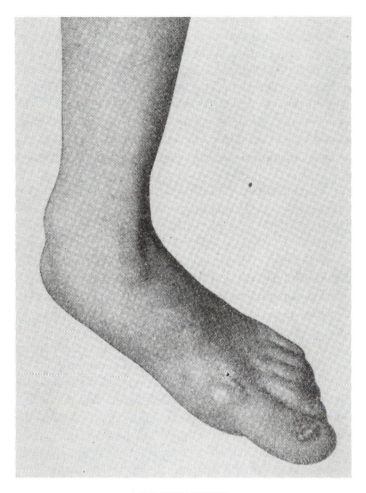

PLATE FIVE

The image of a flat foot illustrating Gustav Muskat's essay on the diseases of the feet in Max Joseph, *Handbuch der Kosmetik* (Leipzig: Veit & Comp., 1912) (Source: National Library of Medicine, Bethesda, MD).

suffered horribly. His feet were open sores. And yet he fought in the burning sun from the beginning to the end of the battle of Gitschin. He could not be persuaded to go into hospital before the battle."[9] For Fontane, the Jewish foot serves as a sign of the suffering that the Jew must overcome to become a good citizen. This becomes part of the liberal image of the Jew. In America, Mark Twain finds it necessary to place special stress on the role of the Jew as soldier in his 1898 defense of the Jews, noting that the Jew had to overcome much greater difficulties in order to become a soldier than did the Christian.[10]

In 1867 Austria institutionalized the ability of the Jews to serve in the armed services as one of the basic rights of the new liberal constitution. This became not only one of the general goals of the Jews but also one of their most essential signs of acculturation. But, as in many other arenas of public service, being "Jewish" (here, espousing the Jewish religion) served as a barrier to status. Steven Beller points out that at least in Austria there was "in the army evidence [that there was] a definite link between conversion and promotion."[11] István Deák observed that "of the twenty-three pre-1911 Jewish generals and colonels in the army's combat branches, fourteen converted at some point during their career, although some only at the very end."[12] Indeed, one of the legends which grew up about the young, "liberal" monarch Franz Joseph of the 1850s, was that he promoted a highly decorated corporal from the ranks when he discovered that the soldier had not been previously promoted because of the fact that he was a Jew. Franz Joseph is said to have remarked: "In the Austrian army there are no Jews, only soldiers, and a soldier who deserves it becomes an officer."[13] Evidently it was difficult but not impossible to achieve the rank of officer. And Jews wanted to be officers. Theodor Fontane observed that "it seemed as if the Jews had promised themselves to make an end of their old notions about their dislike for war and inability to engage in it."[14] The status associated with the role of the Jew as soldier was paralleled by the increasingly intense anti-Semitic critique of the Jewish body as inherently unfit for military service. This critique became more and more important as the barriers of Jewish entry into the armed services in Germany and Austria were

PLATE SIX

The Jew as soldier in the frontispiece to H. Naudh [i.e., H. Nordmann], *Israel im Heere* (Leipzig: Hermann Beyer, 1893). His body and his physiognomy set him apart as different and as diseased (Source: Private Collection, Ithaca).

lessened in the closing decades of the nineteenth century. What had been an objection based on the Jew's religion came to be pathologized as an objection to the Jewish body. Images of Jewish difference inherent within the sphere of religion become metamorphosed into images of the Jew within the sphere of public service.

In 1893 H. Nordmann published a pamphlet on "Israel in the Army" in which the Jew's inherent unfittedness for military service is the central theme **[PLATE 6].**[15] The title image stressed the Jew's badly formed, unmilitary body. At the same time a postcard showing an ill-formed "little Mr. Kohn," the eponymous Jew in German caricatures of the period, showing up for his induction into the military was in circulation in Germany **[PLATE 7].**[16] And in the Viennese fin-de-siècle humor magazine, *Kikeriki*, the flat and malformed feet of the Jew served as an indicator of the Jewish body almost as surely as the shape of the Jewish nose **[PLATE 8].**[17] By

PLATE SEVEN

German postcards represented the body of the Jew as deformed and unsoldierly. Here "little Mr. Kohn" is about to be inducted into the armed services. (Source: Private Collection, Ithaca).

the 1930s the image of the Jew's feet had become ingrained in the representation of the Jewish body. The Nazi caricaturist Walter Hofmann, who drew under the name of "Waldl," illustrated how the Jew's body had been malformed because of the Jew's own refusal to obey his own God's directives.[18] Central to his representation are the Jew's flat feet. The foot became the hallmark of difference, of the Jewish body being separate from the real "body politic" **[PLATE 9]**. These images aimed at a depiction of the Jew as unable to function within the social institutions, such as the armed forces, which determined the quality of social acceptance. "Real" acceptance would be true integration into the world of the armed forces.

The Jewish reaction to the charge that the Jew cannot become a member of society because he cannot serve in the armed services is one of the foci of the Jewish response to turn-of-the-century anti-Semitism. The "Defense Committee against Anti-Semitic Attacks in Berlin" published its history of "Jews as soldiers" in 1897 in order

Ein Albumblatt für den „Kunstkritiker" der „Neuen Freien Presse"

PLATE EIGHT

The notorious, anti-Semitic Viennese fin-de-siècle humor magazine, *Kikeriki*, presented its image of the art critic of the *New Free Press* (Vienna), a liberal paper with a Jewish owner. Bearing a scroll with the motto, "anything for money," the Jewish critic was given the essential image of the Jew's body. From Eduard Fuchs, *Die Juden in der Karikatur* (Munich: Langen, 1921) (Source: Private Collection, Ithaca).

Was kann der Sigismund dafür, daß er so schön ist?...

Als der liebe Gott den Juden schuf, formte er ihn, gleich Adam, aus feuchtem Lehm. Dann ließ er ihn in der Sonne liegen zu bleiben, damit er trockne.

Weil aber der Jude von Anfang an das Licht scheute und das Dunkel vorzog, pfiff er auf das Gebot des wahren Gottes und verduftete lieber vorzeitig.

Da der Lehm noch feucht und welch war, bekam der Fürwitzige gleich nach den ersten Schritten nicht nur abnorme O-Beine, sondern auch Plattfüße.

Als der Schöpfer dieses Zerrbild seines „Ebenbildes" sah, ergrimmte er und schleuderte dem Flüchtenden so heftig einen Meteor nach, daß dieser aufs Gesicht fiel.

Der Jude erhob sich wieder. Nun war er auch im Gesichte gezeichnet. Was Wunder, wenn er da noch heute flucht und sich durch „Gottlosenverbände" zu rächen sucht.

PLATE NINE

The Nazi caricaturist Walter Hofmann, who drew under the name of "Waldl," presented a series of images of the construction of the Jewish body in a cartoon strip ironically entitled "What can Sigismund do about the fact that he is so pretty?" The body of Sigismund, the archetypal Jew was literally constructed, like that of Adam or the golem, from wet clay, but the Jew disobeyed the divine order and arose before his body was truly formed: "Since the clay was still damp and soft, the smarty developed after the first few steps extraordinary bandy legs, but also flat feet." Walter Hofmann, *Lacht ihn tot! Ein tendenziöses Bilderbuch von Waldl* (Dresden: Nationalsozialistischer Verlag für den Gau Sachsen, n.d.) (Source: Private Collection, Ithaca).

to document the presence of Jews in the German army throughout the nineteenth century.[19] After the end of World War I, this view of Jewish non-participation became the central topos of political anti-Semitism. It took the form of the "Legend of the Stab in the Back" (*Dolchstosslegende*) which associated Jewish slackers (war profiteers who refused to serve at the front) with the loss of the war.[20] In 1919 a brochure with the title "The Jews in the War: A Statistical Study using Official Sources" was published by Alfred Roth which accused the Jews of having systematically avoided service during the war in order to undermine the war effort of the home front.[21] On the part of the official Jewish community in Germany, Jacob Segall in 1922 provided a similar statistical survey to the 1897 study in which he defended the role of the Jewish soldier during the World War I against the charge of feigning inabilities in order to remain on the home front.[22] In the same year, Franz Oppenheimer drew on Segall's findings in order to provide an equally detailed critique of this charge, a charge which by 1922 had become a commonplace of anti-Semitic rhetoric.[23]

There were also attempts on the part of Jewish physicians to counter the argument about the weakness of the Jewish body within the body politic. Their arguments are, however, even more convoluted and complicated, because of the constraints imposed by the rhetoric of science. As Jewish scientists, they needed to accept the basic "truth" of the statistical arguments of medical science during this period. They could not dismiss published statistical "facts" out of hand and thus operated within these categories. Like Segall and Oppenheimer, who answer one set of statistics with another set of statistics, the possibility of drawing the method of argument into disrepute does not exist for these scientists, as their status as scientists rested upon the validity of positivistic methods. And their status as scientists provided a compensation for their status as Jews. As Jews, they were the object of the scientific gaze; as scientists, they were themselves the observing, neutral, universal eye.

German-Jewish scientists attempted to resolve this dilemma. In 1908 the German-Jewish eugenist Dr. Elias Auerbach of Berlin undertook a medical rebuttal, in an essay entitled "The Military Qualifications of the Jew," of the "fact" of the predisposition of the

47

Jew for certain disabilities which precluded him from military service.[24] Auerbach begins by attempting to "correct" the statistics which claimed that for every 1000 Christians in the population there were 11.61 soldiers, but for 1000 Jews in the population there were only 4.92 soldiers. His correction (based on the greater proportion of Jews entering the military who were volunteers and, therefore, did not appear in the statistics) still finds that a significant portion of Jewish soldiers were unfit for service (according to his revised statistics, of every 1000 Christians there were 10.66 soldiers; of 1000 Jews, 7.76). He accepts the physical differences of the Jew as a given, but questions whether there is a substantive reason that these anomalies should prevent the Jew from serving in the military. He advocates the only true solution that will make the Jews of equal value as citizens: the introduction of "sport" and the resultant reshaping of the Jewish body.[25] Likewise, Heinrich Singer attributes the flat feet of the Jew to the "generally looser structure of the Jews' musculature."[26]

More directly related to the emblematic nature of the Jewish foot is the essay by Gustav Muskat, a Berlin orthopedist, which asks the question of "whether flat feet are a racial marker of the Jew?"[27] He refutes the false charge that "the clumsy, heavy-footed gait of the Semitic race made it difficult for Jews to undertake physical activity, so that their promotion within the military was impossible." While seeing flat feet as the "horror of all generals," he also refutes the charge that Jews are particularly at risk as a group from this malady. Like Auerbach, Muskat sees the problem of the weaknesses of the Jewish body as a "real" one. For him, it is incontrovertible that Jews have flat feet. Thus the question he addresses is whether this pathology is an inherent quality of the Jewish body which would preclude the Jew from becoming a full-fledged member of secular (i.e., military) society. For Muskat the real problem is the faulty development of the feet because of the misuse of the foot. The opinion that it is civilization and its impact on the otherwise "natural" body which marks the Jew becomes one of the major arguments against the idea of the sign value of the Jewish foot as a sign of racial difference.[28] The Jew is, for the medical literature of the nineteenth century, the ultimate example of the effect of civilization (i.e., the city and "modern life") on the individual.[29] And civilization in the form of the Jewish-dominated city, "is the real center for the degeneration of the race and the reduction of military readiness."[30] The Jewish foot, like the foot of the criminal and the epileptic, becomes a sign of Jewish difference. **[PLATE 10]** The Jew is both the city dweller par excellence as well as the most evident victim of the city.[31] And the occupation of the Jew in the city, the Jew's role as merchant, is the precipitating factor for the shape of the Jew's feet.[32]

For nineteenth-century medicine cities are places of disease and the Jews are the quintessential city dwellers. It is the "citification" of the Jew, to use Karl Kautsky's term, which marks the Jewish foot.[33] The diseases of civilization are the diseases of the Jew. In 1940 Leopold Boehmer can speak of the "foot as the helpless victim of civilization."[34] The shape of the Jew's foot is read in this context as the structure of the Jewish mind, the pathognomonic status of the Jew's body as a sign of the Jew's inherent difference. The Jew's body can be seen and measured in a manner which fulfills all of the positivistic fantasies about the centrality of physical signs and symptoms for the definition of pathology. It can be measured as the mind cannot.

Muskat's argument is a vital one. He must shift the argument away from the inherited qualities of the Jewish body to the social anomalies inflicted on the body (and feet) of all "modern men" by their lifestyle. He begins his essay with a refutation of the analogy present within the older literature which speaks about the flat foot of the black (and by analogy of the Jew) as an atavistic sign, a sign of the earlier stage of development (in analogy to the infant who lacks a well-formed arch). Muskat notes that flat feet have linked the black and the Jew as "throw-backs" to more primitive forms of life. He quotes a nineteenth-century ethnologist, Karl Hermann Burmeister, who in 1855 commented that "Blacks and all of those with flat feet are closest to the animals." Muskat begins his essay by denying that flat feet are a racial sign for any group, but rather a pathological sign of the misuse of the feet. (But he carefully avoids the implications that this misuse is the result of the urban location of the Jew or the Jew's inability to deal with the benefits of civiliza-

PLATE TEN

The gait of the criminal and the epileptic marked them as degener-
ates as surely as did their physiognomy. From Cesare Lombroso,
*Der Verbrecher (Homo Delinquens) in anthropologischer, ärztlicher
und juristischer Beziehung*, trans. M. O. Fraenkel (Hamburg: Actien-
Gesellschaft, 1890) (Source: National Library of Medicine,
Bethesda, MD).

tion.) He cites as his authorities a number of "modern" liberal commentators such as the famed Berlin physician-politician Rudolf Virchow, who had examined and commented on the feet of the black in order to refute the implication that flat feet are a sign of racial difference. Like other Jewish commentators, Muskat is constrained to acknowledge the "reality" of the "flat feet" of both the Jew and the black, but cites the renowned orthopedist Albert Hoffa[35] to the effect that only four percent of all flat feet are congenital. Flat feet are not a racial sign, they are "merely" a sign of the abuse of the foot. That 25% of all recruits in Austria and 30% in Switzerland were rejected for flat feet is a sign for Muskat that the Jewish recruit is no better nor worse than his Christian counterpart. (He never cites the rate of the rejection of Jewish recruits.) Muskat's rebuttal of the standard bias which sees the foot as a sign of the racial difference of the Jew still leaves the Jew's foot deformed. What Muskat has done is to adapt the view of the corruption of the Jew by civilization (and of civilization by the Jew) to create a space where the Jew's foot has neither more nor less signification as a pathological sign than does the flat foot in the general population. This attempt at the universalization of the quality ascribed to the Jewish foot does not however counter the prevailing sense of the specific meaning ascribed to the Jew's foot as a sign of difference.

Moses Julius Gutmann repeats the association between the classical image of the flat foot and the new neurological syndrome in his 1920 dissertation which attempted to survey the entire spectrum of charges concerning the nature of the Jewish body. Gutmann dismisses the common wisdom that " 'all Jews have flat feet' as excessive."[36] He notes, as does Muskat, that Jews seem to have a more frequent occurrence of this malady (8 to 12% higher than the norm for the general population). And his source, like that of Muskat, are the military statistics. But Gutmann accepts the notion that Jews have a peculiar pathological construction of the musculature of the lower extremities.

In a standard handbook of eugenics published as late as 1940, the difference in the construction of the musculature of the foot is cited as the cause of the different gait of the Jew.[37] The German physician-writer Oskar Panizza, in his depiction of the Jewish body, observed that the Jew's body language was clearly marked: "When he walked, Itzig always raised both thighs almost to his mid-rift so that he bore some resemblance to a stork. At the same time he lowered his head deeply into his breast-plated tie and stared at the ground. Similar disturbances can be noted in people with spinal diseases. However, Itzig did not have a spinal disease, for he was young and in good condition."[38] The Jew looks as if he is diseased, but it is not the stigmata of degeneracy which the observer is seeing, but the Jew's natural stance.

This image of the pathological nature of the gait of the Jews is linked to their inherently different anatomical structure. Flat feet remain a significant sign of Jewish difference in German science through the Nazi period. And it is always connected with the discourse about military service. According to the standard textbook of German racial eugenics by Baur, Fischer and Lenz in 1936: "Flat feet are especially frequent among the Jews. Salaman reports during the World War that about a sixth of the 5000 Jewish soldiers examined had flat feet while in a similar sample of other English soldiers it occurred in about a fortieth."[39] In 1945 Otmar Freiherr von Verschuer can still comment without the need for any further substantiation that great numbers of cases of flat feet are to be found among the Jews.[40]

The debate about the special nature of the Jew's foot and gait enters into another sphere, that of neurology, which provides a series of links between the inherent nature of the Jew's body and his psyche. This concept, too, has a specific political and social dimension. The assumption, even among those physicians who saw this as a positive quality was that the Jews were innately unable to undertake physical labor:

> In no period in the history of this wonderful people since their dispersion, do we discover the faintest approach to any system amongst them tending to the studied development of physical capacity. Since they were conquered they have never from choice borne arms nor sought distinction in military prowess; they have been little inducted, during their pilgrimages, into the public games of the countries in which they have been located; their own

ordinances and hygienic laws, perfect in other particulars, are indefinite in respect to special means for the development of great corporeal strength and stature; and the fact remains, that as a people they have never exhibited what is considered a high physical standard. To be plain, during their most severe persecutions nothing told so strongly against them as their apparent feebleness of body.[41]

It is within such a medical discourse about the relationship between the Jews' inability to serve as a citizen and the form of the Jews' body that the debate about Jews and sport can be located. Elias Auerbach's evocation of sport as the social force to reshape the Jewish body had its origins in the turn-of-the-century call of the physician and Zionist leader Max Nordau for a "new Muscle Jew."[42] This view became a commonplace of the early Zionist literature, which called upon sport, as an activity, as one of the central means of shaping the new Jewish body.[43] Nordau's desire was not merely for an improvement in the physical wellbeing of the Jew, but rather an acknowledgment of the older German tradition which saw an inherent relationship between the healthy political mind and the healthy body. It was not merely *mens sana in corpore sano*, but the sign that the true citizen had a healthy body which provided his ability to be a full-scale citizen, itself a sign of mental health. Nordau's cry that we have killed our bodies in the stinking streets of the ghettoes and we must now rebuild them on the playing fields of Berlin and Vienna, is picked up by the mainstream of German-Jewish gymnastics.

In Vienna, at the third "Jewish Gymnastics Competition" a series of lectures on the need for increased exercise among the Jews departed from the assumption of a statistically provable physical degeneration of contemporary Jewry.[44] The medicalization of this theme is continued by M. Jastrowitz of Berlin in the *Jewish Gymnastics News*, the major Jewish newspaper devoted to gymnastics in 1908.[45] Jastrowitz accepts the basic premise of Nordau's conviction, that the Jewish body is at risk for specific diseases, and attempts to limit and focus this risk. For Jastrowitz the real disease of the Jews, that which marks their bodies, is a neurological deficit which

53

has been caused by the impact of civilization. Jastrowitz, like most of the Jewish physicians[46] of the fin de siècle, accepts the general view that Jews are indeed at special risk for specific forms of mental and neurological disease. He warns that too great a reliance on sport as a remedy may exacerbate these illnesses. For Jastrowitz, the attempt to create the "new muscle Jew" works against the inherent neurological weaknesses of the Jew. This is the link to the general attitude of organic psychiatry of the latter half of the nineteenth century which saw the mind as a product of the nervous system and assumed that "mind illness is brain illness." Thus the improvement of the nervous system through training the body would positively impact on the mind (so argued Nordau). Jastrowitz's view also assumes a relationship between body and mind and he fears that, given the inherent weakness of the Jewish nervous system, any alteration of the precarious balance would negatively impact on the one reservoir of Jewish strength, the Jewish mind. The Jew could forfeit the qualities of mind which have made him successful in the world by robbing his brain of oxygen through overexercise. For Nordau and Jastrowitz the relationship between the healthy body, including the healthy foot and the healthy gait, and the healthy mind is an absolute one. The only question left is whether the degeneration of the Jewish foot is alterable. For neurologists this problem could not simply be limited to orthopedic theory and treatment. More than that was at stake, as is clear from the debate (in which Sigmund Freud was involved) over the new diagnostic category of intermittent claudication.

"Claudication intermittente" was created by Jean Martin Charcot at the beginning of his medical career in 1858.[47] (Charcot taught not only Freud but also was Max Nordau's doctoral supervisor.) This diagnostic category was described by Charcot as the chronic reoccurrence of pain and tension in the lower leg, a growing sense of stiffness and finally a total inability to move the leg, which causes a marked and noticeable inhibition of gait. This occurs between a few minutes and a half hour after beginning a period of activity, such as walking. It spontaneously vanishes only to be repeated at regular intervals.

Charcot determined that this syndrome seems to be the result of the reduction of blood flow through the arteries of the leg leading to the virtual disappearance of any pulse from the four arteries which provide the lower extremity with blood. The interruption of circulation to the feet then leads to the initial symptoms and can eventually lead to even more severe symptoms such as spontaneous gangrene. Charcot's diagnostic category was rooted in work done by veterinarians, such as Bouley and Rademacher, who observed similar alterations in the gait of dray horses.[48] Charcot did not himself speculate on any racial predisposition for this syndrome, as he did on the origin of hysteria and diabetes.[49] Nevertheless, the image of the Jew's foot as an atavistic structure similar to the flat feet of the horse soon appeared at the very heart of neurological research on this syndrome. Like flat feet, intermittent claudication is a "reality," i.e., it exists in the real world, but, like flat feet, it was placed in a specific ideological context at the turn of the century.

What is vital is that this diagnostic category soon after Charcot's identification of it became one of the markers in neurology for the difference between the Jewish foot and that of the "normal" European. Intermittent claudication became part of the description of the pathological difference of the Jew. And it was, itself, differentiated from other "racially" marked categories which evoked the impairment of gait as part of their clinical presentation. Charcot clearly differentiated intermittent claudication from the chronic pain associated with the diabetic's foot (a diagnostic category so closely associated with Jews in nineteenth-century medicine that it was commonly called the "Jewish disease"[50]). In 1911 Dejerine also differentiated this syndrome from "spinal intermittent claudication."[51] This was one of the syndromes associated with syphilis, a disease which also had a special relationship to the representation of the Jew in nineteenth-century and early twentieth-century medicine. What is clear is that the sign of the "limping Jew" was read into a number of diagnostic categories of nineteenth-century neurology.

Very quickly intermittent claudication became one of the specific diseases associated with Eastern European Jews. H. Higier in Warsaw published a long paper in 1901 in which he summarized the state of the knowledge about intermittent claudication as a sign of the racial makeup of the Jew.[52] The majority of the 23 patients he examined were Jews and he found that the etiology of the disease was "the primary role of the neuropathic disposition [of the patients] and the inborn weakness of their peripheral circulatory system." By the time Higier published his paper at the turn of the century this was a given in the neurological literature. The debate about the flat feet of the Jews as a marker of social stigma gave way to the creation of a scientific discourse about the difference of the Jew's feet, a discourse which does not merely rely on the argument of atavism (which had been generally refuted in the neurological literature of the fin de siècle), but on the question of the relationship between the Jew's body and the Jew's mind through the image of the deficits of the neurological system. Intermittent claudication became a sign of inherent constitutional weakness, so that it was also to be found as a sign for the male hysteric.[53] Hysteria was, of course, also understood as a neurological deficit, one which, it was believed in the fin de siècle, was primarily to be found among Eastern European Jewish males. (The association of hysteria with impairment of gait has remained a truism of medical science for many decades. It can, in fact, be traced back to the eighteenth century.[54]) The hysterical and the limping Jew are related in the outward manifestation of their illness: both are represented by the inability of the limbs to function "normally," by the disruption of their gait, as in Sigmund Freud's case of "Dora" (1905 [1901]).[55]

The link between the older discussion of "flat feet" and the new category of intermittent claudication was examined by a number of sources. H. Idelsohn in Riga made the association between the Jews, Charcot's category of intermittent claudication, and flat feet overt when he examined his Jewish patients to see whether there was any inherent relationship between the fabled Jewish flat feet and inherent muscular weakness.[56] Idelsohn placed the discussion of the special nature of the Jewish foot into the context of a neurological deficit. While he did not wish to overdetermine this relationship (according to his own statement), he did find that there was reason to grant flat feet a "specific importance as an etiological moment." He described the flat foot, citing Hoffa, as "tending to sweat, often blue colored and cold, with extended veins . . . People with flat feet are often easily tired, and are incapable of greater exertion and marches."[57] He saw in this description a visual and structural analogy to Charcot's category of intermittent claudication. Heinrich Singer picked up Idelsohn's and Higier's views concerning the relationship between intermittent claudication and flat feet and repeated them as proof of the "general nervous encumbrance born by the Jewish race . . . ."[58] This conviction is echoed by Gustav Muskat in a paper of 1910, in which he made the link between the appearance of intermittent claudication and the pre-existing pathology of flat feet.[59]

One of Idelsohn's major sources for his attitude was a paper by Samuel Goldflam in Warsaw.[60] Goldflam was one of the most notable neurologists of the first half of the century and the co-discoverer of "Goldflam-Oehler sign" (the paleness of the foot after active movement) in the diagnosis of intermittent claudication.[61] Goldflam stressed the evident predisposition of Jews for this syndrome. What was also noteworthy in Goldflam's discussion of his patients was not only that they were all Eastern Jews, but that they almost all were very heavy smokers. He does attribute a role in the etiology of the disease to tobacco intoxication.[62] Idelsohn argued that since *all* of Goldflam's patients were Jews, it is clear that intermittent claudication was primarily a Jewish disease and that this is proven by the relationship between the evident sign of the difference of the Jewish foot, the flat foot, and its presence in a number of his own cases. Its absence in the clinical description given by Goldflam (and others) was attributed by him to its relatively benign and usual occurrence, which is often overlooked because of the radical problems, such as gangrene, which occur with intermittent claudication.

In a major review essay on the "nervous diseases" of the Jews, Toby Cohn, the noted Berlin neurologist (long the assistant of the noted Emanuel Mendel at the University of Berlin), included intermittent claudication as one of his categories of neurological deficits.[63] While commenting on the anecdotal nature of the evidence, and calling on a review essay by Kurt Mendel (who does not discuss the question of "race" at all[64]), he accepted the specific nature of the Jewish risk for this syndrome while leaving the etiology open. Two radically different etiologies had been proposed: the first, as we have noted in Higier, Idelsohn and Singer, reflected on the neuropathic qualities of the Jewish body, especially in regard to diseases of the circulatory system. (Hemorrhoids, another vascular syndrome, were also identified as a "Jewish" disease during this period). The second, noted by Goldflam and Cohn, did not reflect on the inherent qualities of the Jewish foot, but on the Jewish misuse of tobacco and the resulting occlusion of the circulatory system of the extremities. It is tobacco which, according to Wilhelm Erb, played a major role in the etiology of intermittent claudication.[65] In a somewhat later study of forty-five cases of the syndrome, Erb found, to his own surprise, that at least thirty-five of his patients showed an excessive use of tobacco.[66] (This meant the consumption of 40–60 cigarettes or 10–15 cigars a day.) Indeed, the social dimension which the latter provide in their discussion of the evils of tobacco misuse supplies both an alternative and an explanation for the neurological predisposition of the Jew's body to avoid military service.[67] But according to all of these Western (or Western-trained) Jewish physicians, the misuse of tobacco is typical of the Eastern Jew, not of the Western Jew. Some years earlier, the noted Berlin neurologist Hermann Oppenheim also made the East-West distinction when he observed that of the cases of intermittent claudication in his practice (48 cases over five years) overwhelming majority, between 35 and 38, were Russian Jews.[68] For Oppenheim and many others, the Eastern Jew's mind is that of a social misfit and his body reifies this role, but this is not a problem of Western Jewry— except by extension.

Here the parameters of the meaning ascribed to the Jewish foot are set: Jews walk oddly because of the form of their feet and legs. This unique gait represents the inability of the Jew to function as a citizen within a state which defines full participation as military service. Jewish savants who rely on the status of science as central to their own self-definition, who cannot dismiss the statistical evidence of Jewish risk as nonsense, seek to "make sense" of it in a way which would enable them (as representatives of the authoritative voice of that very society) to see a way out. The "way out" is, in fact, the acceptance of difference through the attribution of this difference to social rather than genetic causes and its projection on to a group labeled as inherently "different," the Eastern Jews. This is an important moment in the work of these scientists—for the risk which they see lies in the East, lies in the "misuse" of tobacco by Eastern Jews. It is not accidental that the major reports on the nature of the Jew's gait come from Eastern Europe and are cited as signs of the difference in social attitudes and practices among Eastern European Jews. The rhetorical movement which these scientists undertook, implied an inherently different role for the Western Jew, serving in the armed forces of the Empire, whether German or Austrian. This movement was important, because the clean line between "nature" and "nurture" was blurred in nineteenth-century medicine. The physician of the nineteenth and early twentieth century understood that the appearance of signs of degeneration, such as the flat foot, may have been triggered by aspects in the social environment but was, at its core, an indicator of the inherent weakness of the individual. The corollary to this is the inheritance of acquired characteristics—that the physiological changes which the impact of environment triggers become part of the inheritance of an individual. This view can be found in the work of C. E. Brown-Séquard, who, as early as 1860, had argued that there were hereditary transmissions of acquired injuries, as in the case of "animals born of parents having been rendered epileptic by an injury to the spinal cord."[69] The damage rendered by environmental factors ("tobacco") to the Jewish foot thus mark the next generation. The loop is thus complete: whether hereditary or environmental, the qualities of "poor citizenship" are marked by the Jewish foot. For non-Jewish scientists of the late nineteenth century, this marker exists as a sign of the Jewish body. For Jewish scientists, whose orientation is Western (no matter what their actual geographic locus), these qualities are a sign of the atavistic nature of the Eastern Jews and serve as a boundary between the degenerated Jews in the East and the Western Jew.

3

THE JEWISH PSYCHE

Freud, Dora, and the
Idea of the Hysteric

◆

Sigmund Freud's reading of the ancient Greek myth of the wandering womb, which, when lodged in the throat, created the *globus
hystericus*, can serve us as a detailed example of the problems
attendant to "seeing" the hysteric.[1] It is well known that Freud, in
the autobiographical account he wrote of the occasion some forty
years after the event, recalled the "bad reception" which his initial
paper on male hysteria had when he presented it before the Viennese Society of Physicians on October 15, 1886.[2] Returning from
his work with Jean Martin Charcot in Paris and desiring to present
his newly acquired insights about male hysteria to his home audience in Vienna, Freud's powerful memory was that his hearers
thought what he "said was incredible. ... One of them, an old
surgeon, actually broke out with the exclamation: 'But, my dear
sir, how can you talk such nonsense? *Hysteron* (sic) means the
uterus. So how can a man be hysterical?'"[3] Freud's angry memory
was aimed at the narrow-minded claim of the Viennese establishment, that it, and it alone, had command of Greek. It was the young,
French-trained Freud who knew that the concept of hysteria was
tied to universals (which, at that point, he understood as trauma)

and was not merely a reflex of the biological uniqueness of a sub-group. It was hysteria (the hallmark of the new science) that Freud wished to rescue from the crabbed claws of a Viennese medical establishment which could not even get its Greek correct, for *hustera* is the correct form of the Greek noun for uterus. Thus the young Jew (and Freud understood himself from his exposure to the virulent "scientific" anti-Semitism of the Viennese University as a Jew) showed his command over not only the language of science (represented by Charcot's discourse on hysteria) but also the language of culture (Greek). (The significance of this factor will be shown in the course of this analysis.) Freud's understanding as the understanding of his time was that hysteria did not manifest itself as a disease of the "womb" but of the imagination. This did not absolve the female from being the group most at risk, however, for the idea of a pathological human imagination structurally replaced the image of the floating womb as the central etiology of hysteria. What was removed from the category of hysteria as Freud brought it back to Vienna was its insistence on another group, the Jews, which replaced the woman as essentially at risk.

Hysteria was a disease which, according to nineteenth-century science, had to be seen to be understood. This Lineannean means of describing illnesses through their visible signs and symptoms (to use Jean Martin Charcot's term, taken from the witch-hunting manuals of the Inquisition, the *stigmata* of the illness, from the *stigmata diaboli* which marked the bodies of the witch) dominated nineteenth-century European, but especially French, psychiatry. To describe was to understand, to describe in the most accurate manner meant to avoid the ambiguity of words and rely on the immediate, real image of the sufferer.

But the malleability of the symptoms in hysteria troubled the fin-de-siècle scientist. As Charcot noted "symptoms . . . have their destiny: *Habent sua fata.*"[4] Symptoms, "after having enjoyed a certain degree of favour, doubtless on account of the theoretical considerations connected with [them, have] gone somewhat out of fashion. . . ." But this is to be understood from the standpoint only of the physician-nosologist; from the standpoint of the patient, the symptoms are real, even if the patients are duplicitous: "You will meet with [simulation] at every step in the history of hysteria, and one finds himself sometimes admiring the amazing craft, sagacity, and perseverance which women, under the influence of this great neurosis, will put in play for the purposes of deception—especially when the physician is to be the victim. . . . It is incontestable that, in a multitude of cases, they have taken pleasure in distorting, by exaggerations, the principal circumstances of their disorder, in order to make them appear extraordinary and wonderful" (230). This deception is, for Charcot and his time, an absolute sign of the hysteric and it can only be read correctly by a "good" diagnostician.

For hysteria must be "seen" to have observable symptoms, such as the changes of the skin or the wasting of the body to be understood as a real disease: "Hysteria is a real disease, as real as smallpox or cancer, and . . . it has a physical basis, probably of a chemical nature, although this is yet very imperfectly understood."[5] As an early review of the first major journal from the Salpêtrière devoted to the visual representation of the insane noted, the camera was as necessary for the study of hysteria as the microscope was for histology.[6] This fantasy of "realism" captured the belief of the nineteenth century for both the doctor and—the patient. For the doctor, the image *is* the patient, as it is for the patient. This search for an ontological representation of illness parallels the undertaking of the exemplary contemporary scientist of the fin de siècle, Louis Pasteur, whose germ theory of contagious disease relied on the visibility of the germ for its power.[7] As Georges Canguilhem notes: "After all, a germ can be seen, even if this requires the complicated mediation of a microscope, stains and cultures, while we would never be able to see a miasma or an influence."[8] To see the patient means to develop the technique for seeing, a technique which is "scientific"; the patient, in turn, as the object of the medical gaze, becomes part of the process of the creation of an ontological representation of the disease, a representation which is labeled "hysteria." This does not deny the underlying "pathology" of the hysteric; it reflects only the "meaning" attributed to the symptoms created to represent the "pathology" as a disease.

The idea of the hysteric was a central one for the imaginative world of Sigmund Freud, as it was close to his self-definition. For at the end of the nineteenth century the idea of seeing the hysteric was closely bound to the idea of seeing the Jew—and very specifically the male Jew.[9] For if the visual representation of the hysteric within the world of images of the nineteenth century was the image of the female, its subtext was that feminized males, such as Jews, were also hysterics, and they too could be "seen." The face of the Jew was as much a sign of the pathological as was the face of the hysteric. But even more so, the face of the Jew became the face of the hysteric. Let us quote from one of the defenders of the Jews against the charge of being tainted by hysteria. Maurice Fishberg's *The Jews: A Study of Race and Environment* (1911) states the case boldly: "The Jews, as is well known to every physician, are notorious sufferers of the functional disorders of the nervous system. Their nervous organization is constantly under strain, and the least injury will disturb its smooth workings." But it is not *all* Jews, according to Fishberg, paraphrasing Raymond's study of mental illness in Russia: "The Jewish population of [Warsaw] alone is almost exclusively the inexhaustible source for the supply of specimens of hysterical humanity, particularly the hysteria in the male, for all the clinics of Europe."[10] It is the male Jew from the East, from the provinces, who is most at risk for hysteria. This remains a truism of medical science through the decades. Professor H. Strauß of Berlin, in one of the most cited studies of the pathology of the Jews, provides a bar chart representing the risk of the Jews for hysteria.[11] Here the relationship between men and women indicates that male Jews suffer twice as often from hysteria than do male non-Jews. While it is clear that women still are the predominant sufferers from the disease, it is evident from the visual representation of the cases of hysteria that there is a clear "feminization" of the male Jew in the context of the occurrence of hysteria. Freud's teacher, the liberal-Jewish neurologist Moriz Benedikt, also links the "American" quality of life with the appearance of hysteria, a disease which is understood by him as "a uniquely feminine nervous disease"—in men.[12] It is the struggle for life in the city which causes the madness of the male Jew: "Mental anxiety and worry are the most frequent causes of mental breakdown. They are all excitable and live excitable lives, being constantly under the high pressure of business in town."[13] The reason for this inability to cope with the stresses of modern life lies in "hereditary influences," i.e., in their being Jews.[14]

And that is written on their faces, as on the faces of women. William Thackeray, in *Codlingsby*, his parody of Disraeli's novels, has his eponymous protagonist revel in the aestheticized sight of the "ringlets glossy, and curly, and jetty—eyes black as night—midsummer night—when it lightens; haughty noses bending like beaks of eagles—eager quivering nostrils—lips curved like the bow of Love" of the Jews.[15] "Every man or maiden," looks Jewish—but also looks feminine—"every babe or matron in that English Jewry bore in his countenance one or more of these characteristics of his peerless Arab race." Codlingsby muses: "How beautiful they are!" when the jarring voice of Rafael Mendoza breaks his revery: "D'you vant to look at a nishe coast?" But the accent is not a true sign of the Jew's difference: "All traces of the accent with which he first addressed Lord Codlingsby had vanished, it was disguise: half the Hebrew's life is a disguise. He shields himself in craft, since the Norman boors persecuted him." The association between the falsity of the language of the Jews (which is not merely accented but duplicitous) is balanced by the "true" sight of the Jews—a factor which Thackeray parodies. This is equally true in a contemporary image of the Jew taken from *Punch*. **[PLATE 11]** What remains is that the "sight" of the Jew—the registration of the external signs of Jewishness—is a "truer" indicator of the nature of the Jew (or at least the perception of the Jew's nature in Thackeray's relativistic manner of representing the Jew) than is the mutable sign of the Jews' language, a language which is corrupted as well as corrupting by the world in which the Jew in the Diaspora lives.

The Jew was immediately visible. Francis Galton, the founder of "eugenics," tried to capture this "Jewish physiognomy" in his composite photographs of "boys in the Jews' Free School, Bell Lane."[16] Galton photographed a number of pupils in this school and used a form of multiple exposure to create an image of the "essence" of the Jew—not just the Jew's physiognomy but the Jews very nature. **[PLATES 12–13]** There he sees the "cold, scanning gaze" of the Jew as the sign of their difference, of their potential pathology.

WHAT'S IN A NAME?

" WHAT A PRETHUTH NOOTHENTH IT ITH ! JUTHT BECAUTH MA THIRNAME
HAPPENTH TO BE ABRAMTH, AND MA PARENTH CHRITHENED ME MOTHETH,
LOTTH O' PEOPLE THEEM TO THUTHPECT I MUTHT BE O' HEBREW ECTHTRACTHION !
WHEREATH A THWEAR A HAVEN'T GOT A THINGLE DROP O' HEBREW BLOOD IN
ALL MA VEINTH, 'THELPME ! "

PLATE ELEVEN

The physiognomy of the Jew matches the Jew's voice and this at a time when British Jews were becoming more and more acculturated. *Punch, or the London Charivari* (October 27, 1883) (Source: Private Collection, Ithaca).

PLATE TWELVE

Francis Galton's original photographs of Jewish students at a London school. From Joseph Jacobs, *Studies in Jewish Statistics* (London: D. Nutt, 1891) (Source: Private Collection, Ithaca).

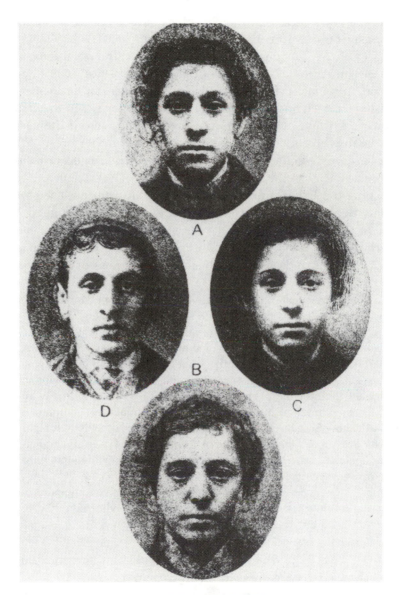

PLATE THIRTEEN

Galton then superimposed the original photographs to produce a form of multiple exposure and created an image of the "essence" of the Jew. From Joseph Jacobs, *Studies in Jewish Statistics* (London: D. Nutt, 1891) (Source: Private Collection, Ithaca).

It is in the Jews' gaze that the pathology can be found.[17] This view is at least as old as Robert Burton's *Anatomy of Melancholy*, where he writes of the "goggle eyes" of the Jews as a sign of "their conditions and infirmities."[18] But it is not merely that Jews "look Jewish" but that this marks them as inferior: "Who has not heard people characterize such and such a man or woman they see in the streets as Jewish without in the least knowing anything about them? The street arab who calls out 'Jew' as some child hurries on to school is unconsciously giving the best and most disinterested proof that there is a reality in the Jewish expression."[19] The gaze of the non-Jew seeing the Jew is immediate translated into action; the gaze of the Jew becomes the functional equivalent of the damaged language of the Jew.

As the Jewish social scientist Joseph Jacobs notes in his discussion of Galton's finding of the absolute Jewishness of the gaze:

> Cover up every part of composite A but the eyes, and yet I fancy any one familiar with Jews would say: "Those are Jewish eyes." I am less able to analyze this effect than in the case of the case of the nose. . . . I fail to see any of the cold calculation which Mr. Galton noticed in the boys at the school, at any rate in the composites A, B, and C. There is something more like the dreamer and thinker than the merchant in A. In fact, on my showing this to an eminent painter of my acquaintance, he exclaimed, "I imagine that is how Spinoza looked when a lad," a piece of artistic insight which is remarkably confirmed by the portraits of the philosopher, though the artist had never seen one. The cold, somewhat hard look in composite D, however, is more confirmatory of Mr. Galton's impression. It is noteworthy that this is seen in a composite of young fellows between seventeen and twenty, who have had to fight a hard battle of life even by that early age."[20]

For the Jewish social scientist such as Jacobs the inexplicable nature of the Jewish gaze exists (even more than the "nostrility" which characterizes the Jewish nose) to mark the Jew. His rationale is quite different than that of Galton—he seeks a social reason for the "hard and calculating" glance seen by Galton, but claims to see it never the less. The Jewish "race," as was the commonplace in the anthropological literature of the age, could never be truly beautiful.[21] And it is the Jewish gaze which most of the writers fix on. Arthur de Gobineau noted that "the . . . French, German and Polish Jews—they all look alike. I have had the opportunity of examining closely one of the last kind. His features and profile clearly betrayed his origin. His eyes especially were unforgettable" [PLATE 14].[22] It is the meaning of these eyes which haunt the Jewish scientist. Jacobs noted in the essay on "Anthropological Types" in the *Jewish Encyclopedia* that these "eyes themselves are generally brilliant, both eyelids are heavy and bulging, and it seems to be the main characteristic of the Jewish eye that the upper lid covers a larger proportion of the pupil than among other persons. This may serve to give a sort of nervous, furtive look to the eyes, which, when the pupils are small and set close together with semistrabismus, gives keenness to some Jewish eyes."[23] And yet hidden within those claims for universality are the images of race which Galton produces parallel to his other composites, in which the eyes of the Jew and his gaze are pathologized.

This view reappears within the medical literature in the work of Jewish physicians, such as Moses Julius Gutmann who writes of the structure of the Jewish face, of its typical form, as being the result of a combination of features which produce "the melancholy, pained expression (the 'nebbich' face)" which is associated with the Jew. For Gutmann, and others, it is the result of the "psychological history of the Jew."[24] Sigmund Freud's own fantasy about the Jew also reflects the question of the meaning of the Jews' eyes. Freud tells of dreaming about Theodore Herzl sometime between 1905 and 1907: "a majestic figure, with a pale, dark-toned face framed by a beautiful, raven-black beard, with infinitely sad eyes. The apparition strove to explain to . . . [Freud] the necessity of immediate action if the Jewish people was to be saved."[25] Here the reversal of the image of the "nebbich" face reflects the reversal of the classical, negative visual image of the Jew. Parallel images can be found at the fin de siècle in the work of the Viennese-Jewish artist Ephraim Moses Lilien, whose idealized images of the Jews were all of Eastern Jews (often in historical settings) [PLATE 15].

The clinical gaze of the Jewish physician now becomes the object

PLATE FOURTEEN

The Polish Jew from Maurice Fishberg, *The Jews: A Study of Race and Environment* (New York: Walter Scott, 1911). This American-Jewish social scientist attempted to counter many of the prevalent views about the degenerate nature of the Jewish race. Still, note the piercing stare. His images are typical of the range of visual representations of the Jew in the anthropological literature of the nineteenth and early twentieth centuries (Source: Private Collection, Ithaca).

PLATE FIFTEEN

Ephraim Moses Lilien's image of idealized Eastern Jews attempted to counter the image of the Jew as diseased. Note the beneficent look of the eyes. From Maurice Fishberg, *The Jews: A Study of Race and Environment* (New York: Walter Scott, 1911) (Source: Private Collection, Ithaca).

of the gaze of study. The image of the eyes attributed to the Jew reappears in the context of the science of race. When the Jewish physician looks into the mirror he sees the person at risk, he sees the Jew; he also sees the physician, the healer. How can the image of the healer be the same as the image of the patient? How can the gaze which is pathological also be the gaze which diagnoses in order to cure? It is this biological definition of all aspects of the Jew which helps form the idea of the Jew in the fin de siècle. The scientific gaze should be neutral. The scientific gaze should be beyond or above all of the vagaries of individual difference.[26] As George Herbert Mead put it: "Knowledge is never a mere contact of our organisms with other objects. It always takes on a universal character. If we know a thing, explain it, we always put it into a texture of uniformities. There must be some reason for it, some law expressed in it. That is the fundamental assumption of science."[27]

But the Jews' gaze is not neutral. It is a gaze which forms the structure of psychoanalysis. As Victor Tausk, one of the earliest followers of Freud, commented to Lou Andreas-Salomé "on the nearly exclusive involvement of Jews in the progress of psychoanalysis. It was understandable, he said, that we could see the fabric more clearly in ancient and dilapidated palaces through their crumbling walls and could gain insights which remain hidden in fine new houses with smooth façades revealing only their color and their outward shape."[28] The Jews' gaze was that of the extraordi-

71

nary physician; this simple reversal of the "cold, scanning gaze" of
the Jew made into a diagnostic virtue of precisely what the eugenist
labeled as pathology. For Freud the composite photograph is virtually the representation of the dream in his *Interpretation of Dreams*
(1900). It is an obsessive metaphor, which recurs throughout the
course of his work.[29] Freud was well aware of the use of such photographs in the work of racial scientists, such as Houston Stewart
Chamberlain.[30] The centrality of this metaphor is a residue of
Freud's earlier acceptance of Charcot's reliance on the act of seeing
as the privileged form of diagnosis. It is not seeing the unique
but rather the universal. And yet hidden within those claims for
universality are the images of race which Galton produces parallel
to his other composites, in which the eyes of the Jew (read: Sigmund
Freud) and his gaze are pathologized. The clinical gaze of the Jewish
physician now becomes the object of the gaze of study. The image
of the eyes, found in the calculating glance of the hysteric and the
epileptic, reappears in the context of race.

In Henry Meige's dissertation of 1893 on the wandering Jew in
the clinical setting of the Salpêtrière, the image of the Jew and
the gaze of the Jew become one.[31] Meige undertakes to place the
appearance of Eastern European (male) Jews in the Salpêtrière as
a sign of the inherent instability of the Eastern European Jew. In
his dissertation he sketches the background to the legend of the
wandering Jew and provides (like his supervisor Charcot) a set of
visual "images of Ahasverus" **[PLATE 16]**.[32] He then provides a
series of case studies of Eastern (male) Jews, two of which he illustrates. The first plate is of "Moser C. called Moses," a forty-five-
or forty-six-year-old Polish Jew from Warsaw who had already
wandered through the clinics in Vienna and elsewhere **[PLATE
17]**.[33] The second plate is of "Gottlieb M.," a forty-two-year-old
Jew from Vilnius, who likewise had been treated in many of the
psychiatric clinics in Western Europe **[PLATE 18]**.[34] Given the
extraordinary movement of millions of Eastern Jews through Western Europe beginning in the early 1880s toward England and
America, the appearance of these few cases of what comes to be
called "Munchausen syndrome" should not surprise. Without any
goal, these Jews "wandered" only in the sense that they were driven

PLATE SIXTEEN

Henry Meige, in his dissertation, *Étude sur certains neuropathes voyageurs: Le juif-errant à la Salpêtrière* (Paris: L. Battaille et cie., 1893), interpreted the legend of the wandering Jew as a psychiatric phenomenon and provided a set of historical "images of Ahasverus," the wandering Jew (Source: National Library of Medicine, Bethesda, MD).

PLATE SEVENTEEN

The image of Henry Meige's case of "Moser
C. called Moses," a forty-five- or forty-six-
year-old Polish Jew from Warsaw who had
already wandered through the clinics in
Vienna and elsewhere. From Henry Meige,
*Étude sur certains neuropathes voyageurs:
Le juif-errant à la Salpêtrière* (Paris: L. Battaille et cie., 1893) (Source: National Library of Medicine, Bethesda, MD).

PLATE EIGHTEEN

Henry Meige's image of of "Gottlieb M.", a forty-two year-old Jew from Vilnius, who likewise had been treated at many of the psychiatric clinics in Western Europe. From Henry Meige, *Étude sur certains neuropathes voyageurs: Le juif-errant à la Salpêtrière* (Paris: L. Battaille et cie., 1893) (Source: National Library of Medicine, Bethesda, MD).

West and that some sought the solace of the clinic where they would at least be treated as individuals, even if sick individuals. What is striking is that Meige provides images and analyses which stress the pathognomonic physiognomy of the Jew—especially his eyes (29). The images gaze at us informing us of their inherent hysterical pathology. The Jew is the hysteric; the Jew is the feminized Other; the Jew is seen as different, as diseased. This is the image of the hysteric with which the Jewish scientist was confronted. His "startle" effect was to see himself as the Other, as the diseased, but most importantly as the feminized Other, the altered form of his circumcised genitalia reflecting the form analogous to that of the woman.

No wonder that Jewish scientists such as Jacobs, Fishberg, and Freud—in very different ways—sought to find the hysteric outside of their own self-image. For that image was immutable within the biology of race. Fishberg quotes the accepted wisdom (in order to refute it for himself and project it onto the Eastern Jew) when he cites Richard Andree: "No other race but the Jews can be traced with such certainty backward for thousands of years, and no other race displays such a constancy of form, none resisted to such an extent the effects of time, as the Jews. Even when he adopts the language, dress, habits, and customs of the people among whom he lives, he still remains everywhere the same. All he adopts is but a cloak, under which the eternal Hebrew survives; he is the same in his facial features, in the structure of his body, his temperament, his character."[35] And this constancy of character, with its deviant sexual nature, leads to the disease which marks the Jew, leads to hysteria. Because the etiology of the Jew's hysteria, like the hysteria of the woman, was to be sought in "sexual excess."[36] Specifically in the "incestuous" inbreeding of this endogenous group: "Being very neurotic, consanguineous marriages among Jews cannot but be detrimental to the progeny."[37] Jews (especially male Jews) are sexually different; they are hysterical and they look it.

But race is one of the categories of the visualization of the hysteric which played a role in shaping the image of the hysteric in the course of the nineteenth century. For the construction of seeing the hysteric took many different forms in providing a composite image of the hysteric, an image in bits and snatches, an image which revealed the "truth" about the hysteric's difference to him or herself. The nosology of the "categories" of difference are really quite analogous to Charcot's construction of the visual pattern of the actions of the hysteric. One can argue that Freud's intellectual as well as analytic development in the 1890s was a movement away from the "meaning" of visual signs (a skill which he ascribes to Charcot in his obituary of 1893) and to the interpretation of verbal signs, from the "crudity" of seeing to the subtlety of hearing.[38] Charcot understands the realism of the image to transcend the crudity of the spoken word. In a letter to Freud on November 23, 1891 he commented concerning the transcription of his famed Tuesday lectures that "the stenographer is not a photographer."[39] The assumption of the inherent validity of the gaze and its mechanical reproduction forms the image of the hysteric. The central argument which can be brought is that this vocabulary of seeing remains embedded in Freud's act of understanding the hysteric, who must be seen to be understood. This is not present in the earliest papers on hysteria written directly under Charcot's influence, such as Freud's differential diagnosis of organic and hysterical paralysis written in 1886.[40] For Freud the rejection of Charcot's mode of "seeing" the hysteric is also a rejection of the special relationship which the Jew has with the disease. The theme of the specific, inherited risk of the Jew for hysteria (and other forms of mental illness) was reflected in the work of Charcot which Freud translated.[41] But even more so this general claim about the hereditary risk of the Jew was linked to a diagnostic system rooted in belief of external appearance as the source of knowledge about the pathological. For the "seeing" of the Jew as different was a topos of the world in which Freud lived. Throughout Europe satirical caricatures were to be found which stressed the Jew's physical difference and in the work of Charcot (and his contemporaries) these representations took on pathological significance.[42]

Indeed, Freud's purchase of a lithograph of Brouillet's painting of Charcot in August of 1889 can well be understood as a compensation for Freud's rejection of Charcot's mode of "seeing" and "representing" the hysteric. Indeed, it must also be understood as a com-

77

pensation for his abandonment of his identification with the anti-Semitic Jean Martin Charcot[43]—for whom Jews, as the essential "moderns,"—were at special risk as hysterics—and his new alliance with the provincial Jew Hippolyte Bernheim.[44] Such a movement is paralleled to the abandonment of ideas of trauma—still for Charcot the cause of hysteria (in women as well as in Jews) and its replacement with the etiology of hysteria in the psyche. As Freud states:

> For [the physician] will be able to convince himself of the correctness of the assertions of the school of Nancy [Bernheim] at any time on his patients, whereas he is scarcely likely to find himself in a position to confirm from his own observation the phenomena described by Charcot as "major hypnotism," which seem only to occur in a few sufferers from *grande hystérie*.[45]

It is the scientific "observation," the gaze of the Jew rather than the gaze directed at the Jew, which marks the distinction between Charcot and Bernheim. Freud's "conversion" to Bernheim's mode of seeing the "usual" rather than seeing the "unique" also marks the beginning of his rejection of reducing the origin of hysteria to the single, traumatic event.

This returns us to the problem of defining the visual precursors for Charcot and for Freud. We must trace the image of the epileptic and the meaning of trauma—two clearly linked images in Freud's vocabulary of the hysteric—and see how Freud's reading of the hysteric is linked through these images of trauma to the central image of difference—the Eastern European Jew as hysteric (or perhaps more accurately, the provincial Jew as parvenu, out of his mind because he is out of his natural place). It is the discourse on the relationship between "trauma" and "hysteria" which provides the key to Freud's—and many of his contemporaries'—ambivalence concerning models for therapy.

"Trauma" is not a neutral concept. "Railway spine," the hysterical trauma resulting from railway accidents, was the model for understanding the traumatic origin of hysteria at the turn of the century.[46] Indeed, in much of the early work on hysteria these

images haunt the literature. The hysteric is the sufferer from traumatic neurosis similar to that caused by experiencing a train accident, as outlined by Herbert Page in his classic work on *Injuries of
the Spine and Spinal Cord* (1883) and accepted in toto by Charcot in
his work on the neurosis of fright or shock. Both men and women
are therefore equally at risk for such forms of psychopathology.
Hysteria is thus merely the direct (brain or spinal cord lesion) or
indirect (shock) result of trauma. And here the confusion between
the models of hysteria evolved by Charcot and Hughlings Jackson
must be stressed. For the "traumatic" event causes hysteria only in
those who are predisposed to being hysteric (Charcot) but the lesion
caused by trauma also releases those subterranean aspects of our
earlier evolution held in check by the highest order of neurological
organization (Hughlings Jackson). The Jew is predisposed to hysteria both by heredity and consanguinity (incestuous inbreeding)
and, as we shall see, by the trauma of civilization as represented by
the Jews' predisposition to the somatic diseases linked to hysteria—
such as syphilis.

The image of trauma in the fin de siècle is directly tied to modern
civilization and the train. As Sir Clifford Allbutt, Professor of Medicine at Cambridge University, stated in an essay in the *Contemporary Review* of 1895:

> To turn now . . . to nervous disability, to hysteria . . . to the fright-
> fulness, the melancholy, the unrest due to living at a high pressure,
> the world of the railway, the pelting of telegrams, the strife of
> business . . . surely, at any rate, these maladies or the causes of
> these maladies are more rife than they were in the days of our
> fathers? To this question . . . there is, I know, but one opinion on
> the subject in society, in the newspapers, in the books of philoso-
> phers, even in the journals and treatises of the medical pro-
> fession.[47]

Thus the railroad, railway accidents, and the "speed of modern
life" all collaborate to create the hysteric. But nineteenth-century
"railway" medicine faced a dilemma which later faced Sigmund
Freud. Trauma—such as involvement in a railway crash—is the

cause of hysteria, but why do not all individuals who are involved in railway crashes become hysteric? This question was answered in part by the mid-century neurologist C. E. Brown-Séquard, who—as we noted in the matter of the effects of excessive tobacco-smoking on feet—had argued that there were hereditary transmissions of acquired injuries, as in the case of "animals born of parents having been rendered epileptic by an injury to the spinal cord."[48] This view quickly became a standard one in the literature on "railway spine."[49]

The image of the hysteric being at risk because of his/her inheritance limited the field from which the hysteric could be drawn. Thus the physician could—under most circumstances—see him/herself as a separate category, as distanced from the hysteric as the child of alcoholics or criminals. But not the Jewish physician. For the Jewish physician is at risk no matter which theory of hysteria one accepted.[50] Some views using the model of biological determinism had it that the Jew was at risk simply from inheritance; some views sought after a sociological explanation. But both views, no matter what the etiology, saw a resultant inability of the Jew to deal with the complexities of the modern world, as represented by the Rousseauean city. It is the city, the source of the deformation of the foot which also leads to the pathologization of the psyche. And the source of the madness of the Jews lies in the Jew's sexuality—in the sexual practices of the Jews as well as in the configuration of the Jew's sexual drives. They are as perverse as is the form of his circumcised penis.[51] Jewish scientists, when they address this question directly, seek for a developmental rather than a hereditary reason for this, for their, evident higher rate of hysteria. They seek out the "two-thousand-year Diaspora" as the origin of trauma.[52] But this does not free them. Given the views of Brown-Séquard there is really little escape no matter what the cause. The Jew becomes the hysteric and the hysteria is measured by the sexual abnormality of the Jew. Thus the search for the origin of the psychopathological image of the hysteric in the sexual life of the individual has already been undertaken when that individual is a Jew.

Thus when we turn to Freud's case studies, either in the collaborative *Studies on Hysteria* of 1895 or in his later, and much more complex studies, such as his study of Dora (1905 [1901]), we encounter the question of Freud's (and Breuer's) representation of the Jew—of their "seeing" (or perhaps better, "hearing") the Jew. In an earlier study I argued that the image of "Anna O." in Breuer's case-study contribution to the *Studies on Hysteria* masked the "Jewishness" of Bertha Pappenheim.[53] In Freud's own contributions (such as the case of Katharina or Miss Lucy R.) there is an attempt to universalize the image of the hysteric through the citation—not of cases of male hysteria—but of those of non-Jewish hysterics. But the common qualities ascribed to the hysteric and the Eastern, male Jew remain central to the representation of this nosological category for Freud.

This can be seen in a close reading of what has become the exemplary "case of hysteria" for our contemporary reading of the history of hysteria, Freud's case of "Dora."[54] Seen by contemporary feminist critics, such as Hélène Cixous as "the core example of the protesting force of women,"[55] it is also the classic example of the transmutation of images of gender and race (masculinity and "Jewishness") into the deracinated image of the feminine. Freud used the case of Dora to argue for the necessary publication of case studies, but also for the needed masking of the analysand. The disguising of the identity of Dora is complete. There is no sign in the case study of the "racial" identity of Ida Bauer, the Eastern European Jewish daughter of Philip Bauer, whose syphilis was treated by Freud some six years before the beginning of Dora's analysis. Charcot (and Freud) had attempted to distance the diseases of syphilis and hysteria and yet a relationship between the two patterns of illness remained. This omission, like Josef Breuer's omission of his patient's "racial" identity in his narrative of "Anna O's" case, while including it in his casenotes, masks a salient aspect of the case. We can best quote Freud in this regard, when he returns to the 1895 case of "Katharina" in 1924 and observes in reference to his having deliberately identified the patient's father as her uncle: "Distortions like the one which I introduced in the present instance should be altogether avoided in reporting a case history."[56]

Perhaps as important for our reading of the suppressed aspects of the case of Dora (Ida Bauer) is the fact that her beloved brother

The Jewish Psyche

♦

Otto Bauer was one of the founders of the Austrian Socialist Party. His attitude toward his Jewish identity is of importance. For Austro-Marxism advocated cultural-national autonomy for all peoples within the diverse Hapsburg Empire—except for the Jews. It saw assimilation as inevitable and positive; and tied assimilation to a distinct distaste for Yiddish (and subsequently Hebrew) as linguistic signs of a negative separatism (a sign which took on positive meaning when ascribed to Czech or Hungarian as "national" languages). An "Eastern Jew" himself, as he was born of Bohemian ancestry in Vienna, Bauer held an ambivalent relationship to the idea of race. "Race" was an acceptable label for the other national groups—since it was associated by them with positive ideas of autonomy—for the Jews (especially Eastern Jews) it was always a sign of the pathological.[57] Bertha Pappenheim, Breuer's "Anna O.," stated it quite baldly in an essay published at the turn of the century. Raised in an orthodox Jewish home, for her the German-language schools developed in the Eastern reaches of the Hapsburg Empire were "a stronghold, often conquered in battle, in the fight against the malaise from which Galician Jewry suffers as from a hereditary disease."[58] It is the cure of this hereditary disease which Freud undertakes in treating Dora (and thus treating an aspect of his own identity). This is, indeed, the hidden meaning of the development of the idea of transference and counter-transference, one which is nascent in the case of Dora, and why Freud's own understanding of the process is blocked in this case.

The centerpiece of Freud's study of Ida Bauer is, according to Freud's argument, the attempt to explain the origin of a case of hysteria through the analysis of the Oedipal triangle as perceived by a patient whose object of attraction is of the same sex. Dora's familial relationships were complex and strained ones, pulled between her father (Philip), her mother (Käthe), the father's lover (called by Freud, Frau K. and to whom Freud believed Dora to be attracted) and her husband (Herr K., the attempted seducer of Dora, who has traditionally been the focus of the interpretation of the study). Much time and effort has been expended to understand Freud's "misreading" of this case. What is clear is that there are a number of "misreadings" by Freud, and not simply over the matter of Dora's personal sexual dilemma. Jacques Lacan pointed out one of the central ones—that the *globus hystericus* manifested by Dora is interpreted by Freud as the symbolic representation of orality within a specific context in the case study. Frau K's seduction of Dora's impotent father is described in Freud's analysis as an act of fellatio rather than being understood as cunnilingus.[59] This displacement is, however, not merely the shift of Freud's focus from the genitalia of the female to those of the male. Rather it is a double displacement—for the act of fellatio is also the emblematic act of male homosexual contact. What Freud's double displacement means can be found if we look at the "scientific" context of the meaning of the act of fellatio in the medical debates of the nineteenth century. Through such a contextualization we can outline Freud understanding of the transmission of a "disease" (the collapse of language as represented by the symptom of the *globus hystericus* in Ida Bauer) as necessarily associated with the act of sucking a male's penis.

Let us begin with this "misreading" as a sign of Freud's representation of the idea of race in the guise of the representation of the feminine, as it replaces the male's genitalia as the object of attraction and, therefore, sight, with the woman's. For Freud the act of seeing one's genitalia is one which is especially "feminine": "The pride taken by women in the appearance of their genitals is quite a special feature of their vanity; and the disorders of the genitals which they think calculated to inspire feelings of repugnance or even disgust have an incredible power of humiliating them, of lowering their self-esteem, and of making them irritable, sensitive, and distrustful."[60] The special quality of seeing the female's genitalia, genitalia normally understood by Freud as presence in the fantasy of their absence, points towards the *other* genitalia, the male genitalia, seen by the male which when "disordered" points toward pathological nature of the male. But what is this disorder? In the case study it is, on one level, the origin of Ida Bauer's understanding about the diseased nature of her genitalia, the syphilitic infection of her father. One of the most interesting qualities ascribed to the father from the very beginning of the case study is the fact that he was syphilitic. The relationship between the physical trauma of syphilis and the image of the syphilitic is central to understanding the image of the hysteric which Freud evolves in his study. In the case of Dora's father, his "gravest illness . . . took the form of a confusional attack, followed by symptoms of paralysis and slight mental disturbance."[61] Freud diagnoses this as a case of "diffuse vascular affection; and since the patient admitted having had a specific infection before his marriage, I prescribed an energetic course of anti-luetic treatment . . ."[62] Four years later the father brings his daughter to Freud for treatment. Freud argues in a footnote for the retention of the relationship between the etiology of hysteria in the offspring and the syphilitic infection of the "father." "Syphilis in the male parent is a very relevant factor in the etiology of the neuropathic constitution of children."[63] Here is the trauma —this case of hysteria is a form of heredito-syphilis transmitted by the father. Freud's emphasis on this line of inheritance is not solely because Ida Bauer's father had evidently (according to the account in the case study) infected her mother (and therefore his daughter) but because the general laws of the inheritance of disease which were accepted during this period argued that the son inherits the diseases of the mother (and therefore her father) while the daughter inherits the diseases of the father (and therefore his mother).[64] Freud later uncovers another sign of this biological predisposition in the fact that "she had masturbated in childhood."[65] This is the link which brings together the trauma (the syphilitic infection of the father), the mode of transmission (sexual intercourse with a circumcised penis), the Jewishness of the father as represented in his pathological sexuality, and the hysterical neurosis of the daughter. The merging of various forms of illness, from syphilis to hysteria, is through the model of inherited characteristics. The "real" disease is the degeneracy of the parent and its manifestation in specific "illness" can vary from individual to individual.[66] Thus syphilis and hysteria are truly forms of the same pattern of illness.

One reading of the case would be to say that hypersexual Jewish males pass on their Jewish disease to their daughters in the form of hysteria. But this discourse is present in Freud's text only if we contextualize the meaning of syphilis within the context of Freud's self-definition as a Jew and that of his patient, Ida Bauer.

Freud creates very early on a differential diagnosis between "tabes dorsalis" (a label for one of the late manifestations of syphilis) and hysteria, at least when it appears in a woman who is infected with syphilis. He undertakes this in an extended footnote at the very beginning of the study in which he documents the central diagnostic thesis of this case study: that it is the ordered narrative of the patient about her illness which is disrupted in the hysteric. In other words, the hysteric lies—"the patients' inability to give an ordered history of their life in so far it coincides with the history of their illness is not merely characteristic of the neurosis. It also possess great theoretical significance."[67] The relationship between the sexual etiology of the hysteric and the hysteric's discourse represents the underlying shift from an image of race to one of gender (for as we shall see the discourse of the Jew is a primary marker of difference). The counterexample is brought in Freud's notes, a case study of a patient who "had been for years . . . treated without success for hysteria (pains and defective gait)." She narrates her "story . . . perfectly clearly and connectedly in spite of the remarkable events it dealt with . . ." Freud concludes this "could not be . . . [a case] of hysteria, and immediately instituted a careful physical examination. This led to the diagnosis of a fairly advanced stage of tabes, which later was treated with Hg injections (Ol. cinereum) by Professor Lang with markedly beneficial results" (31).[68] Here the image of the "defective gait" which is one of the hallmarks of the "hysteric" in the nineteenth century (and the history which is created for this image at the Salpêtrière), recurs only to be revealed as the final stages of syphilis. The irony is that it is Joseph Babinski whose neurological work at the Salpêtrière provided the clue for such an analysis of the impaired plantar reflex[69] and Charcot himself, in his work on intermittent claudication who provided racial context for such impairment.[70] (And, indeed, there is a link of intermittent claudication to the image of the hysteric.[71])

It is only at the very close of her case that Freud reveals one of Dora's primary symptoms: "she had not been able to walk properly and dragged her right foot. . . . Even now her foot sometimes dragged."[72] Freud sees this "disorder, the dragging of one leg," as having a "secret and possibly sexual meaning of the clinical picture . . ."[73] Freud interprets this as a sign of the "false step" which Dora had imagined herself to have taken during the attempted seduction by Herr K. at the lake. Later, Felix Deutsch, who treated Ida Bauer after she broke off her analysis with Freud, observed that the "dragging of her foot, which Freud had observed when the patient was a girl, should have persisted twenty-five years."[74] This remained a central sign for her affliction, a sign which is not solely the association between an accident which she had as a child and the bed rest which accompanied it. For the incapacity of gait is also a racial sign in Ida Bauer's Vienna, and is associated with the "impairment" of the Jew. For it is the Jew, in a long tradition, who is at greatest risk in having both impaired gait and syphilis. It is this image in the case of Dora which links the impairment of the syphilitic and the hidden image of the Jew. But it is, as we have shown in the preceding chapter, also a sign of the male Jew—it is a sign of masculine insufficiency rather than that of the woman. The limping Jew is the male Jew.

The association of the syphilitic infection of the father and the neurosis of the daughter is linked by Freud in his analysis of the physical symptom of leukorrhea or genital catarrh, an increased "disgust[ing] . . . secretion of the mucous membrane of the vagina . . ."[75] In Freud's reading, Dora associates this with her lesbian "disgust" toward Herr K.'s attempted heterosexual seduction and the feeling of his "erect member against her body."[76] Freud's conclusion is that for Ida Bauer "all men were like her father. But she thought her father suffered from venereal disease—for had he not handed it on to her and to her mother? She might therefore have imagined to herself that all men suffered from venereal disease, and naturally her conception of venereal disease was modeled upon her one experience of it—a personal one at that. To suffer from venereal disease, therefore, meant for her to be afflicted with a disgusting discharge."[77] Freud thus interprets one of the two dreams narrated to him by Dora in terms of the connection between the "disgusting catarrh," the wetness of bedwetting and masturbation, and her mother's compulsive cleanliness. "The two groups of ideas met in this one thought: 'Mother got both things from father: the sexual wetness and the dirtying discharge.' "[78] In the recurrent dream the connection (right word) is made through the symbolic representation of the "drops," the jewels which her mother wishes to rescue from the fire which threatens the family.[79] Freud interprets the "drops"—the jewelry ['Schmuck']" as a " 'switch-word,' while 'jewelry' ['Schmuck'] was taken as an equivalent to 'clean' and thus as a rather forced contrary of 'dirtied.' " [80] Freud stresses that the "jewels" become a "jewelcase" in the dream and that this term ["Schmuckkasten"] is "a term commonly used to describe female genitals that are immaculate and intact."[81]

One can add another layer of misreading. As I have shown, there is a subtext in the hidden language of the Jews. In Viennese urban dialect, borrowed from Yiddish, "Schmock" has another meaning. "Schmock" even in German urban ideolect had come to be a standard slang term for the circumcised male penis.[82] The "hidden" meaning of the language of the Jews is identical to the lying of the hysteric, the central symptom of hysteria according to Freud. This transference can be seen in Freud's early description of the discourse of two Eastern male Jews in a letter to his friend Emil Fluss on the return trip from Freiburg to Vienna in 1872:

> Now this Jew talked the same way as I had heard thousands of others talk before, even in Freiburg. His face seemed familiar—he was typical. So was the boy with whom he discussed religion. He was cut from the cloth from which fate makes swindlers when the time is ripe: cunning, mendacious, kept by his adorning relatives in the belief that he is a great talent, but unprincipled and without character. I have enough of this rabble.[83]

The "misreading" of the text is a repression of the discourse of the male Eastern Jew—the parvenu marked by his language and discourse as different and diseased. Hidden within the female genitalia (the "Schmuckkasten") is the image of the male Jew as represented by his genitalia (the "Schmock"). The replacement of the "Jewish" penis—identifiable as circumcised and, as we shall see, as diseased, by the "German" vagina stands at the center of Freud's revision of the identity of Ida Bauer.

It is the hidden language, Yiddish, which reveals the ground upon which Freud's constructs his idea of the feminine. For the acculturated Eastern Jew in Vienna, *Mauscheln*, the speaking of German with a Yiddish accent, intonation, or vocabulary, is the sign of this difference. And this is the language of Freud's mother, Amalia Freud née Nathanson, the invisible woman in all of his autobiographical accounts. As Freud's son Martin noted, she was a Galician Jew from Brody who remained a typical Polish Jew, "impatient, self-willed, sharp-witted and highly intelligent." She retained the language, manner, and beliefs of Galicia:

> [She was] absolutely different from Jews who had lived in the West for some generations . . . These Galician Jews had little grace and no manners; and their women were certainly not what we should call 'ladies.' 'They were highly emotional and easily carried away by their feelings . . . They were not easy to live with, and grandmother, a true representative of her race, was no exception. She had great vitality and much impatience.[84]

It is in the image of the mother that the qualities ascribed to the hysteric, to Ida Bauer, can be found. In suppressing the shift of language, Freud also suppresses the "hidden" reference to the "Jewish" penis. The hidden discourse of the Jew, hidden within the high German culture discourse, is ignored.

This "misreading" of the female for the male organ is in truth a "mis-seeing" of the genitalia. For Freud traces the origin of Ida Bauer's knowledge of the act of fellatio, the "seeing" as well as sucking of the male member. Freud understands this "so-called sexual perversion" as being "very widely diffused among the whole population, as everyone knows except medical writers upon the subject. Or, I should rather say, they know it too; only they take care to forget it at the moment when they take up their pens to write about it. So it is not to be wondered at that this hysterical girl of nineteen, who had heard of the occurrence of such a method of sexual intercourse (sucking at the male organ), should have developed an unconscious fantasy of this sort and should have given it expression by an irritation in her throat and by coughing."[85] Freud reports that Dora's governess, to whom she was evidently as attracted, as she was to Frau K., "used to read every sort of book on sexual life and similar objects, and talked to the girl about them, at the same time asking her quite frankly not to mention their conversations to her parents, as one could never tell what line they might take about them."[86] But there are contradictions in Ida Bauer's account. Did she only hear about such sexual activities, or did she read about them? What could she have read, and how much? Later in the case study, after Freud had begun to explain the homosexual attraction which Dora felt for Frau K., his narrative shifts away from Dora's "seeing" to her speaking.

After Dora's father writes to Herr K. to demand an explanation of his actions toward his daughter, Herr K. "spoke of her with disparagement, and produced as his trump card the reflection that no girl who read such books and was interested in such things could have any title to a man's respect. Frau K. had betrayed her and had calumniated her; for it had only been with her that she had read Mantegazza and discussed forbidden topics."[87] It is the book, a foreign book, which "infects" her, and makes her "sick," i.e., "hysteric." Like her governess, Frau K. had used her to get access to her father. This "error" in Freud's image of the etiology of hysteria is a displacement of the image of the infected and the infecting on to the world of high culture, of course not "German" high culture (*Bildung*), but the medical culture of the sexologist.

Paolo Mantegazza (1831–1901) was one of the standard "ethnological" sources for the late nineteenth century for the nature of human sexuality. His three-volume study of the physiology of love, the hygiene of love, and the anthropology of love was the standard popular introduction to the acceptable social discourse on sexuality in late nineteenth-century Europe.[88] His importance for Freud should not be underestimated. One of a group of physician-anthropologists (such as Cesare Lombroso), Mantegazza had pioneered the introduction of the study (and enjoyment) of *Erthroxylon coca* and its derivative, cocaine, in the late 1850s. Following the publication of Darwin's *Descent of Man*, Mantegazza became one of Dar-

win's most avid correspondents (and sources), supplying Darwin
with a series of "anthropological" photographs which Darwin used
for his later work.

Mantegazza's work, like that of Charcot's, emphasized the
"seeing" of difference, a view which is epitomized in Mantegazza's
basic study of physiognomy and expression of 1885. But for late
nineteenth-century science the controversial centerpiece of Mantegazza's work is his trilogy on love and sex: *Fisiologia dell' amore*
(1872), *Igiene dell' amore* (1877), and *Gli amori degli uomini* (1885).[89]
Cited widely by sexologists from Cesare Lombroso, Richard Krafft-
Ebing, Havelock Ellis, and Iwan Bloch to Magnus Hirschfeld, Mantegazza remained one of the accessible, "popular" sources for "scientific" knowledge (and misinformation) to the educated public at
the turn of the century. It is clear that Ida Bauer could have read
(and probably did read) either Mantegazza or similar texts, whether
under the tutelage of her companion or on her own initiative. What
is of interest is how Freud reads this contradiction in her account:
Did she read them, or only hear about their content? What is inherently dangerous about Mantegazza from the standpoint of Freud's
refusal to relate to Herr K.'s accusation that Ida Bauer had read
him? If we turn to the trilogy, it is clear (and Madelon Spregnether
agrees[90]) that the text which best fits the pejorative description
of Herr K. is the final text in this series, on the anthropology of
sexuality.[91] There one finds an extended discussion of "the perversions of love" including "mutual onanism," "lesbianism and triba-
dism" as well as "histories" of these practices. (However, there are
similar discussions in the seventh chapter of Mantegazza's study
on the "hygiene of love" which details the "errors of the sexual
drive.")

Now this is clearly what Freud should have understood—given
his reading of this as a case of lesbianism—as of importance to Ida
Bauer; but what in this volume would have been of importance
to Sigmund Freud? If we turn to the chapter after the one on
"perversions" we come to a detailed discussion of the "mutilation
of the genitals" which recounts the history of practices among
"savage tribes," including the Jews. Indeed, it is only in Mantegazza's discussion of the Jews that the text turns from a titillating

account of "unnatural practices" into an Enlightenment polemic against the perverse practices of a people out of their correct "space" and "time"—the Jews:

> Circumcision is a shame and an infamy; and I, who am not in the least anti-Semitic, who indeed have much esteem for the Israelites, I who demand of not a living soul a profession of religious faith, insisting only upon the brotherhood of soap and water and of honesty, I shout and shall continue to shout at the Hebrews, until my last breath: Cease mutilating yourselves: cease imprinting upon your flesh an odious brand to distinguish you from other men; until you do this, you cannot pretend to be our equal. As it is, you, of your own accord, with the branding iron, from the first days of your lives, proceed to proclaim yourselves a race apart, one that cannot, and does not care to, mix with ours. (99)

It is circumcision which sets the (male) Jew apart.[92] In his dissertation of 1897 Armand-Louis-Joseph Béraud notes that the Jews needed to circumcise their young males because of their inherently unhygienic nature but also because the "climate in which they dwelt" otherwise encouraged the transmission of syphilis.[93] The Jew in the Diaspora is out of time (having forgotten to vanish like the other ancient peoples); is out of his correct space (where circumcision had validity). His Jewishness (as well as his disease) is inscribed on his penis.

But what does circumcision mean for a Viennese Jewish scientist of the fin de siècle? The debates within and without the Jewish communities concerning the nature and implication of circumcision surfaced again in Germany during the 1840s. German Jews had become acculturated into German middle-class values and had come to question the absolute requirement of circumcision as a sign of their Jewish identity. Led by the radical reform rabbi Samuel Holdheim in Germany and responding to a Christian tradition which denigrated circumcision, the debate was carried out as much in the scientific press as in the religious one.[94] There were four "traditional" views of the "meaning" of circumcision since the rise of Christianity. Following the writings of Paul, the first saw circumcision as inherently symbolic and, therefore, no longer valid after the rise of Christianity (this view was espoused by Eusebius and Origen); the second saw circumcision as a form of medical prophylaxis (as in the writing of Philo but also in the work of the central German commentator of the eighteenth century, Johann David Michaelis); the third saw it as a sign of a political identity (as in the work of the early eighteenth-century theologian Johann Spencer), and the fourth as a remnant of the early Jewish idol or phallus worship (as in the work of the antiquarian Georg Friedrich Daumer—this view reappears quite often in the literature on Jewish ritual murder).

In the medical literature during the course of the fin de siècle two of these views dominated. They were the views which bracketed the images of "health" and "disease." These views saw circumcision either as the source of disease or as a prophylaxis against disease, and in both cases syphilis and masturbation—the two "diseases" which dominate the case of Dora—play a major role. Mantegazza notes that "the hygienic value of circumcision has been exaggerated by the historians of Judaism. It is true enough that the circumcised are a little less disposed to masturbation and to venereal infection; but every day, we do have Jewish masturbators and Jewish syphilitics. Circumcision is a mark of racial distinction; . . . it is a sanguinary protest against universal brotherhood; and if it be true that Christ was circumcised, it is likewise true that he protested on the cross against any symbol which would tend to part men asunder" (98–99). The opposing view of circumcision in the scientific literature of the time saw circumcision as a mode of prevention which precluded the transmission of sexually transmitted diseases because of the increased capacity for "cleanliness."[95] It is classified as an aspect of "hygiene," the favorite word to critique or support the practice. (This view is closely associated with the therapeutic use of circumcision throughout the nineteenth century as a means of "curing" the diseases caused by masturbation, with, of course a similar split in the idea of efficacy: circumcision was either a cure for masturbation as it eliminated the stimulation of the prepuce and deadened the sensitivity of the penis or it was the source of Jewish male hypersexuality.)

There is a detailed medical literature which links the very act of circumcision with the transmission of syphilis, so that the prophylaxis becomes the source of infection. The literature which discusses the transmission of syphilis to newly circumcised infants through the ritual of *metsitsah*, the sucking on the penis by the *mohel*, the ritual circumciser, in order to staunch the bleeding, is extensive **[PLATE 19]**.[96] The *metsitsah* was understood by the scientific community of the nineteenth century as a "pathological" aspect of the ritual, as it was seen as the source of the transmission of disease from the adult male to the male child. This had been the grounds for its abolition in France in 1844.[97] In the establishment of the Viennese Jewish community during the course of the early nineteenth century the debate on the abolition of circumcision was heard as loudly as anywhere else in Central Europe. Isaac Noah Mannheimer, the rabbi of the Seitenstettengasse synagogue and the de facto "chief rabbi" of Vienna (although this title did not officially exist), while a follower of Reformed Judaism, opposed the more radical "reforms" of theologians such as Samuel Holdheim. He strongly advocated the retention of Hebrew as the language of prayer (even though he had preached in Danish during his tenure in Copenhagen) and opposed mixed marriages and the abolition of circumcision. (The link among these three central issues in the self-definition of Viennese Jewry at mid-century should be stressed.) While no compromise was found on the first two issues (Hebrew was maintained as the language of the liturgy and mixed marriages were not authorized), a striking compromise was found in the third case. Together with Rabbi Lazar Horowitz, the spiritual leader of the orthodox community in Vienna, Mannheimer abolished the practice of the *metsitsah*.[98] Although Horowitz was a follower of the ultra-orthodox Pressburg Rabbi Moses Sofer, the abolition of the *metsitsah* became a marker between the practices of Viennese Jewry (which did not permit it for "hygienic" reasons) and the tradition of Eastern Jewry, such as the Jews of Pressburg and Freiburg (where Freud was circumcised).

Here is the link between the emphasis on fellatio in Freud's reading of the case of Dora and the syphilis which haunts the image of the (male) Jew. It is the male sucking the penis of a male in the

The *CIRCUMCISION* of the *CHILD* on the eighth day as commanded Exod. 17. v.10 &c. Levit.12.v.3.

A The great Father holding ý Child between his Knees. B an empty Chair for ý Prophet Elias. C The Circumciser who holding ý Knife in his hand, says, Blessed be thou O Lord who hast ordained unto us Circumcision. At wᵒ words he cuts off ý thick Skin of ý Prepuce & then nᵒ ý nail of his Thumb tears off ý thinner Skin, & having suckt ý Blood ý runs from it 2 or 3 times, he spits it into a cup of wine, then he lays some dragon's blood powder ý coal &c. on ý uncircumsed part to heal it, & binds up ý whole with a bolster dipt in oyl of roses. After this he says another blessing wᵒ ý Child & gives him ý name his Father intended & pronouncing those words in Ezekiel 16. verses. he wets his Lips with ý wine into wᵒ he has spit ý Blood, after (as the 128ᵗʰ Psalm is repeated intirely, and then the Spectators depart saying to the Father may you be present at his Wedding. The Jewish Women are not admitted to this ceremony. the Women represented in the Cut are Christians.

PLATE NINETEEN

A ritual circumcision in the Sephardi tradition depicted by Bernard Picart in his *Cérémonies et Coutumes Religieuses des tous Peuples du Monde* (1722). This particular engraving is a copy of the British version of the extraordinary eleven-volume set of engravings (1731). Already here the image of the visibility of the male Jew's genitalia becomes part of the visual tradition of Western European art (Source: Historical Library, Cushing/Whitney Medical Library, Yale University, New Haven, CT).

act of circumcision. For Freud the act of fellatio would not only be a sign of "perversion" but a sign of the transmission of disease. It would also be a sign which incorporated his own relationship between his racial identity, with his co-religionists, and indeed, with other male authority figures. Thus the act of the female sucking on the penis of the male, a "pathological" act as it represents the spread of disease (hysteria) to the daughter, is a sublimation of the act of the male sucking upon the penis of the male and spreading another disease, syphilis. It also represents, in the period during which Freud was writing and rewriting the case of Dora, Freud's own articulation of the end of his "homosexual" (i.e., homoerotic) relationship with Wilhelm Fliess, whose theories about the relationship between the nose and the penis are echoed in this case study as well as elsewhere in the work of the fin-de-siècle Freud.[99]

But reading Mantegazza we can go one step further in our analysis of Freud's understanding of the meaning of sexually transmitted disease and its relationship to hysteria. For Mantegazza introduces his discussion of the "exclusivity" of the Jews with the following discussion:

> It is altogether likely that the most important reason which has led men of various ages and of varying civilizations to adopt the custom of cutting off the prepuce has been that it was felt to be necessary to imprint upon the human body a clear and indelible sign which would serve to distinguish one people from another and, by putting a seal of consecration upon nationality, would tend to impede the mixture of races. A woman, before accepting the embraces of a man, must first make sure, with her eyes and with her hands, as to whether he was of the circumcised or the uncircumcised; nor would she be able to find any excuse for mingling her own blood-stream with that of the foreigner. It had, however, not occurred to the legislator that this same indelible characteristic would inspire in the woman a curiosity to see and to handle men of a different sort. (98)

The seduction of the Jewish woman by the Other—whether the non-Jew or the lesbian—is the result of the "seeing" of the difference in the form of the genitalia. The need to "see" and "touch" the Other is the fault of the circumcised (male) Jew whose very physical form tempts the female to explore the Other. Here we have another form of the displacement of the act of touching (sexual contact) with the permitted (indeed, necessary) act of seeing but given a pathological interpretation. The rejection of "mixed marriage" and "conversion" by even "godless" Jews such as Sigmund Freud during the fin de siècle is a sign of the need to understand the separateness of the Jew as having a positive valence. The labeling of converts as "sick" becomes a widely used trope of the fin de siècle.[100]

Ida Bauer's act of seeing her father is the act of seeing the (male) Jew. Central to the definition of the Jew—here to be understood always as the "male" Jew—is the image of the male Jew's circumcised penis as impaired, damaged, or incomplete and therefore threatening. The literature on syphilis—which certainly played a role in Freud's understanding of her father's illness as well as that of the daughter—contains a substantial discussion of the special relationship of Jews to the transmission and meaning of syphilis. For it is not only in the act of circumcision that this association is made—it is in the general risk of the Jews as the carriers of syphilis and the generalized fear that such disease would undermine the strength of the body politic. Central to the case of Ida Bauer is a subtext about the nature of Jews, about the transmission of syphilis, and about the act of circumcision.[101] Both are associated with the image of the hysteric. It is Jewishness which is the central category of "racial" difference for the German reader and writer of the turn of the century.[102]

The Jew in European science and popular thought was closely related to the spread and incidence of syphilis. Such views had two readings. The first model saw the Jews as the carriers of sexually transmitted diseases who transmitted them to the rest of the world. Syphilis had been associated with the Jews from the first appearance in Europe of the disease in the fifteenth century.[103] Indeed, it was "commonly called the Peste of the Marranos," according to the Genoese ambassador to Charles VIII in 1492.[104] The literature on syphilis in the nineteenth century contains a substantial discussion of the special relationship of Jews to the transmission and meaning of syphilis. There is the assumption of the general risk of the Jews as the carriers of syphilis and the generalized fear that such disease would undermine the strength of the body politic. It is Jewishness which is the central category of "racial" difference for the German reader and writer of the turn of the century. The need to "see" and "label" the Jew at a time when Jews were becoming more and more "invisible" in Germany made the association with socially stigmatizing diseases which bore specific visible "signs and symptoms" especially appropriate.

The location of the Jews and the locus of anxiety about disease is the city—is Vienna. Here the link between the idea of the Jew as city dweller and the disease which lurks within the confinement of the urban environment becomes manifest. The source of the "hysteria" of the city is the diseased sexuality of the Jew. This view is to be found in Adolf Hitler's discussion of syphilis in fin-de-siècle Vienna in *Mein Kampf* (1925). There he (like his Viennese compatriot Bertha Pappenheim[105]) links it to the Jew, the prostitute, and the power of money:

> Particularly with regard to syphilis, the attitude of the nation and the state can only be designated as total capitulation. . . . The invention of a remedy of questionable character and its commercial exploitation can no longer help much against this plague. . . . The cause lies, primarily, in our prostitution of love. . . . This Jewification of our spiritual life and mammonization of our mating instinct will sooner or later destroy our entire offspring . . .[106]

Hitler's views also linked Jews with prostitutes and the spread of infection. Jews were the arch-pimps; Jews ran the brothels; but Jews also infected their prostitutes and caused the weakening of the German national fiber.[107] Jews are also associated with the false promise of a "medical" cure separate from the social "cures" which Hitler wishes to see imposed: isolation and separation of the syphilitic and his/her Jewish source from the body politic. (Hitler's reference here draws upon the popular belief that particularly the specialties of dermatology and syphilology were dominated by Jews, who used their medical status to sell quack cures.)

The second model which associated Jews and syphilis seemed to postulate exactly the opposite—that Jews had a statistically lower rate of syphilitic infection—because they had become immune to it through centuries of exposure. In the medical literature of the period, reaching across all of European medicine, it was assumed that Jews had a notably lower rate of infection. In a study undertaken between 1904 and 1929 of the incidence of tertiary lues (the final stage of the syphilitic infection) in the Crimea, the Jews had the lowest consistent rate of infection.[108] In an eighteen-year longitudinal study H. Budel demonstrated the extraordinarily low rate of tertiary lues among Jews in Estonia during the prewar period.[109] All of these studies assumed that biological difference as well as the social difference of the Jews were at the root of their seeming "immunity."

Jewish scientists also had to explain the "statistical" fact of their immunity to syphilis. In a study of the rate of tertiary lues undertaken during World War I, the Jewish physician Max Sichel responded to the general view of the relative lower incidence of infection among Jews as resulting from the sexual difference of the Jews.[110] He uses—out of necessity—a social argument. The Jews, according to Sichel, show a lower incidence because of their early marriage and the patriarchal structure of the Jewish family, and also because of their much lower rate of alcoholism. They were, therefore, according to Sichel's implicit argument, more rarely exposed to the infection of prostitutes whose attractiveness was always associated with the greater loss of sexual control in the male attributed to inebriaty. The relationship between these two "social" diseases is made into a cause for the higher incidence among other Europeans. The Jews, because they are less likely to drink heavily, are less likely to be exposed to both the debilitating effects of alcohol (which increase the risk for tertiary lues) as well as the occasion for infection. In 1927 H. Strauß looked at the incidences of syphilitic infection in his hospital in Berlin in order to demonstrate whether the Jews had a lower incidence but also to see (as in the infamous Tuskegee experiments among African-Americans in the 1930s) whether they had "milder" forms of the disease because of their lifestyle or background.[111] He found that Jews had indeed a much lower incidence of syphilis (while having an extraordinarily higher rate of hysteria) than the non-Jewish control group. He proposes that the disease may well have a different course in Jews than in non-Jews. The marker for such a view of the heightened susceptibility or resistance to syphilis is the basic sign of difference of the Jews, the circumcised phallus.

The Jewish Psyche

Both of these models in the German Empire of the late nineteenth century, then, placed the Jew in a "special" relationship to syphilis and, therefore, in a very special relationship to the "healthy" body politic that needed to make the Jew visible. (The central medical paradigm for the establishment of the healthy state was the public health program which evolved specifically to combat the "evils" of sexually transmitted disease through social control.) Western Jews had been completely acculturated by the end of the nineteenth century and thus bore no easily identifiable external signs of difference (unique clothing, group language, group-specific hair and/or beard style). They had to bear the stigma of this special relationship to their diseased nature literally on the skin, where it could be seen, not only on the penis where (because of social practice) it could be "seen" only in the sexual act. And then, because of the gradual abandonment of circumcision, be "seen" not to exist at all!

Just as the hysteric is constructed out of the perceived ability to categorize and classify categories of difference visually, the syphilitic Jew has his illness written on his skin. The skin of the hysteric, like the physiognomy of the hysteric, reflects the essence of the disease. Thus the skin becomes a veritable canvas onto which the illness of the hysteric is mapped. Seeing the hysteric means reading the signs and symptoms (the *stigmata diaboli*) of the disease and representing the disease in a manner which captures its essence. It is the reduction of the ambiguous and fleeting signs of the constructed illness of the hysteric (constructed by the very nature of the definition of the disease in the nineteenth century). If the idea of the hysteric is tied to the idea of the feminization of the healthy, Aryan male or his "Jewification" (to use one of Adolf Hitler's favorite terms), then the representation of the disease must be in terms of models of illness which are convertible into the images of the feminized male. But these images of feminization are also tied to other, salient images of race in fin de siècle. For Jews bear the salient stigma of the black skin of the syphilitic, the syphilitic *rupia*, "a cutaneous disease, with vesicular formation."[112]

The Jews are black, according to nineteenth-century racial science, because they are not a pure race, because they are a race which has come from Africa. But the blackness of the African,

99

like the blackness of the Jew, was credited to the effect of certain diseases, specifically syphilis, on the skin of the African. (For more on this topic, see Chapter 7.) It is the change in the nature and color of the skin which marks the syphilitic; it is the color and quality of the skin which marks the Jew. This had been true as early as the publication in 1489 of the Spanish-Jewish physician Francisco Lopez de Villalobos's long poem on what comes to be called "syphilis":

> And it makes one dark in feature and obscure in countenance,
> Hunchback'd and indisposed, and seldom much at ease,
> And it makes one pained and crippled in such sort as never was,
> A scoundrel sort of thing, which also doth commence
> In the rascalliest place that a man has.[113]

Beginning as a disease of the genitalia, it soon is written on the sinner's skin. In popular and scientific belief the syphilitic *rupia* is written on the Jew's skin because of his special risk for this disease and because of his long-term exposure to it (and his increased immunity).

There had been a long tradition in Europe which held that of the skin of the Jew is marked by a disease, the "*Judenkratze*" or "*parech*," as a sign of divine displeasure.[114] (*Parech* was a disease long attributed to Eastern Europeans including Jews under the designation "plica polonica."[115]) In the late eighteenth century F. L. de La Fontaine argued that the Jews as suffering an extremely disgusting form of *parech* because of their inherent nature.[116] By the middle of the nineteenth century *parech* had also came to be seen not as the result of God's or Nature's wrath but as the result of syphilis.[117] By the end of the nineteenth century many Western Jews regarded it as one of the signs of difference between themselves and Eastern Jews.[118] Karl Marx, writing in 1861, associates leprosy, Jews, and syphilis (with a hint of "Eastern Jewish" foreignness added in through his use of a biblical reference) in his description of his arch-rival Ferdinand Lassalle: "Lazarus the leper, is the prototype of the Jews and of Lazarus-Lassalle. But in our Lazarus, the leprosy lies in the brain. His illness was originally a badly cured case of syphilis."[119] The pathognomonic sign of the Jew is written on the skin; it is evident to all to see. Here all of the forms of disease are linked in a common symptom, all are written on the skin. It should come as no surprise in this long chain of cultural-medical associations that the blackening of the skin was also reported, in the fin de siècle, as a sign of hysteria.[120] The blackness of the Jew is written on the skin and represents the inherent difference of Jewish scientist as well as Jewish patient.

The pathological image of the Jew was part of the general cultural vocabulary of Germany. Hitler used this image over and over in *Mein Kampf* in describing the Jew's role in German culture:

> If you cut even cautiously into such an abscess, you found, like a maggot in a rotting body, often dazzled by the sudden light—a kike! . . . This was pestilence, spiritual pestilence, worse than the Black Death of olden times, and the people were being infected by it. (57–58)

"Plague" ["Scuche"] and pestilence ["Pestilenz"]—a disease from without which, like syphilis rots the body—is the model Hitler uses to see the role of the Jew. He likens the syphilitic weakening of the racially pure Germans by the Jews to the corruption of the blood of the race through another form of "mammonization," interracial marriage:

> Here we have before us the results of procreation based partly on purely social compulsion and partly on financial grounds. The one leads to a general weakening, the other to a poisoning of the blood, since every department store Jewess is considered fit to augment the offspring of His Highness—and indeed the offspring look it. In both cases complete degeneration is the consequence. (247)

If the Germans (Aryans) are a "pure" race—and that is for turn-of-the-century science a positive quality—then the Jews cannot be a "pure" race. Their status as a mixed race became exemplified in the icon of the *Mischling* during the 1930s. According to the biological literature of the day, a person of "mixed" ancestry manifests the inferior race in an overt manner. The Jewishness of the *Mischling* "looks" and sounds degenerate. This is often represented by their facile use of language, "the use of innumerable foreign words and newly created words to enrich the German language in sharp contrast to the necessary simplicity of the language of Germanic students."[121] The Jew's language reflects the corruption of the Jew and his/her discourse. It is the sign of the "pathological early development" of the *Mischling*, who, as an adult, is unable to fulfill the promise of a member of a pure race. The weakness, but also the degenerate facility of the "Mischling," is analogous to the image of the offspring of the syphilitic. And thus we come full circle. For the Jew is contaminated by hysteria whether it is the result of the trauma of infection or of heredity. And this weakness of the race is hidden within the corrupted (and corrupting) individual. Thus Hitler's image of the *Mischling* is of the offspring of a "Jewish" mother and an "Aryan" father: hidden within the name and Germanic lineage of the child is the true corruption of the race, the maternal lineage of the Jew. And as Jews claimed their lineage through the mother (rather than through the father, as in German law) the *Mischling* becomes the exemplary hidden Jew waiting to corrupt the body politic.

The image of the *Mischling*, the individual impaired because of his/her inheritance, brings us back to the world of Ida Bauer. For here we have all of these themes of Jewish disposition and racial diagnosis summarized. The images which haunt Freud's representation of Ida Bauer: her language, the sexual acts of her imagination, their source, the relationship between pathology and infection, are all "racially" marked (at least notionally) in turn-of-the-century medical culture. For Freud, abandoning the act of seeing—an act made canonical in the work of his anti-Semitic mentor Charcot—is an abandonment of the associations of sight within this discourse of sexual difference. The case of Dora is an example of the power over language, of Freud's control over the language of his text which reveals him *not* to be an Eastern Jew. Like his critique of the "bad" Greek of his critics when he held his first talk on male hysteria in Vienna, Freud is the master of the discourse of science and culture. Freud is a scientist who uses language as a scientist. In introducing the question of the nature of Ida Bauer's attraction to Frau K. he remarks: "I must now turn to consider a further complication, to which I should certainly give no space if I were a man of letters engaged upon the creation of a mental state like this for a short story, instead of being a medical man engaged upon its dissection" (77). The act of writing the story is the sign of his special control of a "neutral" language, one which, as we have shown, is hardly neutral when it comes to placing Freud, the Eastern, male Jew, at its center of risk. The meaning of the act of seeing for the Jewish physician shows the inherent truth of Robert Reininger's claim that "Unser Weltbild ist immer zugleich ein Wertbild,"[122] that we construct our understanding of the world from our internalized system of values.

4

THE JEWISH MURDERER

Jack the Ripper, Race, and Gender

◆

"I am down on whores and I shan't quit ripping them till I do get buckled," wrote Jack the Ripper to the Central News Agency on September 18, 1888.[1] The question I want to raise in this essay reflects not on the reality of Jack the Ripper—real he was, and he never did get buckled—but on the contemporary fantasy of what a Jack the Ripper could have been. To understand the image of Jack, however, it is necessary to understand the image of the prostitute in Victoria's London. It is also necessary to comprehend the anxiety which attended her image in 1888, an anxiety which, like our anxieties a hundred years later, focused on diseases labeled sexual and attempted to locate their boundaries within the body of the Other.[2]

Who could truly kill the prostitute but the prostitute herself, who could expiate her sins against the male but she herself? For the prostitute's life must end in suicide. In Alfred Elmore's image *On the Brink*, exhibited at the Royal Academy in 1865, we see the initial step before the seduction of the female, the beginning of the slide toward prostitution and eventual self-destruction **[PLATE 20]**.[3] Alone, outside of the gambling salon in Bad Homburg, having lost her money, the potential object of seduction (Everywoman) is

PLATE TWENTY

The moment of seduction from Alfred Elmore, *On the Brink*, 1865 (Source: Fitzwilliam Museum, University of Cambridge, Cambridge).

tempted by the man to whom she is indebted. Women, all women, were seen as potentially able to be seduced, as having a "warm fond heart" in which "a strange and sublime unselfishness, which men too commonly discover only to profit by" exists, or so writes W. R. Greg in the *Westminster Review* of 1850.[4] The well-dressed woman has come to the spa, has exposed herself to the exploitation of the male, and is caught between the light and darkness of her future, a future mirrored in the representation of her face, half highlighted by the moonlight, half cast in shadow. She is at the moment of choice, a choice between the lily and the passion-flower. According to *The Language of Flowers*, a standard handbook of Victorian culture, she is caught between the lily, signifying purity and sweetness, and the passion-flower, representing strong feelings and susceptibility.[5] The gambling salon was the wrong locus for the female. As early as Hogarth's *The Lady's Last Stake* (1758–59), the female's seduction might be seen as the result of being in the wrong place. Males can gamble; females cannot. Males can indulge their passions; females cannot. Sexuality is a game for the male; it is not for the female. But gambling is also here a metaphor, though a socially embedded one, for the process by which the seduction of the female takes place. Playing upon the innate biological nature of the female makes the seduction possible, but the metaphor of losing at gambling also points to the model of infection and disease.

Alfred Elmore's picture shared this vocabulary of gambling. Gambling is a "fever" (*The* [London] *Times*), the gambler is "infected by the fever of gambling" (Illustrated London News), the gambler is thus "feverish" (*Athenaeum*).[6] Gambling is a disease which infects and makes ill, the infiltration into the purity of the female. Seduction thus has a course of illness: it begins with the signs and symptoms of disease, the fever of gambling, the result of the individual being out of place—much like the colonial explorer expecting to get malaria as a sign of being out of place—and leads inexorably to the next stages of the disease, prostitution and death.[7] The image of the gambler who stands at the moment of choosing between vice and virtue, who is gambling with life itself, is appropriate. Gambling is the sign of the moment before seduction, and thus the male stands in proximity to, but not touching, the female. The sexualized touch is prepared but has not been consummated. Once it is (if it is, and that is the ambiguity of this image), the course is inevitable—at least for the female—for "seduction must, almost as a matter of course, lead to prostitution," as W. W. Sanger observed in 1859.[8]

The appropriate end of the prostitute is suicide, "deserted to a life of misery, wretchedness, and poverty . . . terminated by self-destruction."[9] This is the penalty for permitting oneself to be seduced by immoral men, to be infected, and thus to spread infection to—innocent men? This is the chain of argument which places the seducer and the prostitute beyond the boundary which defines polite sexuality, and into the realm of disease, as in the case of Victoria's Prime Minster William Gladstone's fascination with prostitutes, which led him to attempt their conversion at his own hearthside and simultaneously undertake to have sexual contact with them. The seducer and the prostitute are the defining borders of diseased sexuality. The seducer is parallel to the image of Bram Stoker's *Dracula* (1897). For in the act of seduction he transforms the innocence of the female into a copy of himself, just as Dracula's victims become vampires. She becomes the prostitute as seductress, infecting other males as he had infected her with the disease of licentiousness (and, not incidentally, syphilis). Sexuality, disease, and death are linked in the act of seduction. As a contemporary reformist source noted, in this image "the Deceiver recognizes the Deceived . . . he, the tempter, the devil's agent . . . Men, seducers, should learn from this picture and fallen women, look at this, and remember 'the wages of sin is death.' "[10] The sign of the moment of the transmission of the disease of polluted (and polluting) sexuality, the sexualized touch, is just about to take place in Elmore's icon of seduction.[11] In Thomas Hood's widely cited poem on the death of the prostitute, "The Bridge of Sighs" (1844), the sexualized touch, the source of disease, is dramatized in its moment of passing away; when the prostitute's body dies, so does her contamination:

> Take her up instantly,
> Loving not loathing.

The Jewish Murderer

Touch her not scornfully;
Think of her mournfully,
Gently and humanly;
Not of the stains of her,
All that remains of her
Now is pure womanly . . . [12]

Death seems to purge the dead prostitute of her pollution, in a series of images of dead prostitutes in the nineteenth century from George Frederic Watt's *Found Drowned* (1848–50) through to the ubiquitous death mask of the *Beautiful Dead Woman from the Seine* which decorated many bourgeois parlors in France and Germany during the fin de siècle. The touching of the dead body is not merely a piteous gesture toward the "fallen," it is a permitted touching of the female, a not contagious, not infecting touching, a control over the dead woman's body.

Once dead by her own hand it was the physician who could touch the body. His role was to examine and dissect the body condemned to death by its fall from grace. And that body becomes the object of study, the corpse to be opened by the physician. For one of the favorite images of late nineteenth-century medical art is the unequal couple transmogrified into the image of the aged pathologist contemplating the exquisite body of the dead prostitute before he opens it. In the striking image by Enrique Simonet (1890) we are present the moment when the body has been opened and the pathologist stares at the heart of the whore [**PLATE 21**]. What will be found in the body of these drowned women? Will it be the hidden truths of the nature of the woman, what women want, the answer to Freud's question to Marie Bonaparte? Will it be the biological basis of difference, the cell with its degenerate or potentially infectious nature which parallels the image of the female and its potential for destroying the male? Will it be the face of the Medusa, with all of its castrating power? Remember that in that age of "syphiliphobia" the "Medusa" masks the infection hidden within the female. In Louis Raemaker's 1916 Belgian poster representing the temptation of the female as the source of syphilis, much of the traditional imagery of the seductress can be found [**PLATE 22**].

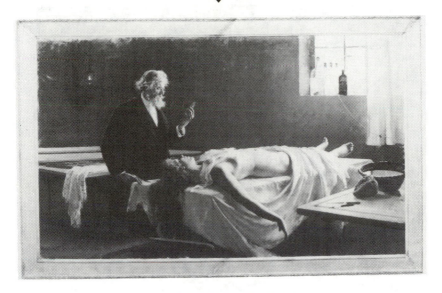

PLATE TWENTY-ONE

The beautiful dead woman during the autopsy in Enrique Simonet, *Tenía corazón*, 1890 (Source: Museo de Bellas Artes provincial, Malaga, Spain).

Standing among rows of graves, wearing a black cloak, and holding a skull which represents her genitalia, she is the essential femme fatale. But there is a striking fin-de-siècle addition to the image—for here "la syphilis" is the medusa. Her tendril-like hair, her staring eyes, present the viewer with the reason for the male's seduction: not his sexuality, but her vampiric power to control the male's rationality. The medusa is the genitalia of the female, threatening, as Sigmund Freud has so well demonstrated, the virility of the male, but also beckoning him to "penetrate" (to use Freud's word) into her mysteries.[13]

What will be found in the body of these drowned women? If we turn to the German expressionist Gottfried Benn's 1912 description of the autopsy of a beautiful drowned girl, we get an ironic, twentieth-century answer to this question:

> The mouth of a girl, who had long lain in the reeds
> looked so gnawed upon.

109

PLATE TWENTY-TWO

A woman with spiderlike hair, wearing a black cloak, stands among rows of graves. She holds a skull in her hands in this powerful illustration of the evils of syphilis in Louis Raemaker's *L'Hécatombe. La Syphilis*, ca. 1916 (Source: University of Wisconsin Medical School Library Collection, Madison).

The Jewish Murderer

When they finally broke open her chest, the esophagus
was so full of holes.
Finally in a bower below the diaphragm
they found a nest of young rats.
One of the little sisters was dead.
The others were living off liver and kidneys,
drinking the cold blood, and had
here spent a beautiful youth.
And death came to them too beautiful and quickly
We threw them all into the water.
Oh, how their little snouts squeaked![14]

The physician-poet Benn ironically transfers the quality of the aesthetic ascribed to the beautiful dead prostitute to the dead and dying rats. What is found within the woman is the replication of herself: the source of disease, of plague, the harbor rats, nestled within the gut. The birthing of the rats is the act of opening the body, exposing the corruption hidden within. The physician's eye is always cast to examine and find the source of pathology. This is the role assigned to the physician by society. Here, again, it is the male physician opening the body of the woman to discover the source of disease, here the plague, hidden within the woman's body.

But in the fantasy of the nineteenth century the physician could not remove the prostitute from the street. Only the whore could kill the whore. Only the whore, and Jack—killing and dismembering, searching after the cause of corruption and disease, Jack could kill the source of infection because, like them, he too was diseased. The paradigm for the relationship between Jack and the prostitutes can be taken from the popular medical discourse of the period: *Similia similibus curantur*, "like cures like," the motto of C.F.S. Hahnemann, the founder of homeopathic medicine. The scourge of the streets, the carrier of disease can only be eliminated by one who is equally corrupt and diseased. And that was Jack.

Jack, as he called himself, was evidently responsible for a series of murders which raised the anxiety level throughout London to a fever pitch in the cold, damp fall of 1888. The images of the murders in the *London Illustrated Police News* provide an insight into how the murderer was seen and also how the "real" prostitute, not the icon of prostitution or of seduction was portrayed in mass art. The murders ascribed to Jack the Ripper all took place in the East End of London, an area which had been the scene of heavy Eastern European Jewish immigration. Who, within the fantasy of the thought-collective, can open the body, besides the physician? No one but Jack, the emblem of human sexual perversion out of all control, out of all bounds. Jack becomes the sign of deviant human sexuality destroying life, the male parallel to the destructive prostitute. He is the representative of that inner force, hardly held under control, which has taken form, the form of Mr. Hyde. Indeed, an extraordinarily popular dramatic version of Robert Louis Stevenson's "Dr. Jekyll and Mr. Hyde" was playing in the West End while Jack (that not-so-hidden Mr. Hyde) terrorized the East End.

The images of the victims of "Jack"—ranging in number from four to twenty depending on which tabulation one follows—were portrayed as young women who had been slashed and mutilated. The Whitechapel murders most probably included Emma Smith (April 2, 1888), Martha Tabram (August 7, 1888), Mary Ann Nichols (August 31, 1888), Annie Chapman (September 8, 1888). Elizabeth Stride and Catherine Eddowes were both murdered on September 30, 1888. But, because of the sensibilities of even the readers of the *Illustrated Police News*, the mutilation presented is the mutilation of the face (as in the image of Annie Chapman). The reality, at least that reality which terrified the London of 1888, was that the victims were butchered. Baxter Philips, who undertook the postmortem description of Mary Ann Nichols described the process:

> The body had been completely disembowelled and the entrails flung carelessly in a heap on the table. The breasts had been cut off, hacked for no apparent purpose, and then hung on nails affixed to the walls of the room. Lumps of flesh, cut from the thighs and elsewhere, lay strewn about the room, so that the bones were exposed. As in some of the other cases, certain organs had been extracted, and, as they were missing, had doubtless been carried away.[15]

The medical literature of the time was more specific: "The Whitechapel monstrosity . . . invariably removes one kidney, the ovaries, uterus and labia."[16] These images of Jack's victims appeared at the time only within "scientific" sources such as Alexandre Lacassagne's 1889 study of sadism **[PLATE 23]**.[17]

In the public eye the prostitutes were their faces, the faces of the prostitute in death. But the true fascination was with those "certain organs [which] had been extracted" and had "been carried away." The whore's body had not merely been opened, but her essence, her sexuality, had been removed. These images are quite in contrast to those of the contemporary "Whitehall" murder where a decapitated torso was discovered and reconstructed from limbs found throughout the city. The mutilated body was understood over the course of the further killings to be one of Jack's victims, even though it contrasted with the bodies of the prostitutes whom Jack killed. In the case of Jack, the bodies were opened and their viscera were removed. Such sexual disfigurement, along with the amputation of the breasts of some of the victims, made it clear to both the police and the general public that Jack's actions were sexually motivated. And, indeed, most of the theories concerning Jack's identity assumed that he (or a close family member) had been infected with syphilis by a prostitute and was simply (if insanely) taking his revenge. But the vague contours of Jack the "victim" soon gave way to a very specific visual image of Jack.

What is striking is that the image of "Jack" is also set. He is the caricature of the Eastern Jew. Indeed, the official description of "Jack" was of a man "age 37, rather dark beard and moustache, dark jacket and trousers, black felt hat, spoke with a foreign accent" **[PLATE 24]**.[18] There appeared scrawled on the wall in Goulston Street near where a blood-covered apron was discovered the cryptic message: "The Juwes are The men That Will not be Blamed for nothing." The image of the Jews as sexually different, the Other even in the killing of the Other, led to the arrest of John Pizer, "Leather Apron," a Polish-Jewish shoemaker **[PLATE 25]**. Pizer was eventually cleared and released. But a high proportion of the 130 men questioned in the Ripper case were Jews. Sir Robert Anderson, the police official officially in charge of the case, noted in his memoir that:

PLATE TWENTY-THREE

Jack the Ripper's last victim, Catherine Eddowes, murdered
on September 30, 1888. The post-autopsy photograph of the
victim. From Alexandre Lacassagne, *Vacher l'éventreur et les
crimes sadiques* (Lyons: A. Storck, 1889) (Source: National
Library of Medicine, Bethesda, MD).

PLATE TWENTY-FOUR

The image of the Jewish Jack the Ripper from the *Illustrated Police News* (September, 1888) (Source: Olin Library, Ithaca, NY).

One did not need to be a Sherlock Holmes to discover that the criminal was a sexual maniac of a virulent type; that he was living in the immediate vicinity of the scenes of the murders; and that, if he was not living absolutely alone, his people knew of his guilt, and refused to give him up to justice. During my absence abroad the Police had made a house-to-house search for him, investigating the case of every man in the district whose circumstances were such that he could go and come and get rid of his blood-stains in secret. And the conclusion we came to was that he and his people were low-class Jews, for it is a remarkable fact that people of that class in the East End will not give up one of their number to

PLATE TWENTY-FIVE

The arrest of an Eastern Jew for the Whitechapel murders. *Illustrated Police News* (September 1888) (Source: Olin Library, Ithaca, NY).

Gentile justice. . . . I will only add that when the individual whom we suspected was caged in an asylum, the only person who had ever had a good view of the murderer at once identified him, but when he learned the suspect was a fellow-Jew he declined to swear to him.[19]

The claim that Jack the Ripper was a "sexual maniac" and a Jew lead to repercussions within the East End community. When the body of Catherine Eddowes was found on September 30th outside

116

the International Working Men's Educational Club by a Jew, a pogrom almost occurred in the East End, at least according to the *East London Observer* (October 15, 1888). "On Saturday the crowds who assembled in the streets began to assume a very threatening attitude towards the Hebrew population of the District. It was repeatedly asserted that no Englishman could have perpetrated such a horrible crime as that of Hanbury Street, and that it must have been done by a JEW—and forthwith the crowds began to threaten and abuse such of the unfortunate Hebrews as they found in the streets" [PLATE 26]. The powerful association between the working class, revolutionaries, and the Jews combined to create the visualization of Jack the Ripper as a Jewish worker, marked by his stigmata of degeneration as a killer of prostitutes. Here Jack had to intervene. In one of his rhyming missives sent to Sir Melville MacNaghten, the chief of the Criminal Investigation Division at Scotland Yard in 1889, he wrote:

> I'm not a butcher, I'm not a Yid
> Nor yet a foreign skipper,
> But I'm your own light-hearted friend,
> Yours truly, Jack the Ripper.[20]

When during the 1890s the German playwright Frank Wedekind visualized his Jack the Ripper killing the arch-whore Lulu he represented him as a degenerate, working-class figure: "He is a square-built man, elastic in his movements, with a pale face, inflamed eyes, thick arched eyebrows, drooping moustache, sparse beard, matted sidewhiskers and fiery red hands with gnawed finger nails. His eyes are fixed on the ground. He is wearing a dark overcoat and a small round hat."[21] This primitive figure was quite in line with the views shared by the Italian forensic psychiatrist, Cesare Lombroso, and his French opponent, Alexandre Lacassagne, as to the representative image (if not origin) of the criminal, very specifically the sadist.[22] For the Germans, at least for liberals such as Wedekind, Jack was also seen as a member of the lumpenproletariat in reaction to the charge, made in 1894 in the anti-Semitic newspapers in Germany, that Jack was an Eastern European Jew functioning as

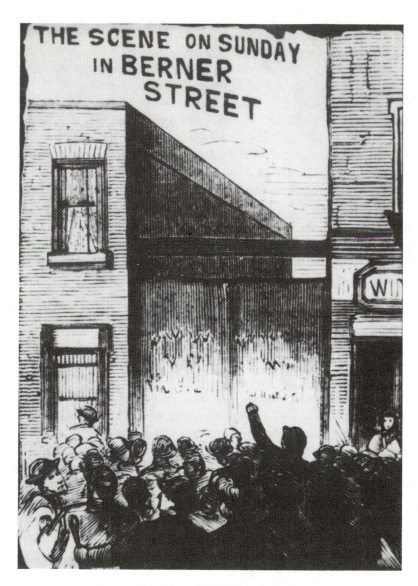

PLATE TWENTY-SIX

A mob threatens the East End Jewish community in response to the Whitechapel murders. *Illustrated Police News* (September 1888) (Source: Olin Library, Ithaca, New York).

118

part of the "International Jewish conspiracy."[23] This view echoed Sir Robert Anderson's comment on the conspiratorial nature of the "low-class" Jews in the East End. But in Britain this image evoked a very specific aspect of the proletariat, that of London's East End, the Eastern Jew.[24]

But why Eastern European Jews? The charge of ritual murder, the murder of Christian women by Polish Jews, appeared in the Times during this period. But this was but a sub-issue or perhaps a more limited analogy to the events in Whitechapel. Nor can we simply recall the history of British anti-Semitism, from the Norwich pogrom of 1144, caused by the charge of the ritual murder of a child, to the King's Road murders of 1771, which were laid at the feet of the Jews. The search for Jack the Ripper was the search for an appropriate murderer for the Whitechapel prostitutes. The murderer had to be representative of an image of sexuality that was equally distanced and frightening. Thus the image of Jack the Ripper as the *shochet*, the ritual butcher, arose at a moment during which there was a public campaign of the anti-vivisectionists in England and Germany against the "brutality" of the ritual slaughter of kosher meat.

This image of the Jack as the *shochet* rested on a long association in the Western imagination between Jews and the mutilated, diseased, different-looking genitalia. The Jewish mark of sexual difference—circumcision—was closely associated with the popular notion of Jack as syphilitic so that Jack the Ripper evoked in the minds of many the image of a foreign, syphilitic, mutilated butcher-Jew. The Jew remains the representation of the male as outsider, the act of circumcision marking the Jewish male as sexually apart, as anatomically different. It is important to remember that there is a constant and purposeful confusion through the late nineteenth and early twentieth centuries of circumcision and castration. This association is made within psychoanalytic theory at the fin de siècle, but it is present within the general culture of the nineteenth century, specifically in the medical debates about the origin of circumcision as a symbolic substitution for castration. It even permeated the ethnological literature of the period. In the Viennese yearbook of sexual folklore, *Anthropophyteia*, edited by the folklorist Friedrich Salamo Krauss which began publication in 1904, there is a small collection of tales, all with sexually explicit themes, which reflect the nightside of Jewish humor. (Sigmund Freud both informally contributed to this journal as well as sat on the board of editors. He also used it extensively for a number of his studies.) One of these jokes relates directly to the linkage of circumcision and castration, the text is in Yiddish, the bracketed comments are in German in the original:

> There is a *briss* (ritual circumcision) at the home of a *gwir* (rich man) in town. The *sandok* (godfather) sits on a chair and covers his *ponim* (face) with a *taliss* (prayer shawl). The *mohel* (ritual circumciser) also covers himself with a *taliss*, takes a knife, makes a *brocho* (blessing), sticks his hand into the half darkness and cuts. "Oi," the godfather leaps up with a scream, the *mohel* had accidently reached into his *tachtonim* (trousers) and cut off his *vechores* (penis).—"Oi, oi," the *mohel* begins to cry, "*a brocho l'va-tolo!*" (I have used the name of God in vain as I made a useless blessing!)[25]

The removal of the prepuce becomes the amputation of the penis. This association is a longstanding one within Western anti-Semitism and, as can be seen here, even infiltrates Jewish self-awareness.

The prostitute is, as has been shown, the embodiment of the degenerate and diseased female genitalia in the nineteenth century. From the standpoint of the normative perspective of the European middle class, it is natural that the Jew and the prostitute must be in conflict and that the one "opens up" the Other, as they are both seen as "dangers" to the economy, both fiscal and sexual, of the state. This notion of the association of the Jew and the prostitute is also present in the image of "spending" semen (in an illicit manner) which dominates the literature on masturbation in the eighteenth and early nineteenth centuries.[26] For the Jew and the prostitute are seen as negating factors, outsiders whose sexual images represent all of the dangers felt to be inherent in human sexuality. And consciously to destroy, indeed, to touch the polluting force of the Other, one must oneself be beyond the boundaries of acceptability.

The Jewish Murderer

The linkage between Jew and prostitute is much older than the 1880s. This association is related to the image of the black and the monkey (two icons of "deviant" sexuality) in the second plate of Hogarth's *A Harlot's Progress* [**PLATE 27**]. Here Moll Hackabout, the harlot, has become the mistress of a wealthy London Jew. The Jew has been cheated by the harlot, her lover is about to leave the scene. But her punishment is forthcoming. She will be dismissed by him and begin her slow slide downwards. Tom Brown, Hogarth's contemporary and the author of "A Letter to Madam—,kept by a Jew in Covent Garden," which may well have inspired the plate, concludes his letter on the sexuality of the Jew by asking the young woman "to be informed whether Aaron's bells make better music than ours."[27] It is this fascination with the sexual difference of the

PLATE TWENTY-SEVEN

Moll Hackabout as the Jew's mistress, the second plate of William Hogarth's *A Harlot's Progress* (1731) (Source: Private Collection, Ithaca).

Jew, parallel to the sexual difference of the prostitute, which relates them even in death. Each possesses a sexuality which is different from the norm, a sexuality which is represented in the unique form of their genitalia.

The relationship between the Jew and the prostitute also has a social dimension. For both Jew and prostitute have but one interest, the conversion of sex into money or money into sex. "So then," Brown writes to the lady, "'tis neither circumcision nor uncircumcision that avails any thing with you, but money, which belongs to all religions ..." (200). The major relationship, as Tom Brown and Hogarth outline, is a financial one; Jews buy specific types of Christian women, using their financial ability as a means of sexual control. "I would never have imagined you ... would have ever chosen a gallant out of that religion which clips and diminishes the current coin of love, or could ever be brought to like those people that lived two thousand years on types and figures" (199).

By the end of the nineteenth century this linkage had become a commonplace in all of Christian Europe. In 1892 there reappears in London an early nineteenth-century (1830s) pornographic "dialogue between a Jew and a Christian, a Whimsical Entertainment, lately performed in Duke's Palace," the "Adventures of Miss Lais Lovecock."[28] This dialogue represents the Jew and represents him in a very specific manner. First, the Jew speaks in dialect. By 1888 the British Jewish community had become completely acculturated. With Disraeli's terms as Prime Minister, as well as the Prince of Wales (later King Edward VII) attending the wedding of Leopold de Rothschild on January 14, 1881 at a London synagogue, the boundary between the "native" Jew and the "foreign" Jew had to be drawn. This explains the use of dialect, which, in 1892, would point toward the Eastern Jew, toward Jack the Ripper, who could not command written English at least about the "Juwes."[29] The text may well have reflected the image of the Jew in the 1830s, but it clearly had a very different set of associations after Jack the Ripper's appearance. The Jew, Isaac, describes his seduction of his father's Jewish (and, therefore, since all Jews are deviants in one way or another, hermaphroditic) maid who has a "clitoris, which was hard and shaped like a penis," while he seduces the Christian

122

prostitute, Polly. She is described by him as having "little feet and ankles, I think of your pretty legs, and den I think of your snowy thighs, and den my fancy glowing hot got to de fountain of bliss, and dere I vill go immediately" (66). She is the object of the Jew's desire, for his women (servant girls or whores) are as sexually marginal as he is himself. But it is only for money that Polly is willing to ring "Aaron's bells," for "nothing under three hundred a year . . ." (62). The prostitute is little more than a Jew herself. Both are on the margins of "polite" society. And, as we know, from the degeneration of Hogarth's Moll Hackabout following her relationship with the Jewish merchant, such sexuality in women leads to corruption and physical decay. The Jew, with all of his associations with disease, becomes the surrogate for all marginal males, males across the boundary from the (male) observer, males who, like women, can be the source of corruption, if not for the individual, then for the collective.

The association of the venality of the Jew with capital is retained even into the latter half of the twentieth century. In a series of British comic books from the 1980s in which an anthropomorphized phallus plays the central role, the Jew is depicted as masturbating, committing an "unnatural" act (while all of the other phalluses are depicted having a potential female partner) while reading a financial journal.[30] What is striking in these comics is that all of the phalluses are circumcised. This is a problem of contemporary culture. In the post-World-War-II decades, circumcision became a commonplace—even among non-Jews—in the United States and (less so, but more prominently than before World War II) Great Britain. How then to differentiate between the Jew and the non-Jew, between the "deviant" and the "normal"? We are faced with an analogous problem as to why George Eliot's eponymous character Daniel Deronda did not know he was a Jew. Did he never look at his penis? Here the hidden is not marked upon the skin, for the skin hides rather than reveals. It is the Jew within which surfaces. Here, in seeing a financial journal as the source of power and therefore of sexual stimulation; in Eliot's novel, with the "natural" sexual attraction between the crypto-Jew Deronda and the beautiful Jewess, Mirah Cohen.[31] (Deronda never defines himself as sexually different, for his own body is the baseline which defines for him the sexually "normal." His circumcised penis is not a sign of difference, until he understands himself to be a Jew.)

The image of the Jew revealed in his sexuality seems to be an accepted manner of labeling the image of the deviant. Even his phallus does not know for sure until he performs a "perverse" act. Here the icon is a reversal of the traditional image of the phallus as the beast out of control. In this image it is the man, not his phallus, who is bestial (read: Jewish). The perversion of the Jew (and thus the "humor" of this depiction of the phallus) lies in his sexualized relationship to capital. This, of course, echoes the oldest and most basic calumny against the Jew, his avarice, an avarice for the possession of "things," of "money," which signals his inability to understand (and produce) anything of transcendent aesthetic value. The historical background to this is clear. Canon law forbade the taking of interest. The taking of interest, according to Thomas Aquinas, was impossible, for money, not being alive, could not reproduce.[32] Jews, in taking money, treated money as if it were alive, as if it were a sexualized object. The Jew takes money as does the prostitute, as a substitute for higher values, for love and beauty. And thus the Jew becomes the representative of the deviant genitalia, the genitalia not under the control of the moral, rational conscience.

But the image of the Jew as prostitute is not merely one that draws an economic parallel between the sexuality of the Jew and that of the prostitute. It also reveals the nature of the sexuality of both Jew and prostitute as diseased, as polluting. Just as the first image of Jack the Ripper was that of the victim of the prostitute, the syphilitic male, so too were the Jews closely identified with sexually transmitted diseases. For the Jew was also closely related to the spread and incidence of syphilis. This charge appeared in various forms, as in the anti-Semitic tractate *England under the Jews* (1901) by Joseph Banister, in which there is a fixation on the spread of "blood and skin diseases."[33] Such views, as we have seen in the previous chapter, had two readings. Banister's was the more typical. The Jews were the carriers of sexually transmitted diseases

124

and transmitted them to the rest of the world. This view is also to be found in Hitler's discussion of syphilis in *Mein Kampf*.

This view of the Jew as syphilitic was not limited to the anti-Semitic fringe of the turn of the century. It possessed such power throughout the West that even "Jewish" writers (i.e., writers who felt themselves stigmatized by the label of being "Jewish") such as Marcel Proust (whose uncomfortable relationship to his mother's Jewish identity haunted his life almost as much as did his gay identity) presented it in their work.[34] In Proust's *Remembrance of Things Past*, a series of novels written to recapture the world of the 1880s and 1890s, one of the central characters, Charles Swann, is a Jew who marries a courtesan. Proust's linkage of Jew and prostitute is mirrored in his manner of representing the sexuality of the Jew. For Proust, being Jewish is analogous to being homosexual—it is "an incurable disease."[35] But what marks this disease for all to see? In the *mentalité* of the turn of the century, syphilis in the male must be written on the skin, just as it is hidden within the sexuality of the female. Proust, who discusses the signs and symptoms of syphilis with a detailed clinical knowledge in the same volume, knows precisely what marks the sexuality of the Jew upon his physiognomy.[36] It is marked upon his face as "ethnic eczema."[37] It is a sign of sexual and racial corruption as surely as the composite photographs of the Jew made by Francis Galton at the time revealed the "true face" of the Jew.[38] This mark upon the face is Hitler's and Banister's sign of the Jew's sexual perversion. It is the infectious nature of that "incurable disease," the sexuality of the Jew, Proust's Jew fixated upon his courtesan. (This is an interesting reversal of one of the sub-themes of Zola's *Nana*. There, Nana, like Moll Hackabout, is first the mistress of a Jew, whom she, quite easily reversing the role of Jack the Ripper, bankrupts and drives to suicide.) The Jew's sexuality, the sexuality of the polluter, is written on his face in the skin disease which announces the difference of the Jew. For Proust, all of his Jewish figures (including Swann and Bloch) are in some way diseased, and in every case, this image of disease links the racial with the sexual, much as Proust's image of the homosexual links class (or at least, the nobility) with homosexu-

125

ality. ("Homosexuality" is a "scientific" label for a new "disease" coined by Karoly Benkert in 1869 at the very same moment in history that the new "scientific" term for Jew-hating, "anti-Semitism," was created by Wilhelm Marr.) The image of the infected and infecting Jew also had a strong political as well as personal dimension for Proust. For the ability to "see" the Jew who was trying to pass as a non-Jew within French society is one of the themes of the novels, a theme which, after the Dreyfus Affair, had overt political implications. Seeing the Jew was seeing the enemy within the body politic, was seeing the force for destruction. And Proust's "racial" as well as sexual identity was tied to his sense of the importance of class and society for the definition of the individual. Thus Proust's arch-Jew Swann was visibly marked by him as the heterosexual syphilitic, as that which Proust was not (at least in his fantasy about his own sexual identity).

A contrary model was also present which stated that Jews were immune to the ravages of the disease because of centuries of exposure. The reason given by non-Jewish scientists was the inherited tendency of male Jews to be more "immune." Just as "Jewishness" was an inherited tendency, so too was the nature of a "Jewish sexuality," a sexuality so markedly different that it was claimed that some Jewish male infants were even born circumcised![39]

Both of these arguments saw the Jew as having a "special" relationship to syphilis through the agency of the prostitute. And this special relationship could literally be seen on the Jew. Joseph Banister saw the Jews as bearing the stigmata of skin disease (as a model for discussing sexually transmitted disease): "If the gentle reader desires to know what kind of blood it is that flows in the Chosen People's veins, he cannot do better than take a gentle stroll through Hatton Garden, Maida Vale, Petticoat Lane, or any other London 'nosery.' I do not hesitate to say that in the course of an hour's peregrinations he will see more cases of lupus, trachoma, favus, eczema, and scurvy than he would come across in a week's wanderings in any quarter of the Metropolis."[40] The image of the Jew's nose is a "delicate" anti-Semitic reference to the phallus. For the "nose" is the iconic representation of the Jew's phallus throughout the nineteenth century. Indeed, Jewish social scientists such as the British savant Joseph Jacobs, spent a good deal of their time denying the meaning of "nostrility" as a sign of the racial cohesion of the Jews.[41] It is clear that for Jacobs (as for Wilhelm Fliess in Germany[42]) the nose is the displaced locus of anxiety associated with the marking of the male Jew's body through circumcision—an anxiety which was fueled by the late nineteenth-century debate about the "primitive" nature of circumcision and its reflection on the acculturation of the Western Jew. Indeed, as we noted in Chapter 3, even the color of the Jew's skin, the blackness, of the Jew, was spoken of as if it was a sign of syphilis. Like the leper, Jews bear their diseased sexuality on their skin.[43]

Jews=lepers=syphilitics=prostitutes=blacks. This chain of association presents the ultimate rationale for the Jewish Jack the Ripper. For the diseased destroy the diseased, the corrupt the corrupt. They corrupt in their act of touching, of seducing, the pure and innocent, creating new polluters. But they are also able in their sexual frenzy to touch and kill the sexual pariahs, the prostitutes, who like Lulu at the close of Frank Wedekind's play (and Alban Berg's opera) go out to meet them, seeking their own death. Being unclean, being a version of the female genitalia (with their amputated genitalia), the male Jew is read (as Jack's Viennese contemporary Otto Weininger read him) as really nothing but a type of female. The pariah can thus touch and kill the pariah; the same destroy the same. Wedekind's Lulu dies not as a suicide but as the victim of the confrontation between two libidinal forces—the unbridled, degenerate sexuality of the male and the sexual chaos of the sexually emancipated female. But die she does, and Jack leaves the stage, having washed his hands, like Pontius Pilate, ready to kill again.

5

THE JEWISH GENIUS

Freud and the
Jewishness of the Creative

◆————————◆

The "intellectual attributes of the Jews," whether in the desert or in the banks of Europe, "have remained constant for thousands of years."[1] The qualities of the Jewish mind, of the "common mental constructions" which define the Jew, usually are understood in fin-de-siècle culture as negative and destructive.[2] The Jews "possess no imagination . . . All who have any claim at all to speak, testify unanimously that lack—of let us say poverty—of imagination is a fundamental trait of the Semite."[3] The "Jewish mind does not have the power to produce even the tiniest flower or blade of grass that has grown in the soil of another's mind and to put it into a comprehensive picture."[4] "Hence the Jewish people, despite all apparent intellectual qualities, is without any true culture, and especially without any culture of its own. For what sham culture the Jew today possesses is the property of other peoples, and for the most part it is ruined in his hands."[5]

Jewish scientists, such as the founder of the "sociology of the Jews," Arthur Ruppin, found it necessary to counter this view constantly: "It is incorrect to accuse the Jews of having talent but producing no geniuses. Genius is sown thinly among all peoples.

... Certainly the number of highly gifted individuals among the Jews will increase as soon as the Jews are able to leave the merchant class in larger numbers, for it is clear that the education to acquisitiveness certainly hinders the creative gift."[6] This view was to be found as well within the medical literature of the age. Jews were neurasthenic or hysteric and evidenced the signs and symptoms of these debilitating diseases in terms of the language which they employed. Their aesthetic creations were therefore inherently flawed, as they reflected a diseased mind.

That the Jew could not produce transcendental works of aesthetic value was a commonplace in Germany from the Enlightenment on. That this inability was a psychological fault resulting from their Jewishness was a discovery of the medical science of the nineteenth century. This medicalization of the lack of true creativity on the part of the Jews became part of the discourse of degeneration. For the racial biologist of the fin de siècle the Jews could evidence no true genius and, therefore, their creations could have no true originality. Indeed, any seeming genius shown by the Jew was a mark of his degeneracy. Medical literature of the time tended to show that behind the Jews' supposed intellectual superiority was an inferior ability to perform measurable tasks, such as schoolwork.[7] It was the superficiality of the Jew, the Jew's mimicry of a world which he could never truly enter, which produced works which were felt to be creative but, in fact, were mere copies of the products of *truly* creative individuals. And this degenerate creativity was marked by the stigmata of disease, of madness.

But are "madness" and "creativity" necessarily linked? Aristotle believed that they were. In the *Problemata* he asked the question, "Why are men of genius melancholics?"[8] Melancholia, the dominance of one of the humors, the mythic black bile, was seen as the root of most mental illnesses from the ancient Greeks through the Renaissance. Aristotle saw figures such as Heracles as possessing a melancholic constitution but also saw "most of the poets" as being "clearly melancholics." "Creative" minds are diseased or, at least according to the ancients, are housed in a body dominated by black bile, the source of madness. The special role, closely associated with that of the priest, attributed to the artist and poet by the

Greeks demanded a specific type of insight, an insight which was unique. Aristotle, who sought to determine the boundary between the "normal," observing member of society (defined by himself) and the "poet," employed a materialistic, strictly somatic definition of "creativity." For him, "creativity" is the product of the imbalance of the natural forces (the humors), forces which the Greeks believed created the stasis of daily life. "Creativity" is not the inspiration or punishment of the gods, but a product of the body and a sign of its pathology. The "creative" individual is thus "different" from the observer, diseased and productive.

This view of the relationship between "madness" and "creativity" has been sporadically accepted in Western culture since the Greeks. On one level or another, or at some remove, "creative" individuals are set apart from the normal not only by their actions but also by the source of these actions. The uniqueness of the "creative" individual is perceived as the result of some greater, overwhelming force which places the ordinary observer in a position removed from the wellspring of "creativity." This view is generally accepted throughout the nineteenth century and attains the status of a truism. Whether in the works of the Romantic psychiatrists of the early nineteenth century, who sought after a metaphysical answer to the idea of madness, or in the work of the biologically oriented psychiatrists who see mind (and, therefore, "creativity") as a simple product of the brain, the "creative" individual is labeled as drawing on resources (or errors) which are not present in the "normal" individual. And that "normal" individual is silently assumed to be the physician, scientist, or philosopher who is describing "creativity!"

In framing the debates about the nature of "creativity" in the medical sciences of the twentieth century, we can see how the very object and meaning of the "creative" has shifted over time. "Creativity" is a universal category of Western thought, but what it means is historically and culturally determined in an absolute manner. Each age invents, to fulfill its own needs, what the truly "creative" is and each time constructs a working definition which satisfies its own need to place itself in relationship to the "creative."

The dominant theory of the relationship between creativity and

130

disease in the late nineteenth century was those of Cesare Lombroso. Lombroso, in his first major work on the subject, *Genius and Madness* (1864), drew analogies between the products of genius and works made by the insane which he had seen during in his practice in the Turin psychiatric clinic.[9] Lombroso's book, and his subsequent fame as the best-known medical champion of the concept of "degeneracy" as the central explanation of deviancy (from sociopathic and psychopathic to creative acts), moved this question into the center of the concerns of modern clinical and asylum psychiatry. It was only following Lombroso that the two questions were clearly separated: one line led to the examination of the "great" in order to find the psychopathological origin of their greatness; the other to examine the aesthetic products of the mentally ill to establish the nature of the creativity of the mad (and discover the "creativity" in their illness).

One issue which Lombroso addressed quite directly is the relationship between race, insanity, and genius. Jews, following the accepted wisdom of the age, evidenced a "curious" overabundance of "lunatics," "four or even six times . . . as [many as] the rest of the population." Lombroso was forced to separate this "fact" from its use: "This fatal privilege has not attracted the attention of the leaders of that anti-Semitic movement which is one of the shames of contemporary Germany. They would be less irritated at the success of this race if they had thought of all the sorrows that are the price of it, even at our epoch; for if the tragedies of the past were more bloody, the victims are not now less unhappy, struck at the source of their glory, and because of it deprived even of the consolation of being able, as formerly, to contribute to the most noble among the selections of species."[10] This is very much in line with Wilhelm Wundt's view that "care and tragedy can influence nutrition by limiting the entrance of air and blood" and can thus affect the psyche.[11] Jews evidence greater levels of genius because of "the bloody selection of medieval persecutions, and owing also to the influence of temperate climate, the Jews of Europe have risen above those of Africa and the East, and have often surpassed the Aryans."[12] At least one Jewish physician in Vienna agreed with Lombroso's claims. The young Arthur Schnitzler, writing in his father's medical journal in 1891, commented that Lombroso's information about the heightened risk of Jews for mental illness as the cost of the greater genius of the race is "of special interest for our times."[13]

Lombroso's statistical work relied on Joseph Jacobs, who attributed the Jews' talent to their religious traditions.[14] But Lombroso could not see any connection between "this rhythmical caterwauling and the sublime notes of Meyerbeer and Mendelssohn."[15] While Jews have a much higher rate of men of genius, they have yet to produce "men like Newton, Darwin, and Michelangelo, . . . because they have not yet accomplished their ethnic evolution, as they show by the obstinacy with which they cling to their ancient beliefs."[16] In the work of Lombroso (himself an Italian Jew), the category of the creative was contaminated by the pathological, for him, "religious" identity (as for Mantegazza the practice of circumcision) contaminates the pure genius of the Jew. Lombroso expresses this attitude when he stresses that the genius of the Jew in its positive appearance brings a new level of creativity into the Aryan race.[17]

The question of the relationship between the idea of madness and the meaning of creativity was much discussed at the turn of the century. That Jews were active within the spheres of culture and science could not be contradicted—but was their activity to be understood as "creative"? The seemingly central role of Jews in culture was put into question by the argument that this type of art was superficial or perhaps even corrupting. Indeed, it was all to often argued, that the "creativity" of the Jew was really a sign of his diseased, "mad" state. Thus Lombroso's evocation of Heinrich Heine reflected a central motif in the work of fin-de-siècle scientists. For them, the ill Heine became the exemplary image of the diseased Jew. (According to Lombroso, Heine's illness was not madness *per se*, but a disease of the spinal cord, which "may have given a morbid character" to Heine's writing.[18] Arthur Schnitzler, in his review of Lombroso, countered with the claim that Lombroso was misreading Heine's "hatred" for Germany as a sign of his pathology; what Heine desired, according to Schnitzler, was his desire to be healed of his love for Germany.[19] The impossibility of being both a Jew and a German lead, in Schnitzler's reading, to a true madness.)

The debate about the nature of the Jews' creativity ran through the medical as well as the popular literature of the fin de siècle. Freud's younger Viennese contemporary, the self-hating Jew Otto Weininger, presented the dichotomy between the Jew and the Aryan in his *Sex and Character* (1903).[20] Otto Weininger had been a student of philosophy and biology at the University of Vienna at the fin de siècle. He published his revised dissertation, *Sex and Character*, in 1903 and killed himself shortly thereafter in the house in Vienna in which Beethoven had died.[21] Weininger was both a baptized Jew and a repressed homosexual.[22] His book became an immediate best-seller and established him as a serious contributor to the discourse about the relationship between race and gender at the beginning of the century.[23] This is a work of intensive self-hatred which, however, had an unprecedented influence on the scientific discourse about Jews and women at the turn of the century. Why, it might well be asked? Weininger's suicide shortly after the publication of this book helped to publicize his ideas, but they were hardly new ones to his contemporaries. The appeal of Weininger's work was not innovation but summation. To the end of a century he held up a polemical mirror that many found to contain truths of their times. (Read by Freud in an early draft, the book was fundamental in shaping at least some of his attitudes toward the nature of the body. And, indeed, it was seen as a serious work of science after its publication by radical thinkers of the time, such as the American arch-feminist Charlotte Perkins Gilman.[24] Ludwig Wittgenstein, confronted with his "Jewish" nature and his Catholic upbringing, accepted and incorporated aspects of Weininger's "philosophy" into his world view.[25] Its influence extended to the most original and influential work by Japan's leading fin-de-siècle philosopher Kitâro Nishida.[26]) What *Sex and Character* did was to restate in a scientific, i.e., biological context Arthur Schopenhauer's views on women and simply extend the category of the feminine to the Jew. It argued, within the rhetoric of contemporary science, that there is a psychological scale which runs from the Jewish mind on one end to the Aryan at the other. This scale is parallel to another, the "feminine" and the "masculine."

Weininger stressed that categories such as the "Jew" and the "Woman" were psychological states always found in tension with the "Christian" and the "Male." Weininger, the converted Jew, saw himself as less "Jewish" than the arch-anti-Semite Richard Wagner, whom he labels as "having an accretion of Jewishness in his art" (305). Jewishness is a "common mental construction." It does "not refer to a nation or to a race, to a creed or to a scripture. When I speak of the Jew I mean neither an individual nor the whole body, but mankind in general, in so far as it has a share in the platonic idea of Judaism" (306). Weininger constructs the image of the Jew like that of the woman as inherently negative, as necessarily to be transcended.

For Weininger Jews and women have "no genius." He attacks Spinoza and Heinrich Heine as the representative Jewish thinkers who are viewed by his contemporaries as "creative" geniuses. They are for him incapable of true genius: "The philosopher Spinoza, about whose purely Jewish descent there can be no doubt, is incomparably the greatest Jew of the last nine hundred years, much greater than the poet Heine (who indeed was destitute of any quality of true greatness) . . . ." (216). Nevertheless, Spinoza lacks genius. What passes for genius in the Jew—and the woman—is but "exaggerated egotism" (317). Jewish creativity is inherently superficial.

What characterizes the woman is her language: "The impulse to lie is stronger in woman, because, unlike that of man, her memory is not continuous, whilst her life is discrete, unconnected, discontinuous, swayed by the sensations and perceptions of the moment instead of dominating them" (146). Women's language is lies; Jews' language is *Mauscheln*, speaking so distinctively that it marks the speaker as a Jew:

> Just as the acuteness of Jews has nothing to do with the true power of differentiating, so his shyness about singing or even about speaking in clear positive tones has nothing to do with real reserve. It is a kind of inverted pride; having no true sense of his own

worth, he fears being made ridiculous by his singing or his speech. (324)

Jews and women, for example, have no "true humor," for true humor must be transcendent; Jews "are witty only at [their] own expense and on sexual things" (318). Jews are inherently more preoccupied by the sexual but less potent than Aryans (311). Their obsession is rooted in the fact that sex breaks down boundaries between individuals. Jews like women are "devoid of humor and addicted to mockery" (319). "The Jew who does not set out, like the humorist, from the transcendental, and does not move towards it, like the erotic, has no interest in depreciating what is called the actual world, and that never becomes for him the paraphernalia of a juggler or the nightmare of a mad-house" (319).

The Jews' supposed predilection for mockery became a leitmotif in the fin de siècle, one that was was related to the very nature of the Jewish body. The psychoanalyst and first biographer of Freud, Fritz Wittels, argued, in reference to Freud's great opponent, the hunchbacked Karl Kraus, that Kraus's sense of satirical wit rested on his deformity: "Mockery seems to be linked with physical deformity, and in that way to be suitable as a special domain of the Jews," as Freud showed ... "in the analysis of the phobia of a five-year-old boy [Little Hans] with its stress on castration and circumcision."[27] The "Kraus-neurosis" was supposedly the result of Kraus's deformity, but Wittels directly related this to the overall perception of the difference attributed to the body of the Jew. And the most evident reflex of these physical attributes, according to Wittels, is to be found in the nature of the Jew's language. It is the hidden language of the Jews, it is *Mauscheln*, which is related to the physical nature of the Jews. They mock others because of their own physical infirmity, because of their circumcised penis.

Otto Rank reverses this view in his essay on "The Essence of Judaism" (1905) when he notes that "where the religion [of the Jews] is insufficient to do this [to maintain psychic balance], Jews resort to wit; for they do not have their own 'culture.'"[28] By "culture" Rank is adapting and reversing Weininger's theory of the centeredness of the Christian. "Culture," for Rank, is an advanced state of sexual repression. The Jews exist in a state much more "primitive" and "natural," in which this level of repression has not yet taken place. Humor becomes an atavistic sign of the sexuality of the Jews.

Continuing Weininger's argument, Jews are historically extremely adaptable, as can be shown by their talent for the superficial areas of "creativity" such as journalism. But in their essence they are truly unchangeable. They lack deep-rooted and original ideas. (320) The Jews are the essential unbelievers; not even believing in themselves. (321) The Jew has no center. He is critical, not a critic. He is not merely a materialist; he doubts all and any truths. He is irreligious; indeed, his religion is not even a real religion. It is a reflection of the Jewish mind which always demands multiple choices. It is not the historical treatment of the Jews which has made them what they are: "Outward circumstances do not mould a race in one direction, unless there is in the race the innate tendency to respond" (308). And the Jewishness of the Jew is immutable. The Jew is a "parasite." He is "a different creature in every host and yet remains himself" (320). The Jew is the disease in the body politic.

It is in one arena that this immutability of mind and spirit, this moral "madness," most clearly manifests itself and that is within science, most specifically within the world of medicine. For the Jews there is no transcendentalism, everything is as flat and commonplace as possible. Their effort to understand everything robs the world of its mystery. (314) Evolutionary theory ("the ridiculous notion that men are derived from monkeys" [314–15]), for example, is mere materialism.

The development of nineteenth-century medicine from its focus on bacteriology in the 1880s to its focus on biochemistry at the turn of the century meant a real shift of interest from the "organic" to the "inert" on the part of the medical scientist. For Weininger, Jews are natural chemists, which explains why medicine has become biochemistry: "The present turn of medical science is largely due to the influence of the Jews, who in such numbers have embraced the medical profession. From the earliest times, until the dominance of the Jews, medicine was closely allied with religion. But now they make it a matter of drugs, a mere administration of chemicals. . . . The chemical interpretation of organisms sets these on a level with their own dead ashes" (315). This Weininger interprets as a "Jewification" of medicine. For the Jews focus on the dead, the inert.

For Weininger the turn of the century is the age of feminization, a corruption of society (including medicine) by the Jews: "This is the age which is most Jewish and most feminine. . . . It is a time when art is content with daubs and seeks its inspiration in the sports of animals; . . . a time for originality and yet with the most foolish craving for originality. The choice must be made between Judaism and Christianity, between business and culture, between male and female, between the race and the individual, between unworthiness and worth . . . Mankind has the choice to make. There are only two poles, and there is no middle way." (329–30). Jewishness, like the feminine, is a state condemned to be "uncreative." This litany of hate places the Jew in an antithetical relationship to true "creativity." And as bearing a great risk for "madness." As we have seen elsewhere, Weininger's position is hardly unique. It reflects the general view of anti-Semitic racial science about the special nature of the Jew. Thus "creativity" is linked to Jews, their "madness," and the ultimate source of their madness, their sexuality.

Now we must try to imagine Freud confronted with this view. Of all of the topics he could have addressed about the nature of the psyche, why was it "creativity" which captured him? This choice seems as idiosyncratic as a means of discussing the normal structure of the psyche as those of dreams, or jokes, or slips of the tongue. One answer is that each of these can be linked to debates within the racial science of the late nineteenth century.[29]

Sigmund Freud's view was, on the surface, quite different from Lombroso's or Weininger's. In his writings from the close of the nineteenth century through the onset of World War I, he saw "creativity" (as he did dreams or slips of the tongue or neurotic symptoms) not as a set of formal processes or disease mechanisms in a sub-set of the population but as clues to the normal functioning of the unconscious in everyone. Where Lombroso saw the "mad" and

137

their aesthetic productions as "throwbacks" to an earlier, more primitive state of development or as a sign of the diseased nature of the Jew, Freud saw all "creativity" as a sign of the universal, underlying forces which make all human beings human. He, too, saw it as pathological in that it was the result of deviation from "normal" psychological development, but as such, this pathology was a potential of all human beings, not merely a predestined sub-set. He studied the creative to understand the centrality of unconscious processes, especially the role of unconscious motivation in human action.

Freud, in his case studies of Leonardo (1910) and Michelangelo (1914), as well as in his critical readings of the creative works of Wilhelm Jensen (1907) and the strange autobiography of the "psychotic" Dr. Daniel Schreber (1911), looked at the "creative" work as a sign of the displacement of psychic (and for Freud that means sexual) energy into a different, seemingly unrelated undertaking.[30] The "creative" impulse is a form of displacement or repression analogous to the symptoms of the neurotic. The symptoms of the neurotic parallel the experiences or fantasies which underlie them but do not directly represent the underlying conflict which gives rise to them. For Freud, it is the sphere of the sexual in which these products (whether symptoms or works of art) always arise. For the "creative" individual is by Freud's definition one who *must* sublimate his sexual drive into the realm of fantasy. The truly creative individual represses all of his latent instinctual drives. Like the Jew in Viennese society, the creative figure must deny his essence to become what he can become. And like the Jew, that which is repressed in these creative individuals is the atavistic sexual drive. The reason for this sublimation, as in the case of the artists and authors listed above, is because of the socially unacceptable direction of the expression of their sexuality (from the homosexuality of Leonardo to the incestuous leanings of Jensen). All of these individuals represent sexuality on an earlier plane of development than the sexuality of the heterosexual.

In certain individuals, Freud argued, the active, social repression of these drives leads to the total sublimation of sexual curiosity and, thereby, to the creative process and the true work of art.[31] The "creative" object thus represents the fixed fantasies of the individual. The essential nature of the process of "creativity" is to mask the inherently objectionable (from the standpoint of society) nature of its origin. Works of art "conceal their personal origin and, by obeying the laws of beauty, bribe other people with a bonus of pleasure."[32] The overarching "laws of beauty," the technique of the aesthetic, are the means by which the "creative" works. It is the universal mask which hides and manipulates. It is separate from the "creative" impulse and shapes how the observer sees the work of art. "Creativity" is seen in terms of the "creator" who produces a product, which is implicitly a commodity, as value is inherently attached to it. That product is cast in a form which is universal, and it manipulates the reader or viewer through its evocation of some universal law (the aesthetic). The "creativity" of the artist consists of placing a repressed aspect of the artist's psyche into the realm of the aesthetic. As Josef Breuer—focusing on the ultimate "creative" figure for nineteenth-century German culture—said in the *Studies on Hysteria* (jointly authored with Freud in 1895): "Goethe did not feel he had dealt with an experience till he had discharged it in a creative artistic activity."[33]

But it is the act of seeing—the observer's act of seeing and responding to the creative product of the artist—which defines "creativity" for Freud. To use one of his examples, we—the naive viewer—look at Leonardo's image of the *Holy Family* and "see" the perfection and beauty of the work, but also are instructed in its "meaning" by the psychoanalyst. The psychoanalyst is able to see beneath the initial evocation of the aesthetic (which disguises the motivation of the author) and provide an interpretation of the work of art and of the psyche of the artist. The uninformed viewer's response is aesthetic; with the aide of the interpreter (Freud) we can understand the source of the artist's "creativity" and thus truly understand the "unseen" aspect of the work of art. Analogous to the psychoanalyst's explaining to the patient the typography of the dynamic unconscious, the critic explains to the viewer what he or she is observing. It is here that we learn to distrust the initial act of seeing and to link the act of seeing, not with a visceral response, but with the act of knowing. Freud's focus seems to be solely on the motivation which underlies "creativity." It is the discovery that the "creative" individual is "subject to the laws which govern both normal and pathological activity with equal cogency" which Freud illustrates.[34] But his hidden agenda is to undermine our sense that we can see the world directly.

This is clearest in Freud's popular essay on "Creative Writers and Day-Dreaming" which was presented as a lecture to a lay (i.e., non-medical) audience in Vienna during 1907.[35] Freud's overt intention is to present the parallels between "creativity" and childhood play. In this essay Freud defines "creativity" and the special status of the "creative" artist: "We laymen have always been intensely curious to know—like the Cardinal who put a similar question to Ariosto—from what sources that strange being, the creative writer, draws his material, and how he manages to make such an impression on us with it and to arouse in us emotions which, perhaps, we had not thought ourselves capable."[36] Freud places himself as a "layman" in opposition to the "creative" individual who makes a world which seems complete and who uses that world to manipulate our ("lay" or "non-creative") emotions. But it is a very special "lay" observer, one who has the insight to understand the underlying meaning as well as the immediate effect of the "creative." Freud's initial analogy is to the play of the child. Play is rooted in childhood fantasies of being able to control at least the immediate world of toys in opposition to the real world which is beyond the manipulation of the child.[37] It is into this universe, in which uncontrollable realities are transmuted into manipulable fantasies, that the child escapes: "for many things which, if they were real, could give no enjoyment, can do so in the play of fantasy."[38] It is "humor" which is for Freud the ultimate example of how the healthy adult can escape back into this world of playfulness: "by equating his ostensibly serious occupations of to-day with his childhood games, he can throw off the too heavy burden imposed on him by life and win the high yield of pleasure afforded by *humor*."[39]

Fantasy is like dreaming. It uses everyday impressions which are related to earlier (infantile) experience and "creates a situation relating to the future." Thus, the "creative" individual is like the playful child, but also like the neurotic in another central aspect.[40]

Like the neurotic, the "creative" individual has the compulsion to tell (represent) his or her fantasies: "there is a class of human beings upon whom, not a god, indeed, but a stern goddess—Necessity—has allotted the task of telling what they suffer and what things give them happiness. These are the victims of nervous illness, who are obliged to tell their fantasies. . . ."[41] In paraphrasing Goethe's *Torquato Tasso* in this passage ("and when a man falls silent in his torment/A god granted me to tell how I suffer"), Freud elides the artist as figure (Tasso) and the artist as author (Goethe) with the "mad person" as figure (Tasso) and the healer of the "mad" (Freud). The artificial line which Freud drew between the "creative" individual as neurotic on the one side and himself (and his listeners) on the other at the beginning of his essay is shown at its close to be a false dichotomy. The informed, psychoanalytically instructed observer "sees" below the surface. Freud joins the world of art as artifact and inspiration in his "creative" role as the psychoanalyst, but only in the most hidden and covert way.

In this essay of 1907 the "creative" individual is also not gender neutral. Young women have more erotic fantasies than do young men, who have in turn more fantasies of ambition. Both must learn to conceal and repress these drives, as they are unacceptable in polite society: "the well-brought-up young woman is only allowed a minimum of erotic desire, and the young man has to learn to suppress the excess of self-regard which he brings with him from the spoilt days of his childhood, so that he may find his place in a society which is full of other individuals making equally strong demands."[42] Human sexuality, the wellspring of "creativity," is initially and more strongly present in the fantasy world of the female. And while these trends merge at some point early in the life cycle, the female is the gender whose fantasies are the more sexualized in their most primitive (i.e., earliest) form.

Thus Freud in this text provides a set of working hypotheses about "creativity." First, that "creativity" has to do with the representation of internal stories in a highly affective and effective manner; second, that "creativity" is parallel to the states of "childhood" and "neurosis," in that it is an attempt to gain control over the real world by creating a fantasy world over which one can have control

141

(and "humor" is the prime example of this control); third, that there is a difference, but also a similarity, between the fantasy life (and therefore the "creativity") of men and of women. All of this is framed by a most ambiguous narrative voice which claims that the "creative" artist is different than the author of the text that we are reading (this is made evident in the banality of the hypothetical novel which Freud outlines in his essay), yet which draws parallels between his experience and that of both the artist in reality and in the work of art.

Freud is, however, not interested in the problem of "creativity" for its own sake. He sees his explanation of the nature of "creativity" as one of the central proofs for the validity of his science, psychoanalysis. In the programmatic text of 1913, "The Claims of Psycho-Analysis to Scientific Interest," Freud outlines the theory of repression as the key not only to an understanding of the production of the "beautiful" but also as one of the substantial pieces of evidence of the explanatory power (read: scientific validity) of his views. The power of the aesthetic on the viewer is stressed. Freud, however, leaves the door open to yet further meaningful contributions to the understanding of the aesthetic through the science of psychoanalysis:

> ... Most of the problems of artistic creation and appreciation await further study, which will throw the light of analytic knowledge on them and assign them their place in the complex structure presented by the compensation for human wishes. Art is a conventionally accepted reality in which, thanks to artistic illusion, symbols and substitutes are able to provoke real emotions. Thus art constitutes a region half-way between a reality which frustrates wishes and the wish-fulfilling world of the imagination—a region in which, as it were, primitive man's strivings for omnipotence are still in force.[43]

Freud's reading of the work of art is clearly both within the paradigm of late nineteenth-century visual and literary art and, more importantly, still bound by Lombroso's association of the "creative" and the "primitive." But it is not the "primitive" localized in the inhabitants of the asylum or of the prison, the throwback, but the "primitive" within each and every human being. Freud seems to need to associate the "creative" with the universal and with a universal science, psychoanalysis.

What is clear is the basic difficulty of Freud's argument: if sexual repression is the key to "creativity," why are not all individuals who are sexually repressed "creative"? After World War I Freud himself became quite aware of this objection, as he later noted in his study of "Dostoevsky and Parricide" (1928): "Before the problem of the creative artist analysis must, alas, lay down its arms."[44] Or, as he states in his "Autobiographical Study" (1925): "[Psychoanalysis] . . . can do nothing towards elucidating the nature of the artistic gift, not can it explain the means by which the artist works—artistic technique."[45] But I would rather ask the question in reverse. Why is it that Freud's early categories of "creativity" are so constructed to make all human beings potentially "creative"? Why does Freud need to universalize the question of the "creative"? Why does he need to place "creativity" within those sexual drives and psychic phenomena which are, according to Freud, present in all human beings, not merely the "insane"? Why is it the feminine which seems to have the closest relationship to the wellspring of the "creative"? What do "sexuality," "creativity," and "madness" have to do with one another at the turn of the century? Why must Freud still maintain that "creativity" is like "neurosis" in its inherent characteristic of repression?

The meaning of Freud's representation of the "creative," not as Lombroso's "throwback" or deviant but as a reflection of universal processes, can be understood in the context of Freud's role as a scientist and a Jew in fin-de-siècle Vienna. We can assume that the question of "creativity" had a special significance for Freud, especially during the period from 1903 to 1910, the period when Weininger's views were most widely circulated and discussed in the culture of Vienna. These views were being read against the more general debates within psychiatry about the special status of Jewish genius.[46] Freud needed to move the question of the Jew's "madness" and the Jew's "creativity" onto another level of debate. What he did was to take the special definition of these concepts and their relationship and make them part of his proof for the universality of the human psyche. Freud's stress on the sexual etiology of all neurosis led to his view that creativity is analogous to neurosis in its repression of conflicted sexual identity. The fin-de-siècle subtext which links the creative, the psychopathological, and the sexual to the portrait of the psyche of the Jew, is precisely what Freud was battling—covertly—in his work on the "creative."

Freud's response to this subtext was to separate the question of Jewish "madness" and Jewish "creativity" from the universal laws which he saw as causing psychopathology. These laws are parallel to the laws which determine the "creative." It is not surprising that Freud would focus so much attention on refashioning Lombroso's separate categories of the "normal" and the "abnormal." Unlike the Italian Jew Lombroso, Freud (according to his own account) only first began to sense his "racial" difference from everyone else when he began to study medicine. For him, science and race were linked experiences, and for him it would become a lifelong struggle to separate the two.[47] (Seen in this context, Weininger also offered Freud a major challenge in his view of "Jewish" medicine as a purely mechanistic, materialistic medicine, more chemistry than the art of healing. Jews are not "creative" in the realm of science, Weininger argued, but rather destructive.)

Freud first struggles to show how everyone who is creative or dreams or is "mad" responds to the same, universal rules of psychic organization. Freud's science, the science of psychoanalysis—which evolves over the closing decade of the nineteenth century, while rooted in a materialistic paradigm—self-consciously attempts to move medicine toward an understanding of the dynamic processes of the psyche, the immaterial aspect of the human being. Freud abandons "chemistry" for "metapsychology." This he is constrained to do because of his certainty that human sexuality—associated with the obsessive hypersexuality of the Jews, the very source of their perverse "madness"—lies at the center of human experience. Freud positions himself (more and more successfully as his thought develops after World War I) in opposition to the positivistic clinical gaze of Jean Martin Charcot and the materialistic brain mythology of Moriz Benedikt. His is not the "Jewish" medicine castigated by Weininger and has, therefore, at least the potential to claim a position as "creative." But Freud does not do this unambiguously, as we have seen in his 1907 essay on "creativity." For in openly labeling himself as "creative" he would be labeling himself as a Jew. He would be setting himself off from the universal role of the "layman" (to use his word) as the observer. But he is not the "layman," he is the scientist-physician. And his science must be universal, not particular, in its claims for "creativity." The scientist-physician lays claim to the universal gaze, unencumbered by national or racial perspective—especially in the arena of sexology, where the accusation is that Jews, by their very nature, are predisposed to seeing the sexual everywhere.

Freud thus has the "creative" operate as a reflex of that force which is present in all human beings—sexuality. As we have seen, it was this force that was used to label the Jew as different; for Freud, it now becomes the source of all human endeavors including the truly "creative." That this sexuality is present more in the feminine phantasy than in the masculine, is a reverse-mirror view of Weininger's dismissal of Jews' sexually contaminated "creativity." In fact, Freud reverses all of the poles of Weininger's anti-Semitic discourse on "creativity," and while he does maintain the link between "madness" and "creativity," he sees these tendencies as a product of universal rather than racial psychology. What is striking in all of Freud's discussions of "creativity" during the period from 1900 to 1919 is that he never cites any Jewish writer or painter—not his contemporary and neighbor, the playwright Arthur Schnitzler or the best-known German artist of his day, the Impressionist Max Liebermann, or the classic examples of Jewish creativity, Spinoza and Heine—in his discussions of "creativity" and the nature of the "creative." "Creativity" is universal; Freud's examples are not. They self-consciously eliminate the "Jewish" component in European culture.[48]

Freud's work on "madness" and "creativity" in this period was limited by the anti-Semitic fantasies of fin-de-siècle medicine and culture. It was only with the political triumph of the German Nazis in 1933 that Freud openly praised the Jews as a superior people: "when one thinks that ten or twelve percent of the Nobel Prize

winners are Jews and when thinks of their other great achievements
in sciences and in the arts, one has every reason to think them
superior."[49] In 1938, Freud, writing in a German emigré magazine
directly confronted the question of Jewish creativity. His answer
to the rise of anti-Semitism is a paraphrase of a lost or invented
essay reputedly by a non-Jew, in which the contributions of the
Jews to the Diaspora are evaluated: "Nor can we call them [the
Jews] in any sense inferior. Since we have allowed them to co-
operate in our cultural tasks, they have acquired merit by valuable
contributions in all the spheres of science, art, and technology,
and they have richly repaid our tolerance."[50] "Science," such as
psychoanalysis, and then "art" represent the Jews' "creative" contributions to German culture. But each are "creative" and each
marks the positive presence of the Jew in European society. The
ambiguity of "creativity" in the fin de siècle vanished in the harsh
light of the Nazi realization of German culture's anti-Semitic phan-
tasies. Against this terrible reality, Freud no longer spoke indirectly.

In the 1950s there was a continuation of the debate about the
meaning of Jewish "creativity." After the Shoah, Silvano Arieti,
certainly the most widely influential psychoanalyst after Freud to
deal with the question of "creativity," reverses the process.[51] Arieti
is fascinated by the relationship between "madness" in its mid-
twentieth century manifestation, schizophrenia, and the "creative."[52] Arieti's interest lies in examining the relationship between
Freud's sense of "creativity" as stemming from the primary processes of psychic development, and reflected in the mechanisms of
the dream, and the higher forms of psychic organization. For Arieti,
the clue to the meaning of "creativity" lies in the psychopathological structures of the schizophrenic, who organizes the world along
quite different structures than that of "normal" consciousness: "The
seriously ill schizophrenic, although living in a state of utter confusion, tries to recapture some understanding and to give organization to his fragmented universe. This organization is, to a large
extent, reached by connecting things that have similar parts in
common. Many patients force themselves to see similarities everywhere. In their relentless search for such similarities they see

strange coincidences; that is, similar elements occurring in two or more instances at the same time or at brief intervals. By considering these similarities as identities they attempt to find some clarity in the confusion of the world, a solution for the big jigsaw puzzle."[53] As one can see this statement, Arieti is expanding upon but continuing Freud's model of the "creative."

But there is also an extraordinary subtext in Arieti's corollary to Freud's argument. For Arieti, an Italian Jew whose study *The Parnas* is one of the most moving accounts of the psychological destruction of Italian Jewry, the Jew becomes the prototypical creative individual.[54] Arieti creates a category which he labels the "creativogenic culture" which encourages the innovation of "creativity." Qualities such as the availability of cultural means, openness to cultural stimuli, emphasis on becoming, not just on being, tolerance for diverging views, freedom following repression all provide the matrix for the "creativity." It is of little surprise that for Arieti the exemplary "creative" individuals are the Jews. And the exemplary Jews whom Arieti choses as his example of the truly creative are the scientists, especially the medical scientists. Like Freud, Arieti tabulates the relationship of "Jewish" Nobel Prizes to "German," "French," "Italian," and "Argentinian" Nobel Prizes and determines that . . . "Jews exceed in all categories with the exception of the Peace Prize, where they are surpassed by the French and the Argentinians. If we examine the five fields in which prizes are assigned, we notice that the greatest Jewish contribution are in the fields of medicine and physics."[55] Of course, no working definition of the Jew can be offered by Arieti, as he rejects any biological definition of the Jew. What he does instead is to construct an ontological category quite similar to that of Weininger, simply reversing the poles of Weininger's argument. For Arieti, the "creative" becomes the Jewish state of mind and the Jew, "creativity" incorporated. But again, it is a specific form of the "creative" it is science and specifically the science of medicine, Arieti's own self-definition.

To contrast Freud and Arieti on the concept of "creativity" is to confront a world in which the question of Jewish particularism is repressed or qualified when "creativity" is addressed and one in which it is celebrated. Both views are answers to the charge that

Jews, through their perverse sexuality, are different, "mad," and inherently "uncreative." Today, we have sufficient distance from the wellsprings of this turn-of-the-century debate about the "creative" and its sequelae to see how Freud and his followers, such as Arieti, found themselves confronted with a need to provide a rationale for their own "creativity" in their construction of the world. What is the truly "creative" in this context becomes the writing of the scientist in his striving to define the "creative."

In the late twentieth century, "madness" and "creativity" are again closely linked within psychiatry as states which differentiate the voice of the observing scientist from the voice of the observed. But these concepts are now totally deracinated. The contemporary argument, like that of classical Greek or late nineteenth-century medicine, associates the two aspects of the mind through a definition which in some manner sees the mind as a reflex of the body. The most radical example of this epiphenomenalism views the mind simply as a product of the brain, much as bile is a product of the liver. (This parallel is the favorite one of the epiphenomenalists of the mid-nineteenth century, such as the French physician P.J.G. Cabanis.) "Creativity" is thus the state which results from some inherent error in the body of the "genius." Exemplary of the most radical position of this view is the work of Nancy Andreasen and I.D. Glick of the University of Iowa's College of Medicine.[56] In a review-essay published in 1988 they argue that there is a clear relationship between "creativity" and affective illness (particularly bipolar illness [manic-depression]). They do not argue a causal relationship between the act of creation and the presence of illness, indeed noting that creative individuals are most productive when their affective symptoms are under control. But they assume that the "creativity" of the artist is a parallel manifestation of the same underlying genetic error which they postulate as "causing" bipolar illness. Thus the "creativity" of the artist is a reflex of his/her underlying biology and is closely linked to the simultaneous potential for illness. This view is qualified by K.R. Jamison of the Johns Hopkins School of Medicine.[57] Citing literature from both popular writing on creativity (such as the work of Arthur Koestler) as well as Nancy Andreasen's earlier essays on the relationship between bipolar disorder and "creativity," he sees the cognitive, perceptual, mood and behavioral implications of "creativity" as analogous to "madness." Jamison's study focuses on a sample of "eminent British writers and artists" in order to study the differences of the experience of "madness" and "creativity" in self-designated "subgroups" (poets, novelists, playwrights, artists) as well as the overall structure of their "creative" experience. This sense of the "creative" is paralleled by him to the nature of the experience of individuals with bipolar illness and he traces similarities as well as differences. Thus Jamison sees the seasonal patterns of moods and productivity as potentially similar to but not identical with the hypomanic ("up") state of bipolar illness.[58] A third position is taken by A.M. Ludwig of the A.B. Chandler Medical Center of the University of Kentucky.[59] Unlike most medical writers on this question who are quite detailed in their definition of psychopathology but unable or unwilling to define "creativity," Ludwig attempts first to define "creativity." Relying on the assumptions of the psychoanalytic discourse about "creativity" (but not using it) he sees it tautologically as the structural relationship between the creative individual, the creative process, and the creative product. While he stresses the cultural context of any creative work, he too assumes that all cultures produce works which are "creative." And while not seeing "madness" as a prerequisite for "creativity," Ludwig argues that a touch of "madness" can enhance the "creative." All of these papers, had they been written at the end of the nineteenth century, would have evoked another variable in the discussion of genius—race. But to link pathology and race in late twentieth-century psychiatry is still a very tricky undertaking. A search of the medical literature for the past decade turned up no scientific studies with this variable. So we return to the age-old parallel between the creative and the mad, but today without any hint of the racial implications of this theme at the close of the last century.

6

THE JEWISH READER

Freud reads Heine reads Freud

◆

One of the salient marks of the Jew is his inability to command the language in which he writes. But this charge is lodged primarily against creative writers during the fin de siècle, rather than scientists. The neutral language of science could serve as a mask for the Jew's supposed scientific creativity, but literary language openly revealed his superficiality. As we have seen, there was one writer in particular cited over and over again as the clearest proof of the special, diseased, degenerate nature of the Jewish genius, Heinrich Heine. Heine becomes, for the scientific literature of the period, the exemplary Jewish genius, with all of the implications for that concept which are present in the fin de siècle.

Of all the creative writers whom Sigmund Freud read and quoted, none has quite as unique a place in his mental library as does Heinrich Heine. Although when Freud was asked in 1907 to compile a list of "*good* books" he did not include any by Heine, he did include Heine as the only German author on his (admittedly short) list of "*favorite*" books.[1] Freud neither quotes Heine more frequently than Goethe nor does Heine have as central a position in Freud's world of metaphors as do the Greeks. But Freud's reading of his "*favorite*" German writer, Heinrich Heine, reflects Freud's confrontation with the literary representation of the Jewish cultural voice in a way not paralleled by his reading of any other writer.

The reason for Freud's fascination with Heine's world of words is quite simple: Heinrich Heine was the exemplary cultural Jew for late nineteenth-century Austria.[2] Heine also becomes the touchstone for the scientific discussion of the relationship between ideas of race, genius, and creativity. Sigmund Freud works out some of the implications of Heine's fin-de-siècle image as the touchstone for questions of Austrian-Jewish identity through his poetics of quoting Heine. This poetics of quotation reflects Freud's reading of Heine as his response to the "meaning" of Heine in Freud's time.[3]

Freud's reading of Heine was very much within the late-nineteenth century image of Heine as the essential erotic and/or ironic writer.[4] As August Forel, the Professor of Psychiatry at Zurich and the author of the most widely read sexual handbook, *The Sexual Question* (1905), observed when distinguishing between erotic and pornographic art: "If we compare Heine with de Maupassant, I think we must admit that, in spite of the refinement of his art, the pornographic trait is comparably stronger in the former, because Heine continually loses the thread of moral sense which impregnates most of the works of de Maupassant."[5] This image was either used as a club to attack Heine as the "Jewish" poet par excellence or as the means of glorifying the poet as not "Jewish" at all, but rather decadent, or European, or . . . ., and here one can fill in the blank, anything but Jewish. Freud's reading of Heine falls within this view and, as such, forms a natural counter-reading of Heine by his Viennese Jewish contemporary Karl Kraus.[6] Freud's counter-reading is not random. Both Kraus and Freud were *Ostjuden*, Eastern Jews, transplanted into Vienna, but each attempted to acquire social status through different modes of self-definition—Kraus as a "writer" and Freud as a "scientist." Freud's quite different perspective on things "erotic" and "Jewish" is to no little degree formed by his self-chosen professional identity as a "physician-scientist." Freud presents a reading of Heine bounded by the sense of "Jewish" identity present in this thought-collective, the shared assumption of nineteenth-century biological science that the biology of race was central to any definition of the human being. Thus the meaning associated with the erotic and the ironic or sexuality and humor (those global categories which span Heine's late nineteenth-century image) can be clearly contextualized within the special discourse on race and disease held by late nineteenth-century Jewish physicians.

Sigmund Freud's reading of Heinrich Heine reveals the core contradiction of the late nineteenth-century Jewish scientist-physician. It is how one can simultaneously be "subject" and "object," how one can be the subject of scientific study at the same time that one has the role of the observer. For the Jewish physician in late nineteenth-century Germany and Austria, the ability to enter into the sphere of "science" meant acknowledging the truth of the scientific project and its rhetoric. No finer an observer of European Jewry than Leopold von Sacher-Masoch makes this the centerpiece of his tale of Austrian Jewry included in his "ethnographic" account of European Jewry.[7] In his story we observe the confrontation between the "scientific" Jewish physician and his primitive, miracle-working counterpart. Only science can win and religion must bow gracefully to its preeminence. Sacher-Masoch's tale of science and the Jews reflects the siren song of the *Haskalah*, which perhaps even more than the general Enlightenment saw science as the path of the escape from the darkness of the ghetto into the bright light of modern culture. It was a modern culture defined very much by d'Alembert's understanding of science and technology as the tools for the improvement of the common man. But science, especially applied science such as medicine, implied the ability to enter into the mainstream of the so-called "free" professions.[8] It implied a type of social mobility increasingly available to Jews, especially in Austria, over the course of the nineteenth century.[9] For the late nineteenth-century Jewish scientist, especially those in the biological sciences, the path of social and cultural acceptance was complex. It entailed, more than in any other arena of endeavor, the acceptance of the contradiction between being "subject" and "object," as one of the basic premises of nineteenth-century biological science was the primacy of racial difference.

For the physician-scientist the case became even more complex. It is not merely that there was a hierarchy of race, with each race higher (or lower) on a "great chain of being," but that patterns of illness were seen as varying group to group and marked the risk which each group had in confronting life, especially "modern" civilized life. The Jewish physician was both the "observer" of this form of disease, and also, because he (and he was almost always male until the very late nineteenth century) entered into the competition of civilized society (i.e., the public sphere of medicine), he was the potential "victim" of the same exact illnesses. The demands of "scientific objectivity" could, therefore, not be met by Jewish physicians, and they were forced to undertake complex psychological strategies to provide themselves with an "objective" observing voice.

Freud attempts to resolve this problem of the identity of subject and object not within the context of the biology of race but of gender. And it is this movement from the rhetoric of race to the rhetoric of gender which marks Freud's citation of the "voice" of Heinrich Heine as the exemplary "Jewish" figure of the time. Drawing on earlier work published in 1925 and 1931, Freud wrote about the role of the scientist in resolving the question of gender in his comprehensive *New Introductory Lectures on Psychoanalysis* (1933 [1932]):

> Today's lecture, too, should have no place in an introduction; but it may serve to give you an example of a detailed piece of analytic work, and I can say two things to recommend it. It brings forward nothing but observed facts, almost without any speculative additions, and it deals with a subject which has a claim on your interest second almost to no other. Throughout history people have knocked their heads against the riddle of the nature of femininity—

> Häupter in Hieroglyphenmützen,
> Häupter in Turban und schwarzem Barett,
> Perückenhäupter und tausend andre
> Arme, schwitzende Menschenhäupter. . .
> [Heads in hieroglyphic bonnets,
> Heads in turbans and black birettas,
> Heads in wigs and thousand other
> Wretched, sweating heads of humans . . .]

Nor will you have escaped worrying over this problem—those of you who are men; to those of you who are women this will not apply—you are yourselves the problem. When you meet a human being, the first distinction you make is 'male or female?' and you are accustomed to make the distinction with unhesitating certainty. Anatomical science shares your certainty at one point and not much further.[10]

For the anti-Semitic Aryan Austrian, as well as for the self-styled "Eastern Jew" longing to erase his origins, Heine's references would evoke quite a different set of associations. They would read the oriental turbans, Egyptian hieroglyphs, the sweat of ghetto poverty, the wigs of the shaved heads of orthodox Jewish brides, as hidden signs of racial, not merely sexual difference. This argument can be read as part of a rhetoric of race. First, let me translate this problem, which Freud articulates within the rhetoric of gender science, into the rhetoric of racial science: "There is an inherent biological difference between Jews and Aryans and this has a central role in defining you (my listener) and your culture." The "you" which the "I" is addressing is clearly the Aryan reader, for the Jewish reader is understood as but part of the problem. The Aryan is the observer; the Jew the observed. Upon seeing someone on the street the first distinction "we" (the speaker and his listener as Aryans) make is to ask: "Jew or Aryan?" and that distinction can be made with certainty based on inherent assumptions about differences in anatomy. Indeed, according to a contemporary guidebook, in Vienna the first question one asks about anyone one sees on the street is: "Is he a Jew?"[11] This biological distinction can be clearly and easily "seen" even through the mask of clothing or the veneer of civilization. Jews are visible and know they are visible.

The false assumption in Freud's text is that the uniformity of the identity of all "males," as opposed to all "females," can be made in terms of the form of the genitalia.[12] Freud continues his argument to show that this physiological determinant is central in any discussion of the nature of sexual difference. He identifies himself as a male in this text, quoting a male author (Heine), about the impossibility of "knowing" the truth about the "dark continent" of the feminine.[13] The voice in Freud's text is that of a male and a participant in the central discourse about gender science of the scientific thought-collective. In my racial rereading, the voice would become that of the Aryan and part of the Aryan thought-collective. The fantasy of Freud's identification with the aggressor in my retelling of this passage as a passage about race seems to be vitiated when Freud transforms the problem of the relationship between the subject and the object into a question of sexual identity. The "male" is the "worrier" (read: subject) and the "female" is the "problem" (read: object). But this assumes that Freud's definition of the male body as uniform and constant is the norm within his fin-de-siècle scientific thought-collective.

There is an anatomical (read: sexual) distinction which sets the male Jew apart from other "males." It is the practice of circumcision which defines the body of the male Jew, at least within the discourse of science. Freud replaces the racial perspective inherent in the science of his time with the perspective of gender. But the central problem is the impossibility which the Jewish male has as being both the "object" of study—inherently different in a way marked on his body—and the observer, neutral, identical in form and voice with all other disembodied voices of science. The Jewish male is not quite a "whole" male, he is different and his difference is what marks the entire category of the Jew, as we found in our discussion of Paolo Mantegazza's views on infant male circumcision in Chapter 2. Circumcision became the key to marking the Jewish body as different within the perimeters of "healthy" or "diseased," and Freud eventually responded to this label of difference.

When we turn to Freud's discussion of the nature and meaning of circumcision in *Moses and Monotheism* (1939 [1934–1938]) the complexity of such a reading becomes clear. Here circumcision is one of the signs which marks the Egyptian body. The Jews, in order to acquire the higher status of the Egyptian, incorporate the act of male infant circumcision into their newly evolving religious practices. Freud states the case in the following manner:

On no account must the Jews be inferior to them. He [Moses] wished to make them into a "holy nation", as is expressly stated in the Biblical text, and as a mark of this consecration he introduced among them too the custom [circumcision] which made them at least the equals of the Egyptians. And he could only welcome it if they were to be isolated by such a sign and kept apart from the foreign peoples among whom their wanderings would lead them, just as the Egyptians themselves had kept apart from all foreigners.

Freud footnotes the following to document and explain his comments on the sexual self-selection and isolation of these newly defined Jews:

Herodotus, who visited Egypt about 450 B.C., enumerates in his account of his journey characteristics of the Egyptian people which exhibit an astonishing similarity to traits familiar to us in later Jewry: "They are altogether more religious in every respect than any other people, and differ from them too in a number of their customs. Thus they practise circumcision, which they were the first to introduce, and on grounds of cleanliness. . . . They look down in narrow-minded pride on other people, who are unclean and are not so close to the gods as they are." . . . And, incidentally, who suggested to the Jewish poet Heine in the nineteenth century A.D. that he should complain of his religion as "the plague dragged along from the Nile valley, the unhealthy beliefs of Ancient Egypt"?[14]

The act of circumcision sets the Jewish male apart (in that he is no longer fully a male). This becomes part of the discourse of biological difference. For Freud, the symbolic context of the sexual organ— the difference in the biological construction of masculinity and femininity—is the basis for the basic symbolic language of difference:

In the antithesis between fire and water, which dominates the entire field of these myths, yet a third factor can be demonstrated in addition to the historical factor and the factor of symbolic phantasy. This is a physiological fact, which the poet Heine describes in the following lines:—

156

The Jewish Reader

◆

Was dem Menschen dient zum Seichen
Damit schafft er Seinesgleichen.
['With what serves a man for pissing
he creates his like.']

> The sexual organ of the male has two functions; and there are those to whom this association is an annoyance. It serves for the evacuation of the bladder, and it carries out the act of love which sets the craving of the genital libido at rest.[15]

Here again it is the image of the "male" as a uniform category. The circumcised phallus has, as we have discussed, another function, at least within the scientific discourse of the nineteenth century: a prophylaxis against disease. Freud presents his discourse as a unified, univocal discourse of "male" sexual difference with reference to the poetry of Heinrich Heine.

In all of these cases, it is the poetry of Heine which links the ideas of sexual difference and the discourse of psychoanalysis. It is in the poetry of Heine that the "appropriate" words of difference are to be found which encapsulate, for Freud, the difference between subject and object, between the male body and that of the female. It is evident that quoting Heine, especially in these contexts, is not merely evoking any poetic voice of the nineteenth century. It is citing the exemplary Jewish (and therefore, erotic) writer of Freud's time. Hidden within the poetics of quoting Heine is the distinction made by Freud's contemporaries between the Jewish body and the body of the Aryan. Freud's citation of Heinrich Heine in these contexts provides a key to reading Freud's repression of the implications of the biology of race. Heine is cited as an authority, a voice of culture which speaks to the universality of the truths which Freud presents. Freud merges Heine's voice into his own text. The confusion between the roles of "observer" and "observed" is eliminated. And Freud, like Heine, becomes a commentator. His role as the object of study, as the pathological specimen under the microscope, is eliminated.

It is within the "voice" of the poet, the texts cited by Freud, that the authority of culture is evoked. The ironic tension in Freud's reading of Heine is generated by the conflict between the universal claims of German culture and the parochial, "Jewish" role attributed to Heine.[16] The shift from ironic observer to the object of analysis, from the "Aryan" to the "Jew" is reflected when Freud confronts this transformation. The distanced, ironic poet who is at the same time the subject of his own poetry becomes for Freud the voice which marks the movement of the category of race into the category of gender.

But it is important to note that the representation of Heine in fin-de-siècle culture is not only that of the "Jewish" and "erotic" poet, but also that of the "diseased" poet. There is rather a complex interrelationship in this representation between ideas of disease (Heine's image of the Jewish disease, Judaism, which Freud evokes in *Moses and Monotheism*), the nature of the Jewish (male) body and the nature of the origins of creativity. (Not surprisingly, Freud's *"favorite"* work of Heine, the section of the *Romanzero* called "Lazarus," concerns Heine's own disease and decay.) The image of Heine as an "ill" poet is linked in the nineteenth-century to the idea of Heine as the syphilitic, as the unclean figure whose eroticism is spoiled by his dangerous, pathological state.[17] The debate about the "meaning" of circumcision and its relationship to syphilis is evoked by the image of the dying Heine. Freud's quotation from Heine in *Moses and Monotheism* is taken from Heine's poem on the dedication of the Jewish Hospital in Hamburg, a hospital supported by Heine's uncle Solomon (to whom Freud was evidently related).[18] Heine's image of the threefold Jewish disease: poverty, illness, and Jewishness, comes to reflect Heine's own status as the syphilitic Jew. For syphilis, like the leprosy which the Jews brought back from Egypt along with monotheism, is a marker of the sexual difference of the Jew.[19] This image of the syphilitic becomes one with that of the poet. The association between the image of corruption, especially sexual corruption, and creativity dominates the late nineteenth-century idea of the poetic.[20]

Heine was understood as a writer whose work and life illustrated an "ever increasing sense of nervousness," according to the most widely read critic of German literature of the fin de siècle, the Danish Jew Georg Brandes.[21] Heine was the most feminized writer of his day because of his illness and his erotic writing. According to his contemporary Heinrich Laube: "He was always afflicted with headaches. He was often like a hysterical woman, eternally having her migraine. Then he spoke in a fragmented and desolate manner, his sentences only partially completed, often seeking the necessary words."[22] According to the literature of fin-de-siècle medicine he was a "neurasthenic, and hysteric, and genetically tainted."[23] The etiology of his disease of the central nervous system was generally assumed to be a result of his predisposition. Jewish writers saw this as a family taint, rather than a question of race. Indeed, Max Kaufmann attacks those who accuse Heine of having been afflicted with his "Jewish descent," arguing that such a claim, based as it is on the belief in a "pure" Jewish race, is incorrect.[24] Being Jewish was, however, not sufficient. Heine's long and lingering illness, his decades of being confined to his "mattress grave," were ascribed by many of his contemporaries to a particularly virulent form of syphilis.[25] This is also hinted at in Francis Galton's discussion of Heine's paralysis in his *Hereditary Genius* (1869).[26] The standard bibliographic handbook of the day attributed this disease to Heine's unbridled sexual life as a student at the University of Göttingen, a life style which, according to the author, is the reason Heine was excluded from his fraternity.[27] (The usual explanation given was the heightened anti-Semitism of the fraternities.) It is only in the work of some Jewish critics, such as the editor of his correspondence, that Heine's disease was attributed to an inherited disposition which was triggered by the force of economic circumstance.[28] Even here the assumption is that it was an inherent quality in Heine which manifested itself in the poet's symptoms as well as in the poet's creativity.

In the medical literature of the day, Heine represents the exemplary Jewish syphilitic as creative force.[29] The assumption in the medical literature is that the locomotor ataxia from which Heine suffered was a symptom of a nervous disease caused by a luetic infection. Indeed, the editor of one of the major Parisian medical journals of the fin de siècle, A. Cabanès, stated this quite directly in his discussion of Heine's life and illness.[30] Lombroso and Weininger, like virtually every other writer on the topic of the creativity of the

Jews evoke the case of Heine. Here the circumcised-Jew-as-writer becomes the exemplary syphilitic. This is precisely the locus in which Freud comprehended him. In a conversation with Giovanni Papini in May 1934, Freud discussed his rejection of the life of letters to which he felt himself drawn as a pupil at the Gymnasium in Vienna: "My family was poor, and poetry, on the testimony of the most celebrated contemporaries, brought in little or was renumerative too late. Moreover I was a Jew which obviously put me in a condition of inferiority under an anti-Semite monarchy. Heine's exile and wretched end discouraged me."[31] It is in this juncture between poetic invention and creativity and the established association of the Jews with forms of disease that Freud's reading of Heine can be located.

In his work Sigmund Freud evokes the image of disease as the concomitant to the image of the creative. He stresses the centrality of the link between the pathological and the creative which haunted the late nineteenth century:

> A strong egoism is a protection against falling ill, but in the last resort we must begin to love in order not to fall ill, and we are bound to fall ill if, in consequence of frustration, we are unable to love. This follows somewhat on the lines of Heine's picture of the psychogenesis of the Creation:
>
> > Krankheit ist wohl der letzte Grund
> > Des ganzen Schöpferdrangs gewesen;
> > Erschaffend konnte ich genesen,
> > Erschaffend wurde ich gesund.
> > [Illness was no doubt the final cause
> > of the whole urge to create.
> > By creating, I could recover;
> > by creating, I became healthy.]
>
> We have recognized our mental apparatus as being first and foremost a device designed for mastering excitations which would otherwise be felt as distressing or would have pathogenic effects.[32]

The link between the creative and the corrupt is found in Heine's "god-like" voice. Here, too, there is a rationale for the disassociation between the "subject" and the "object" of scientific study. In common discourse about Heine in contemporary, anti-Semitic commentators, such as Adolf Bartels, there is a link made between Heine's corrosive style and his racial identity.[33] By implication this identity is manifest in Heine's corrupt and corrupting sexuality. This is clearly labeled as degenerate, as not real poetry, but rather a pathological sign of the Jewishness of the poet.

As we saw in the previous chapter, Freud attempts to undermine this association between "Jewish" creativity and disease in his own studies of creativity (from his study of Leonardo through to that of Schreber). In all of these cases, the wellspring of creativity is the pathology of sexuality not of race, and none of his "subjects" are Jews. There is neither a study of Heine nor of Spinoza. Freud manages to avoid this association completely, for he sees Heine not through the lens of the biology of race but rather as a Jewish anti-Jew, a fellow unbeliever:

> Of what use to them is the mirage of wide acres in the moon, whose harvest no one has ever yet seen? As honest smallholders on this earth they will know how to cultivate their plot in such a way that it supports them. By withdrawing their expectations from the other world and concentrating all their liberated energies into their life on earth, they will probably succeed in achieving a state of things in which life will become tolerable for everyone and civilization no longer oppressive to anyone. Then, with one of our fellow-unbelievers, they will be able to say without regret: "Den Himmel überlassen wir/ Den Engeln und den Spatzen." [We leave Heaven to the angels and the sparrows.][34]

The appropriate voice in this context is that of Heinrich Heine, who becomes here "one of our fellow-unbelievers." The very term as well as the quotation is from Heine. Heine had coined it in his discussion of Spinoza. Freud's own oppositional position to religion is well known. Indeed Peter Gay evoked Freud's description of himself as a "godless" Jew in the title of one of his recent books on Freud.[35] This seems to be a contradiction until we understand that the term "Jew," for the late nineteenth-century scientist is neither a religious

161

nor a social label but a biological one. What Freud (and Gay) cannot do is to remove Freud from the category of the biological and, therefore, potentially diseased Jew. And here the fellow disbeliever, Heine, the diseased Jew becomes the double of Freud. The disease which Heine is reputed to have (syphilis) is not the disease which Freud develops (cancer of the jaw); but the idea of the disease of Judaism, the biological definition of the Jew, as the shared disease of the Jews, links both.

Having set the context for the function which Heine's poetic citation has in determining the link between sexuality and race in Freud's text, let us turn to a still more complicated reading of this association. It is one of the few quotations from Heine to serve as the focus for an analysis on Freud's part. This passage is to be found in his 1904 study of *Jokes and Their Relationship to the Unconscious.*

> In the part of his *Reisebilder* entitled 'Die Bäder von Lucca [The Baths of Lucca]' Heine introduces the delightful figure of the lottery-agent and extractor of corns, Hirsch-Hyacinth of Hamburg, who boasts to the poet of his relations with the wealthy Baron Rothschild, and finally says: 'And, as true as God shall grant me all good things, Doctor, I sat beside Salomon Rothschild and he treated me quite as his equal—quite famillionairely.'[36]

Interestingly, Freud's actual telling of this joke (which "works" only if delivered in Yiddish-accented German) is preceded in his study of *Jokes* by his citation of it.[37] For Freud is not evoking Heine's joke here out of his own reading (though there are certainly sufficient examples of his own reading of Heine noted in the study of *Jokes*) but because it is one of the central jokes—so central that it could have been referred to without quoting it—in the psychological discourse about humor in the 1880s and '90s.[38] Freud cites it from an 1896 essay by G. Heymans on Theodor Lipps's theory of the comic.[39]

Heymans refers to Lipps's use of this joke as a example of a meaningless error or malformation, which suddenly reveals itself as having a double meaning.[40] It is the sudden awareness in the reader of the hidden double meaning which generates the comic response. This Kantian reading of the text goes against the initial reading of this passage by Lipps.[41] For Lipps, the form of an expression and its content are inherently bound together. The comic in Heine's text stems from the masking of this structural relationship and our sudden awareness of the external form of meaning as an absolute reflex of its content. The psychological power of this association remains for Lipps even when the external form (as in Heine's joke) becomes trivialized. What is striking is that Lipps, in his 1898 publication of his earlier essays on the theory of humor, can respond to Heymans without even citing the passage from Heine. He comes to agree with Heymans, but places the moment of the awareness of the disparity between the "meaningless" word and its hidden meaning at a mid-point in the process toward the comic realization. The impact of the humor is the result of the hidden presence of the relationship between the form and the content of the expression, a relationship masked and then revealed by the pun. Lipps notes that "no one can doubt that Heine's joke is comic, only because we are aware or 'understand' that this word ["famillionairely"] should have this meaning, or more precisely, because it truly has, in our eyes, this meaning at that moment."[42] For Sigmund Freud, Lipps has "the clearest mind among present-day philosophical writers."[43] Freud uses Lipps as a sort of scientific and philosophical double when he begins his work on dreams, finding a detailed discussion of the topographic structure of the unconscious in Lipps's work.[44] Lipps's study of the comic is also the prime focus of Freud's own work on humor. Indeed, except for his own publications, Lipps is the most frequently cited "authority" in Freud's study of the comic. Freud's own reading of the Heine passage incorporates Lipps's reading and then departs from it.

What is striking is that when we read Lipps's study of the comic closely, as Freud did, our focus is not on the Jewish lottery-agent Hirsch-Hyacinth whose mangled, Yiddish-tinged speech reveals him as an marginal Jew attempting to infiltrate Western cultural traditions. Lipps cites him and his discourse only in passing. (Unlike in Freud's study which is truly a study of the Jewish joke constructed about material from and about Heine.[45]) And, indeed, in the book version of his essays, Lipps does not even reproduce in full Heine's punning reference to the Rothschilds. Rather there is quite another leitmotif in Lipps's work which Freud never mentions in his own study on humor. The "joke" or, in this case, the proverb, which ties Lipps's volume together, appears early in his text and is used over and over again throughout it: "The peasant laughs about the black when he sees him for the first time." (*Komik und Humor*, 30) Lipps's proverb stresses the role of the "subject" and the "object" in generating the comic.

Let me summarize Lipps's view of the nature of the comic as it is represented in this proverb. The comic is the awareness of sameness in difference, the essence of the humanness of the black hidden within his different-colored skin. For Lipps, it is the color of the skin which gives the human being special value (70). It is not that this value is intrinsic to the color of the skin, but rather that society gives skin color value. "We" (Lipps and his educated reader) begin by associating human form with white skin color (153), and "we" therefore, assume the color of the black skin not only to be comic but also ugly (158). It is in the sudden awareness of the similarity between the black's body (56) and its association with "our own body" that the comic is created. The disparity which creates humor is the awareness that what seems to be different (the essence of the body and its relationship to the idea of "humanness") is not different at all. Blacks are people just like—the peasant. It is because of the naivité (58) of the observer of the body of the black (68) that a comic situation is created. "We" laugh because we "know" that we are superior to the peasant (and to the black) because of our sense of the common humanity of all human beings. Any observer who is directly amused by the body of the black is either a child or a primitive. But the true observer (Lipps) "knows" that the body of the black and the body of the Other are identical and is amused only by the peasant's laughter at the black.[46]

All of Lipps's comments about the aesthetics of blackness reflect his sense that these qualities are those of the "primitive" observer. It is the scientist's task to study the responses of others and remain neutral in his own response. The scientist, the true observer, will not find the body of the black comic. The "we" in Lipps's text distinguishes between the subject, scientist-observer, who is neutral and objective, and the child-peasant, who is the object observed as it observes. This distance is clear in Lipps's writing.

When we turn to Freud's reading of Lipps, this metaphor of the biological basis for the comic, the perception of the body as the locus of difference, is displaced. It is not the body—either of the Jew or of the black—which is the seat of the idea of difference. Given the view in the scientific thought-collective in the nineteenth century that the Jew was black,[47] Lipps's placing of the locus of the comic in an understanding of the black body as the object of the comic gaze has specific meaning for the Jewish reader. Just as the black is not quite a "whole" human being because of his black skin (in the eye of child and the peasant), the male Jew is also not quite a whole human being because of his circumcision (in the eye of the scientist). The "damaged" Jewish phallus becomes the Jew. The relationship between the "body" and the "phallus" is not a post-facto analogy. The thesis of the "body-as-phallus" within the symbolic language of psychoanalysis was put forth by Victor Tausk and was used by him to counter the rather simple reading of Heine's "Lorelei" presented by Hanns Sachs to the Vienna Psychoanalytic Society on February 15, 1911. In Tausk's reading the phallus is represented by the body of the boatman swallowed by the waves. This image "could convey the notion of the whole body engulfed by the organ of the superior female."[48] The link between the black and the Jew can be found throughout Viennese culture in Freud's day. The Austrian exile novelist Jakov Lind puts into the mouth of his father in the 1930s: " 'Vienna is Vienna and Jews are Jews. Black is black and Jew is Jew because we could not afford to be anything else.' "[49] Freud's revision of this association is highly sublimated, but is also to be found in the joke book in the context of his reading of Heine (and Lichtenberg):

> " 'My fellow-unbeliever Spinoza', says Heine. 'We, by the ungrace of God, day-laborers, serfs, negroes, villeins. . .' is how Lichtenberg begins a manifesto (which he carries no further) made by these unfortunates—who certainly have more right to this title than kings and princes have to its unmodified form."[50]

Freud separates the Jew and the black into two parallel textual
worlds: the Jew, Spinoza, within the discourse of the Jew Heine;
the black within the Enlightenment rhetoric of Lichtenberg. For
Freud, the similarity between Jews, especially unbelieving Jews,
and blacks as the object of study is eliminated through this device
of citation. But for his thought-collective, Jews and blacks are identical because of their biology, which no subterfuge can alter. And
Heine becomes the marker for this sense of a difference which
should not be a difference. Heine, about whom one laughs, with
whom one laughs, is seen as the epitome of both subject and object,
both the means of analysis and the object of study.

Freud displaces the idea of the difference of the Jew into the realm
of sexuality, evoking Hirsch-Hyacinth's essential Jewish voice in
the joke discussed earlier in the text. But not the sexuality of the
Jew. The question at the very center of the references to Heine is
the placement of sexuality, deviant sexuality or the sexuality of
difference outside of the world of the Jew as the object of study. In
Heine's own world, Freud notes, the image of deviancy is projected
upon the figure of the arch-Aryan as anti-Semite, the image of the
homosexual August, Count of Platen (1796–1835):

> Heine's "Bäder von Lucca" contains a regular wasp's nest of the
> most stinging allusions and makes the most ingenious use of this
> form of joke for polemical purposes (against Count Platen). Long
> before the reader can suspect what is afoot, there are foreshadow-
> ings of a particular theme, peculiarly ill-adapted for direct repre-
> sentation, by allusions to material of the most varied kind,—for
> instance, in Hirsch-Hyacinth's verbal contortions: "You are too
> stout and I am too thin; you have a good deal of imagination and
> I have all the more business sense; I am a practicus and you are
> a diarrheticus; in short you are my complete antipodex."—"Venus
> Urinia"—"the stout Gudel von Dreckwall" of Hamburg, and so on.
> In what follows, the events described by the author take a turn
> which seems at first merely to display his mischievous spirit but
> soon reveals its symbolic relation to his polemical purpose and at
> the same time shows itself as allusive. Eventually the attack on
> Platen bursts out, and thenceforward allusions to the theme (with
> which we have already been made acquainted) of the Count's love

for men gushes out and overflows in every sentence of Heine's attack on his opponent's talents and character. For instance:

"Even though the Muses do not favour him, he has the Genius of Speech in his power, or rather he knows how to do violence to him. For he does not possess the free love of that Genius, he must unceasingly pursue this young man, too, and he knows how to capture only the outer forms, which, despite their lovely curves never speak nobly."

"He is like the ostrich, which believes he is well-hidden if he sticks his head in the sand, so that only his behind can be seen. Our exalted bird would have done better to hide his behind in the sand and show us his head."[51]

Here Freud moves with Heine from the Jew to the homosexual, from Hirsch-Hyacinth, and his accented German to the homosexual von Platen and his Romantic poetry, to locate the idea of the sexually different as the object of study. The voice we read is that of the observing poet Heine as the accented Jew Hirsch-Hyacinth; the covertly observed "object," the gay poet von Platen. What Freud "hears" in Heine's description of von Platen is a series of anal images, all of which refer to von Platen's homosexuality. The tables here are turned: it is the Jew (Heine-Freud) who sees the "pathology" of the Aryan, his homosexuality. (Heine's own homophobia[52] is translated here into the reification of the early Freud's view [best expressed in his analysis of the Schreber autobiography] that homosexuality is a "disease" or at least, a pathological error in development.)

In a real way Heine's position in late nineteenth-century thought parallels that of Freud within the scientific thought-collective of his time. And Freud sensed that doubling. He writes, calling upon Heine's "Gods in Exile," to describe the "uncanny" nature of the double, the sense of sameness in the concept of difference:

But after having thus considered the manifest motivation of the figure of a 'double', we have to admit that none of this helps us to understand the extraordinarily strong feeling of something uncanny that pervades the conception; and our knowledge of pathological mental processes enables us to add that nothing in this more superficial material could account for the urge towards defence which has caused the ego to project that material outward as something foreign to itself. When all is said and done, the quality of uncanniness can only come from the fact of the 'double' being a creation dating back to a very early mental stage, long since surmounted—a stage, incidentally, at which it wore a more friendly aspect. The 'double' has become a thing of terror, just as, after the collapse of their religion, the gods turned into demons.[53]

Heine's text functions for Freud as his own rhetorical double—the object of his study as well as the voice into which he can slip. What is uncanny in Freud's text is the regularity with which Heine's voice appears in this manner. Freud's poetics of quotations reveal themselves to be a politics of quotation. His appropriation of Heine's voice in the "scientific" context of psychoanalytic theory reveals itself to be a dialogue with the voice of the Jew within a discourse initially labeled as scientific but also understood by Freud and his thought-collective as Jewish as well. Heine remains for Freud the sign of the double bind of being both the authoritative voice of the observer and the ever suspect voice of the patient, a voice which remains one of the signs and symptoms of the disease from which both Heine and Freud suffered, their Jewishness.

7

THE JEWISH NOSE

Are Jews White?
Or, The History of the Nose Job

———————◆———————

The personals columns in the *Washingtonian*, the local city magazine in Washington, D.C., are filled announcements of individuals
"in search of" mates. ("In search of" is the rubric under which these
advertisements are grouped.) These advertisements are peppered
with various codes so well known that they are never really explained: DWM [Divorced White Male] just recently arrived from
Boston seeks a non-smoking, financially secure 40+ who loves to
laugh" . . . or "SJF [Jewish Single Female], Kathleen Turner type,
with a zest for life in search of S/DJM . . . for a passionate relationship." Recently, I was struck by a notice which began "DW(J)F
[Divorced White (Jewish) Female]—young, 41, Ph.D., professional,
no kids . . . seeks S/D/WWM, exceptional mind, heart & soul . . ."[1]
What fascinated me were the brackets: advertisements for "Jews"
or for "African Americans" or for "Whites" made it clear that individuals were interested in choosing their sexual partners from certain designated groups within American society. But the brackets
implied that here was a woman who was both "White" and "Jewish." Given the racial politics of post-civil rights America, where do
the Jews fit in? It made me ask the question, which the woman who

placed the personals advertisement clearly was addressing: are Jews white? and what does "white" mean in this context? Or, to present this question in a slightly less polemical manner, how has the question of racial identity shaped Jewish identity in the Diaspora? I am not addressing what the religious, ethnic, or cultural definition of the Jew is—either from within or without Judaism or the Jewish community—but how the category of race present within Western, scientific, and popular culture, has shaped Jewish self-perception.

My question is not merely an "academic" one—rather I am interested in how the representation of the Jewish body is shaped and, in turn, shapes the sense of Jewish identity. My point of departure is the view of Mary Douglas:

> The human body is always treated as an image of society and . . . there can be no natural way of considering the body that does not involve at the same time a social dimension. Interest in its apertures depends on the preoccupation with social exits and entrances, escape routes and invasions. If there is no concern to preserve social boundaries, I would not expect to find concern with bodily boundaries.[2]

Where and how a society defines the body reflects how those in society define themselves. This is especially true in terms of the "scientific" or pseudo-scientific categories such as race which have had such an extraordinary importance in shaping how we all understand ourselves and each other. From the conclusion of the nineteenth century, the idea of "race" has been given a positive as well as a negative quality. We belong to a race and our biology defines us, is as true a statement for many groups, as is the opposite: you belong to a race and your biology limits you. Race is a constructed category of social organization as much as it is a reflection of some aspects of biological reality. Racial identity has been a powerful force in shaping how we, at the close of the twentieth century, understand ourselves—often in spite of ourselves. Beginning in the eighteenth century and continuing to the present, there has been an important cultural response to the idea of race, one which has stressed the uniqueness of the individual over the uniformity of the group. As Theodosius Dobzhansky noted in 1967: "Every person has a genotype and a life history different from any other person, be that person a member of his family, clan, race, or mankind. Beyond the universal rights of all human beings (which may be a typological notion!), a person ought to be evaluated on his own merits."[3] Dobzhansky and many scientists of the 1960s dismissed "race" as a category of scientific evaluation, arguing that whenever it had been included over the course of history, horrible abuses had resulted.[4] At the same time, within Western, specifically American culture of the 1960s, there was also a transvaluation of the concept of "race." "Black" was "beautiful," and "roots" were to be celebrated, not denied. The view was that seeing oneself as being a part of a "race" was a strengthening factor. We at the close of the twentieth century have, however, not suddenly become callous to the negative potential of the concept of "race." Given its abuse in the Shoah[5] as well as in neo-colonial policies throughout the world,[6] it is clear that a great deal of sensitivity must be used in employing the very idea of "race." In reversing the idea of "race," we have not eliminated its negative implications, we have only masked them. For it is also clear that the meanings associated with "race" impacts on those included within these constructed categories. It forms them and shapes them. And this can be a seemingly positive or a clearly negative response. There is no question that there are "real," i. e., shared genetic distinctions within and between groups. But the rhetoric of what this shared distinction comes to mean for the general culture and for the "group" so defined becomes central to any understanding of the implications of race.

Where I would like to begin is with that advertisement in the *Washingtonian* and with the question which the bracketed (J) posed: are Jews white? To begin to answer that question we must trace the debate about the skin color of the Jews, for skin color remains one of the most salient markers for the construction of race in the West over time. The general consensus of the ethnological literature of the late nineteenth century was that the Jews were "black" or, at least, "swarthy." This view had a long history in European science. As early as 1691 François-Maximilien Misson,

171

whose ideas influenced Buffon's *Natural History*, argued against the notion that Jews were black:

> 'Tis also a vulgar error that the Jews are all black; for this is only true of the Portuguese Jews, who, marrying always among one another, beget Children like themselves, and consequently the Swarthiness of their Complexion is entail'd upon their whole Race, even in the Northern Regions. But the Jews who are originally of Germany, those, for example, I have seen at Prague, are not blacker than the rest of their Countrymen.[7]

But this was a minority position. For the eighteenth-and nine-teenth-century scientist the "blackness" of the Jew was not only a mark of racial inferiority, but also an indicator of the diseased nature of the Jew. The "liberal" Bavarian writer Johann Pezzl, who traveled to Vienna in the 1780s, described the typical Viennese Jew of his time:

> There are about five hundred Jews in Vienna. Their sole and eter-nal occupation is to counterfeit, salvage, trade in coins, and cheat Christians, Turks, heathens, indeed themselves. . . . This is only the beggarly filth from Canaan which can only be exceeded in filth, uncleanliness, stench, disgust, poverty, dishonesty, pushiness and other things by the trash of the twelve tribes from Galicia. Exclud-ing the Indian fakirs, there is no category of supposed human beings which comes closer to the Orang-Utan than does a Polish Jew . . . . Covered from foot to head in filth, dirt and rags, covered in a type of black sack . . . their necks exposed, the color of a Black, their faces covered up to the eyes with a beard, which would have given the High Priest in the Temple chills, the hair turned and knotted as if they all suffered from the "plica polonica."[8]

The image of the Viennese Jew is that of the Eastern Jew, suffering from the diseases of the East, such as the *Judenkratze*, the fabled skin and hair disease also attributed to the Poles under the designa-tion of the "plica polonica."[9] The Jews' disease is written on the skin. It is the appearance, the skin color, the external manifestation of the Jew which marks the Jew as different. There is no question for a non-Jewish visitor to Vienna upon first seeing the Jew that the Jew suffers from Jewishness. The internal, moral state of the Jew, the Jew's very psychology, is reflected in the diseased exterior of the Jew. As we saw in chapter 3, "plica polonica" is a real dermatologic syndrome. It results from living in filth and poverty. But it was also associated with the unhygienic nature of the Jew and, by the mid-nineteenth century, with the Jew's special relationship to the most frightening disease of the period, syphilis.[10] For the non-Jew seeing the Jew it mirrored popular assumptions about the Jew's inherent, essential nature. Pezzl's contemporary, Joseph Rohrer, stressed the "disgusting skin diseases" of the Jew as a sign of the group's general infirmity.[11] And the essential Jew for Pezzl is the Galician Jew, the Jew from the Eastern reaches of the Hapsburg Empire.[12] (This late eighteenth-century view of the meaning of the Jew's skin color was not only held by non-Jews. The Enlightenment Jewish physician Elcan Isaac Wolf saw this "black-yellow" skin color as a pathognomonic sign of the diseased Jew.[13]) Following the humoral theory of the times, James Cowles Pritchard (1808) commented on the Jews' "choleric and melancholic temperaments, so that they have in general a shade of complexion somewhat darker that that of the English people . . ."[14] Nineteenth-century anthropology as early as the work of Claudius Buchanan commented on the "inferiority" of the "black" Jews of India.[15] By the mid-century, being black, being Jewish, being diseased, and being "ugly" come to be inexorably linked. All races, according to the ethnology of the day, were described in terms of aesthetics, as either "ugly" or "beautiful."[16] African blacks, especially the Hottentot, as I have shown elsewhere, became the epitome of the "ugly" race.[17] And being ugly, as I have also argued, was not merely a matter of aesthetics but was a clear sign of pathology, of disease. Being black was not beautiful. Indeed, the blackness of the African, like the blackness of the Jew, was believed to mark a pathological change in the skin, the result of congenital syphilis. (And, as we shall see, syphilis was given the responsibility for the form of the nose.) One bore the signs of one's diseased status on one's anatomy, and by extension, in one's psyche. And all of these signs pointed to the Jews being a member of the "ugly" races of mankind, rather than the "beautiful" races. In being denied any association with the beautiful and the erotic, the Jew's body was denigrated.[18]

Within the racial science of the nineteenth century, being "black" came to signify that the Jews had crossed racial boundaries. The boundaries of race were one of the most powerful social and political divisions evolved in the science of the period. That the Jews, rather than being considered the purest race, are because of their endogenous marriages, an impure race, and therefore, a potentially diseased one. That this impurity is written on their physiognomy. According to Houston Stewart Chamberlain, the Jews are a "mongrel" (rather than a healthy "mixed") race, who interbred with Africans during the period of the Alexandrian exile.[19] They are "a mongrel race which always retains this mongrel character." Jews had "hybridized" with blacks in Alexandrian exile. They are, in an ironic review of Chamberlain's work by Nathan Birnbaum, the Viennese-Jewish activist who coined the word "Zionist," a "bastard" race, the origin of which was caused by their incestuousness, their sexual selectivity.[20]

Jews bear the sign of the black, "the African character of the Jew, his muzzle-shaped mouth and face removing him from certain other races . . . ," as Robert Knox noted at mid century.[21] The physiognomy of the Jew which is like that of the black: ". . . the contour is convex; the eyes long and fine, the outer angles running towards the temples; the brow and nose apt to form a single convex line; the nose comparatively narrow at the base, the eyes consequently approaching each other; lips very full, mouth projecting, chin small, and the whole physiognomy, when swarthy, as it often is, has an African look."[22] It is, therefore, not only the color of the skin which enables the scientist to see the Jew as black, but also the associated anatomical signs, such as the shape of the nose. The Jews were quite literally seen as black. Adam Gurowski, a Polish noble, "took every light-colored mulatto for a Jew" when he first arrived in the United States in the 1850s.[23]

If the Germans (Aryans) are a "pure" race—and that is for the turn-of-the-century science a positive quality—then the Jews cannot be a "pure" race. But what happens when the Jew attempted to stop being a Jew, to marry out of the "race"? Their Jewishness, rather than being diminished, became heightened. Their status as a mixed race became exemplified in the icon of the *Mischling*, the member of the mixed race.[24] The term *Mischling* in late nineteenth-century racial science referred to the offspring of a Jewish and a non-Jewish parent. The Jewishness of the *Mischling* " . . . undoubtedly signifies a degeneration: degeneration of the Jew, whose character is much too alien, firm, and strong to be quickened and ennobled by Teutonic blood, degeneration of the European who can naturally only lose by crossing with an 'inferior type' . . ."[25] They can have "Jewish-Negroid" features.[26] Language and, therefore, thought processes, are a reflex of the racial origin of the "black" Jew. And their "blackness" appears even more strikingly in mixed marriages, almost as nature's way of pointing up the difference and visibility of the Jew. This "taint" can appear among families "into which there has been an infusion of Jewish blood. . . . [It] tends to appear in a marked and intensely Jewish cast of features and expression . . ."[27] It is in the "mixed" breed, therefore, that these negative qualities are most evident. As the quintessential anti-Semite said to the German-Jewish writer Jacob Wassermann in the 1920s, "whether, after conversion, they cease to be Jews in the deeper sense we do not know, and have no way of finding out. I believe that the ancient influences continue to operate. Jewishness is like a concentrated dye: a minute quantity suffices to give a specific character—or, at least, some traces of it—to an incomparably greater mass."[28] Crossing the boundaries of race presented the potential of highlighting the inferiority of the Jews.

So even when the Jew wished to vanish, by marrying out of the "race," his or her blackness was not diminished. Indeed, it was heightened. The power of the image of the "Black Jew," the product of crossbreeding Jew with black, is a powerful one in nineteenth-century Europe, especially for those Jews who desired to see themselves as "white." When, for example, Sigmund Freud, half a century after Knox's work, compared the unconscious with the preconscious he evoked the image of the *Mischling* or "half-breed": "We may compare them with individuals of mixed race who, taken all round, resemble white men, but who betray their colored descent by some striking feature or other, and on that account are excluded from society and enjoy none of the privileges of white people."[29] The Jew remains visible, even when the Jew gives up all cultural signs of his or her Jewishness and marries out of the "race." It is the inability to "pass" which is central here as well as the image of the mixed race. But what is the "striking feature" which marks the Jew as different, what marks the Jew as visible, even in the Jew's desired invisibility?

Jews look different, they have a different appearance, and this appearance has pathognomonic significance. Skin color marked the Jew as both different and diseased. For the Jewish scientist, such as Sigmund Freud, these "minor differences in people who are otherwise alike . . . form the basis of feelings of strangeness and hostility between them."[30] This is what Freud clinically labeled as the "narcissism of minor differences." But are these differences "minor" either from the perspective of those labeling or those labeled? In reducing this sense of the basis of difference between "people who are otherwise alike," Freud was not only drawing on the Enlightenment claim of the universality of human rights, but also on the Christian underpinnings of these claims. For this "narcissism" fights "successfully against feelings of fellowship and overpower[s] the commandment that all men should love one another." It is the Christian claim to universal brotherly love that Freud was employing in arguing that the differences between himself, his body, and the body of the Aryan, are trivial. Freud comprehended the special place that the Jew played in the demonic universe of the Aryan psyche. But he marginalized this role as to the question of the Jew's function "as an agent of economic discharge . . . in the world of the Aryan ideal" rather than as one of the central aspects in the science of his time.[31] What Freud was masking was that Jews are not merely the fantasy capitalists of the paranoid delusions of the anti-Semites, they also mirror within their own sense of selves the image of their own difference.

By the close of the nineteenth century, the "reality" of the physical difference of the Jew as a central marker of race had come more and more into question. Antithetical theories, such as those of Friedrich Ratzel, began to argue that skin color was a reflex of geography, and could and did shift when a people moved from one part of the globe to another. Building on earlier work by the President of Princeton University at the close of the eighteenth century, Samuel Stanhope Smith (1787), the Jews came to be seen as the adaptive people par excellence: "In Britain and Germany they are fair, brown in France and in Turkey, swarthy in Portugal and Spain, olive in Syria and Chaldea, tawny or copper-coloured in Arabia and Egypt."[32] William Lawrence commented in 1823 that "their colour is everywhere modified by the situation they occupy."[33] The questionability of skin color as the marker of Jewish difference joined with other qualities which made the Jew visible.

By the latter half of the nineteenth century, Western European Jews had become indistinguishable from other Western Europeans in matters of language, dress, occupation, location of their dwellings and the cut of their hair. Indeed, if Rudolf Virchow's extensive study of over 10,000 German school children published in 1886 was accurate, they were also indistinguishable in terms of skin, hair, and eye color from the greater masses of those who lived in Germany.[34] Virchow's statistics sought to show that wherever a greater percentage of the overall population had lighter skin or bluer eyes or blonder hair there a greater percentage of Jews also had lighter skin or bluer eyes or blonder hair. But although Virchow attempted to provide a rationale for the sense of Jewish acculturation, he still assumed that Jews were a separate and distinct racial category. George Mosse has commented, "the separateness of Jewish schoolchildren, approved by Virchow, says something about the course of Jewish emancipation in Germany. However, rationalized, the survey must have made Jewish schoolchildren conscious of their minority status and their supposedly different origins."[35] Nonetheless, even though they were labeled as different, Jews came to parallel the scale of types found elsewhere in European society.

A parallel shift in the perception of the Jewish body can be found during the twentieth century in the United States. It is not merely that second- and third-generation descendents of Eastern European Jewish immigrants do not "look" like their grandparents; but they "look" American. The writer and director Philip Dunne commented on the process of physical acculturation of Jews in Southern California during the twentieth century:

The Jewish Nose
◆

> You could even see the physical change in the family in the second generation—not resembling the first generation at all. Of course, this is true all across the country, but it is particularly noticeable in people who come out of very poor families. . . . One dear friend and colleague of mine was a product of a Lower East Side slum. He was desperately poor. And he grew up a rickety, tiny man who had obviously suffered as a child. At school, he told me, the goyim would scream at him. Growing up in California, his two sons were tall, tanned, and blond. Both excelled academically and in athletics. One became a military officer, the other a physicist. They were California kids. Not only American but Californian.[36]

But the more Jews in Germany and Austria at the fin de siècle looked like their non-Jewish contemporaries, the more they sensed themselves as different and were so considered. As the Anglo-Jewish social scientist Joseph Jacobs noted, "it is some some quality which stamps their features as distinctly Jewish. This is confirmed by the interesting fact that Jews who mix much with the outer world seem to lose their Jewish quality. This was the case with Karl Marx . . ."[37] And yet, as we know, it was precisely those Jews who were the most assimilated, who were passing, who feared that their visibility as Jews could come to the fore. It was they who most feared being seen as bearing that disease, Jewishness, which Heinrich Heine, said the Jews brought from Egypt.

In the 1920s, Jacob Wassermann chronicled the ambivalence of the German Jews towards their own bodies, their own difference. Wassermann articulates this difference within the terms of the biology of race. He writes that: "I have known many Jews who have languished with longing for the fair-haired and blue-eyed individual. They knelt before him, burned incense before him, believed his every word; every blink of his eye was heroic; and when he spoke of his native soil, when he beat his Aryan breast, they broke into a hysterical shriek of triumph."[38] Their response, Wassermann argues, is to feel disgust for their own body, which even when it is identical in *all* respects to the body of the Aryan remains different: "I was once greatly diverted by a young Viennese Jew, elegant, full of suppressed ambition, rather melancholy, something of an artist, and something of a charlatan. Providence itself had given him fair hair and blue eyes; but lo, he had no confidence in his fair hair and blue eyes: in his heart of hearts he felt that they were spurious."[39] The Jew's experience of his or her own body was so deeply impacted by anti-Semitic rhetoric that even when that body met the expectations for perfection in the community in which the Jew lived, the Jew experienced his or her body as flawed, diseased.[40] If only one could change those aspects of the body which marked one as Jewish!

But nothing, not acculturation, not baptism, could wipe away the taint of race. No matter how they changed, they still remained diseased Jews. And this was marked on their physiognomy. Moses Hess, the German-Jewish revolutionary and political theorist commented, in his *Rome and Jerusalem* (1862) that "even baptism will not redeem the German Jew from the nightmare of German Jew-hatred. The Germans hate less the religion of the Jews than their race, less their peculiar beliefs than their peculiar noses. . . . Jewish noses cannot be reformed, nor black, curly, Jewish hair be turned through baptism or combing into smooth hair. The Jewish race is a primal one, which had reproduced itself in its integrity despite climactic influences. . . . The Jewish type is indestructible."[41] The theme of the Jew's immutability was directly tied to arguments about the permanence of the negative features of the Jewish race.

On one count, Hess seemed to be wrong—the external appearance of the Jew did seem to be shifting. His skin seemed to be getting whiter, at least in his own estimation, though it could never get white enough. Jews, at least in Western Europe, no longer suffered from the disgusting skin diseases of poverty which had once marked their skin. But on another count, Hess was right. The Jew's nose could not be "reformed." Interrelated with the meaning of skin was the meaning of the Jew's physiognomy, especially the Jew's nose. And it was also associated with the Jew's nature. George Jabet, writing as Eden Warwick, in his *Notes on Noses* (1848) characterized the "Jewish, or Hawknose," as "very convex, and preserves its convexity like a bow, throughout the whole length from the eyes to the tip. It is thin and sharp." Shape also carried here a specific meaning: "It indicates considerable Shrewdness in worldly matters; a deep insight into character, and facility of turning that insight to profitable account."[42] Physicians, drawing on such analogies, speculated that the difference of the Jew's language, the very mirror of his psyche, was the result of the form of the his nose. Thus Bernhard Blechmann's rationale for the *Mauscheln* of the Jews, their inability to speak with other than a Jewish intonation, is that the "muscles, which are used for speaking and laughing are used inherently different from those of Christians and that this use can be traced ... to the great difference in their nose and chin."[43] The nose becomes one of the central loci of difference in seeing the Jew.

It is the relationship between character and physiognomy which led Jewish social scientists, such as Joseph Jacobs, to confront the question of the "nostrility" of the Jews **[PLATE 28]**. He (and other Jewish scientists of the fin de siècle) saw that "the nose does contribute much toward producing the Jewish expression."[44] But how can one alter the "nostrility" of the Jewish nose, a sign which, unlike the skin color of the Jew, does not seem to vanish when the Jew is acculturated. Indeed, a detailed study of the anthropology of the "*Mischlinge* born to Jews and non-Jews" published in 1928 summarized the given view that there was a "Jew nose" and that this specific form of the nose was dominant in mixed marriages and was recognized to be a fixed, inherited sign of being Jewish.[45] In

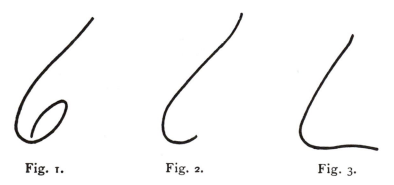

Fig. 1.   Fig. 2.   Fig. 3.

PLATE TWENTY-EIGHT

The creation of the "nostrility" of the Jew and its unmaking, at least in the form of a caricature. From Joseph Jacobs, *Studies in Jewish Statistics* (London: D. Nutt, 1891) (Source: Private Collection, Ithaca).

180

popular and medical imagery, the nose came to be the sign of the pathological Jewish character for Western Jews, replacing the pathognomonic sign of the skin,though closely linked to it. For the shape of the nose and the color of the skin, as we have seen, are related signs.

It seemed that one could "cure" the skin, one could make it less "black" by eliminating the skin diseases which haunted the poverty of the ghetto, or, one could simply see oneself as "white." With this, the "disease" of Jewishness could no longer be seen on the skin. But how could one eliminate the symptom of the "nostrility" of the Jew, that sign which everyone at the close of the nineteenth century associated with the Jew's visibility? An answer was supplied by Jacques Joseph, a highly acculturated young German-Jewish surgeon practicing in fin-de-siècle Berlin [PLATE 29]. Born Jakob Joseph, the physician had altered his Jewish name when he studied medicine in Berlin and Leipzig. Joseph was a typical acculturated Jew of the period. He had been a member of one of the conservative dueling fraternities and bore the scars of his sabre dueling with pride. Like many acculturated Jews, such as Theodor Herzl, Joseph "relished the test and adventure of the duel, the so-called *Mensur*, which was considered manly and edifying."[46] The scars (*Schmisse*) from the *Mensur* were intentionally created. Students challenged each other to duels as a matter of course, without any real need for insults to be exchanged. Being challenged was a process of social selection. "Without exclusivity—no corporation," was the code of the fraternities as late as 1912.[47] The duelists had their eyes and throat protected, but their faces were purposefully exposed to the blade of the sabre. When a cut was made, there were guidelines as to how to repair it so as to maximize the resulting scar. The scar which Joseph bore his entire life marked him as someone who was *Satisfaktionsfähig* (worthy of satisfaction), someone who had been seen as an equal and had been challenged to a duel. Marked on the duelist's face was his integration into German culture. And the more marginal you were the more you wanted to be scarred. In 1874 William Osler, then a young Canadian medical student visiting Berlin, described "one hopeful young Spanish American of my acquaintance [who] has one half of his face—they are usually on

PLATE TWENTY-NINE

Jacques Joseph (1865–1934), the founder of modern cosmetic rhinoplasty. Note the dueling scars in the formal portrait. (Source: National Library of Medicine, Bethesda, MD).

the left half—laid out in the most irregular manner, the cicatrices running in all directions, enclosing areas of all shapes,—the relics of fourteen duels!"[48] This was extreme among the medical students of the day, but not unknown. The scar marked the individual, even within the medical faculty, who was seen as a hardy member of the body politic. Being a member of a Jewish fraternity (most of which did not duel) could reconstitute the sickly Jewish body into what Max Nordau called the "new muscle Jew." The Jewish fraternity organization stated in 1902, that "it desires the physical education of its members in order to collaborate in the physical regeneration of the Jewish people."[49] A dueling scar marks the socially healthy individual.

The social status of the fraternity member, like that of the military officer, was contested for Jews at the close of the nineteenth century. In 1896 the following proposal had been accepted by the dueling fraternities:

> In full appreciation of the fact that there exists between Aryans and Jews such a deep moral and psychic difference, and that our qualities have suffered so much through Jewish mischief, in full consideration of the many proofs which the Jewish student has also given of his lack of honor and character and since he is completely void of honor according to our German concepts, to-day's conference . . . resolves: "No satisfaction is to be given to a Jew with any weapon, as he is unworthy of it.[50]

Jews are different. But with their facial scars, they look just like us. The visibility of the scar is meant as an assurance of the purity of the group. But Jews cannot be pure, so they must be excluded. For a Jew to bear a facial scar is to hide his sickly essence from us. And that is "mischief."

The scarred Jacques Joseph was a trained orthopedic surgeon, who had been the assistant of Julius Wolff, one of the leaders in that field. Among Wolff's most important findings was the establishment of the "law of the transformation of the skeleton," which argued that every function of the skeleton could be described through the laws of mechanics and that any change of the relationship between single components of the skeleton would lead to a functional and physiological change of the external form of the entire skeleton.[51] Wolff's major contribution to the treatment of diseases of the leg was his development of a therapeutic procedure by which a club foot could be corrected through the use of a specialized dressing which altered the very shape of the foot.[52] Orthopedics, more than any other medical speciality of the period, presented the challenge of altering the visible errors of development so as to restore a "normal" function. Wolff's approach also stressed the interrelationship among all aspects of the body. Among his procedures were corrective surgery and the use of appliances. Joseph's interests did not lie with the foot, another sign of Jewish inferiority, but elsewhere in the anatomy. In 1896 Joseph had undertaken a corrective procedure on a child with protruding ears, which, while successful, caused him to be dismissed from Wolff's clinic. This was cosmetic not reconstructive surgery.[53] One simply did not undertake surgical procedures for vanity's sake, he was told. This was not a case of a functional disability, such as a club foot. The child was not suffering from any physical ailment which could be cured through surgery.

Joseph opened a private surgical practice in Berlin. In January 1898, a twenty-eight-year-old man came to him, having heard of the successful operation on the child's ears. He complained that "his nose was the source of considerable annoyance. Where ever he went, everybody stared at him; often, he was the target of remarks or ridiculing gestures. On account of this he became melancholic, withdrew almost completely from social life, and had the earnest desire to be relieved of this deformity."[54] Joseph took the young man's case and proceeded to perform the first, modern cosmetic rhinoplasty. On May 11, 1898 he reported on this operation before the Berlin Medical Society. In that report Joseph provided a "scientific" rationale for performing a medical procedure on what was an otherwise completely healthy individual: "the psychological effect of the operation is of utmost importance. The depressed attitude of the patient subsided completely. He is happy to move around unnoticed. His happiness in life has increased, his wife was glad to report; the patient who formerly avoided social contact now wishes

184

to attend and give parties. In other words, he is happy over the results."[55] The patient no longer felt himself marked by the form of his nose. He was cured of his "disease," which was his visibility. Joseph had undertaken a surgical procedure which had cured his patient's psychological disorder! [**PLATE 30**]

Joseph's procedure was not the first reduction rhinoplasty. Cosmetic nose surgery had been undertaken earlier in the century in Germany and France, before the introduction of modern surgical techniques of anesthesia and antisepsis, by such surgeons as Johann Friedrich Dieffenbach. In the 1880s, John Orlando Roe in Rochester, New York, had performed an operation to "cure" the "pug nose."[56] Based on the profile, Roe divided the image of the nose into five categories: Roman, Greek, Jewish, Snub or Pug, and Celestial. Roe cited the "snub-nose" as "proof of a degeneracy of the human race." It is, of course, the Irish profile which is characterized by the snub-nose in the caricatures of the period.[57] Roe's procedure turned the Irish nose into "a thing of beauty."[58] (In addition, work on reshaping the nose had been done by Robert Weir in New York, Vincenz von Czerny in Heidelberg, George Monks in Boston, and James Israel in Berlin. All of these were primarily forms of reconstructive surgery with the emphasis on correcting underlying somatic rather than aesthetic problems.[59]) However, Joseph's was the first procedure of the type still carried out today. The climate was ripe for the development of a quick and relatively simple procedure to alter the external form of the nose. The earlier procedures were not only more complicated (as well as dangerous) but they also did not come at a time when the need to "cure" the disease of the visibility of the Other was as powerful. Central to Joseph's process of nasal reduction was the fact that there was "no visible scar."[60] Joseph's procedure began the craze for nose jobs in fin-de-siècle Germany and Austria. In the history of medicine, Joseph was the "father of aesthetic rhinoplasty." He came to be nicknamed "Nase-Josef = Nosef" in the German-Jewish community.[61]

It is unclear whether Joseph's first patient was Jewish, but the depiction of his psychological sense of social isolation due to the form of his nose certainly mirrors the meaning associated with anti-Semitic bias at the fin de siècle. It is clear, however, that

185

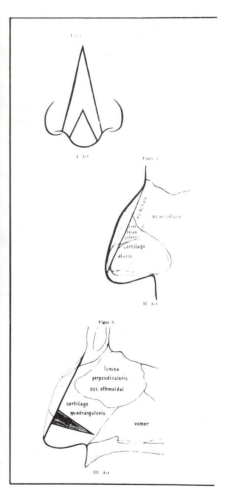

PLATE THIRTY

The first nose job. Before and after photographs and the outline of the surgical procedure. From "Über die operative Verkleinerung einer Nase (Rhinomiosis)," *Berliner klinische Wochenschrift* 40 (1898): 882-85 (Source: National Library of Medicine, Bethesda, MD).

The Jewish Nose

◆

Joseph's initial clientele was heavily Jewish and that he regularly reduced "Jewish noses" to "gentile contours." Many of his patients underwent the operation "to conceal their origins."[62] In justifying the procedure, Joseph called upon the rationale of the psychological damage done by the nose's shape. He cured the sense of inferiority of his patients through changing the shape of their nose. His primary "cure" was to make them less visible in their world. This was one of the rationales cited by the other German-Jewish cosmetic surgeons of the period, such as the art historian-physician Eugen Holländer.[63] Joseph's orthopedic training served him well. He could holistically cure the ailments of the entire patient, including the patient's psyche, by operating on the patient's nose. Here was an extension of Wolff's law into the realm of the psychological. Joseph noted, at the conclusion of his first annual report (1917) as the director of the first department for "facial-plasty" at the *Charité*, the major teaching hospital in Berlin, that "the discharged patients have all been cured of their psychic depression which the consciousness of bodily deformity always involves."[64] These were for the most part patients horribly maimed in the war who were made whole, both physically and psychologically. How equally true of his private patients.

We have one very late case description of one of Joseph's rhinoplasties, dating from January, 1933, soon after the Nazi seizure of power and after Jewish physicians were forbidden to operate on non-Jewish patients except with special permission. The sixteen-year-old Adolphine Schwarz followed the lead of her older brother and had "her nose bobbed." She commented that her brother had written to Joseph and informed him that he had very limited means. "Joseph was very charitable," she later said, "and when he felt that someone suffered from a 'Jewish nose,' he would operate for nothing."[65] The image of "suffering from a 'Jewish nose' " is a powerful one. Young men and women needed to become invisible, needed to alter their bodies, as their visibility became even more marked. For the virtual invisibility of the Jews in Germany vanished with the introduction of the yellow "Jewish star." "Nosef" died in February 1934 from a heart attack, before he was forbidden to practice medicine completely. His scarred face, at the last, did not make him invisible as a Jew, nor did his surgical interventions make those Jews whose noses he "bobbed" any less visible.

But Jacques Joseph was not the only Berlin physician who was operating on noses in the 1890s. Two Jewish scientists of fin-de-siècle Europe who were preoccupied with the nose argued that there is a direct relationship between the "nose" and the "genitalia." For Wilhelm Fliess and his Viennese collaborator, Sigmund Freud, the nose came to serve as a sign of universal development rather than as a specific sign of an "inferior" racial identity.[66] The nose was the developmental analogy to the genitalia. Evolving embryologically at the same stage, there was a shared relationship between the tissue of the nose and that of the genitalia. And, for Fliess and Freud, this was true of all human beings, not merely Jews. Thus one cure for sexual dysfunction, according to Fliess, was to operate on the nose and that he regularly did. Fliess's views were shared by other physicians of the time, such as John Noland Mackensie at The Johns Hopkins University.[67] But their interest was hypothetical; Fliess acted on his theories by operating upon the nose in order to cure perceived "nervous" illnesses. In reviewing the records, it is clear that Fliess's patients did not make up a cross section of society. Of the 156 cases he records (some from the medical literature of the time), only a dozen were men.[68] All of the rest were women, who were operated upon for numerous of complaints, primarily psychological ones. Fliess treated a wide range of mental illnesses, including hysteria, through the extensive use of cocaine, but he also applied acid to the internal structures of the nasal passages or surgically removed them. What Fliess managed to do in these years was to convert a quality of race into an attribute of gender. While his theoretical material covered both males and females, his clinical material (and one assumes this reflected his clinical practice) focused on the female's nasal cavities as the clinical substitute for the Jew's nose.

It was not merely that in turn-of-the-century Europe there was an association between the genitalia and the nose; there was, and had long been, a direct relationship drawn in popular and medical thought between the size of the nose and that of the penis. Ovid wrote: "Noscitur e naso quanta sit hast viro." The link between the

The Jewish Nose

Jew's sexuality and the Jew's nose was a similarly well-established one at century's end, but here the traditional pattern was reversed.[69] The specific shape of the Jew's nose indicated the damaged nature, the shortened form, of his penis. The traditional positive association between the size of the nose and that of the male genitalia was reversed and this reversal was made a pathological sign.[70] The association between the Jewish nose and the circumcised penis, as signs of Jewish difference, was been made in the crudest and most revolting manner during the 1880s. In the streets of Berlin and Vienna, in penny-papers or on the newly installed "Litfassäulen," or advertising columns, caricatures of Jews could be seen.[71] An image of the essential Jew, little "Mr. Kohn," showed him drowned, only his nose and huge, over-sized feet showing above the waterline **[PLATE 31]**.[72] These extraordinary caricatures stressed one central aspect of the physiognomy of the Jewish male, his nose, which represented that hidden sign of his sexual difference, his circumcised penis. The Jews' sign of sexual difference, their sexual selectivity, as an indicator of their identity was, as Friedrich Nietzsche strikingly observed in *Beyond Good and Evil*, the focus of the Germans' fear of the superficiality of their recently created national identity.[73] This fear was represented in caricatures by the elongated nose. It also permeated the scientific discussions of the time. In the "anatomical-anthropological" study of the nose by Viennese anatomist, Oskar Hovorka (1893), the form of the nose is seen as a sign of negative racial difference, as well as a sign of the "idiot and the insane."[74] Look at the nose of the Other and you will see the basic sign of the atavism. Thus, when Wilhelm Fliess attempted to alter the pathology of the genitalia by operating on the nose, at a point in time when national identity was extremely unsure of itself and scapegoats easy to find, he joined together the Enlightenment universalist theory to the German biology of race. Fliess's desire was to make this into a quality of all human beings, male and female, Jew and Aryan, not merely of Jewish males. He succeeded in generating an image of the woman as the sufferer from the pathologies of the nose which was equivalent to the general cultural view of the Jewish male.

Fliess's goal—as that of so many others of the time—was alter

PLATE THIRTY-ONE

A postcard from the fin de siècle showing the flooding in Berlin with the inscription: "In the great flood, little Kohn died!!!" Note the three qualities of the Jew's body: the prominent nose, the large feet, and the "diamond" ring. Here the physical and moral failings of the Jew are equated in the image of the dead Jew (Source: Private Collection, Ithaca).

the Jewish body so that the Jew could become invisible. Some Jews, such as the Berlin literary critic Ludwig Geiger, rebelled against this desire for a Jewish invisibility: "If one desires assimilation—and that can only mean becoming German in morals, language, actions, feelings—one does needs neither mixed marriages nor baptism. No serious person would suggest an assimilation which demanded that all Jews had straight noses and blond hair."[75] But, of course, in arguing the point this way Geiger was reacting to precisely those pressures which caused Jews to dye their hair and "bob" their noses. Geiger implies that the changes are primarily for cosmetic purposes, vanity's sake. What he pointedly avoids discussing is the fact that they were actually meant to "cure" the disease of Jewishness, the anxiety of being seen as a Jew. Being seen as a Jew meant being persecuted, attacked, and harassed. The "cure" for this was the actual alteration of the body. The Jewish mind, which German culture saw as different from that of the Aryan, is afflicted by its sense of its own difference. In order to cure the Jew's mind, Joseph and Fliess had to operate on the Jew's nose.

One can cite another case of the severe psychological damage done by the internalization of this sense of the "Jewish nose," not from the surgical literature but from the psychoanalytic literature of the fin de siècle. It comes from the case file of Freud's first biographer and one of the first psychoanalysts, the Viennese-Jewish physician Fritz Wittels. At the meeting of the Viennese Psychoanalytic Society on December 9, 1908 Wittels recounted a case of a patient who had come to him specifically because of the publication of his polemical work on baptized Jews, on Jews who were trying to pass as Christians.[76] Wittels saw this as a form of insanity. It was a young man of about thirty who suffered from "anti-Semitic persecution, for which he holds his inconspicuously Semitic nose responsible. He therefore plans to have the shape of his nose changed by plastic surgery."[77] Wittels attempted to persuade him that his anxiety about his nose was merely a displacement for anxiety about his sexual identity. "This the patient declared to be a good joke." The evident analogy of Wittel's suggestions does not occur to him. If a patient comes to him expressly because of his writing about the neurosis of conversion and wishes to have his

191

nose rebuilt to hide his Jewishness, then the question of his own "paranoid" relationship to his own circumcised penis, that invisible but omnipresent sign of the male's Jewishness is self-evident. Freud picked up on this directly and notes that "the man is evidently unhappy about being a Jew and wants to be baptized." "At this point Wittels remarks that the patient is an ardent Jew. Nevertheless, he does not undergo baptism. In this fact lies the conflict that has absorbed the meaning of other conflicts." To be a Jew and to be so intensely fixated on the public visibility of that identity is to be ill. Then Wittels revealed the name of the patient to the group and Freud recognized from the name that the patient's father was an engaged Zionist. He then read the desire to unmake himself as a Jew as a sign of the rejection of the father. Freud, however, did not comment on the link between a strong Jewish identity and the rejection of the visibility which that identity entailed. There was a real sense in Freud's comment that the Jewish body, represented by the skin or the nose, could never truly be changed. It was a permanent fixture, forever reflecting the Jew's racial identity. Altering the Jew's external form may have provided a wider margin in which the Jew could "pass," but the Jew could never be truly at peace with the sense of his or her invisibility.

The image of a literally scarred Jacques Joseph operating on the literal image of the Jew is powerfully disturbing. Joseph reshapes the image of the Jew, but even that is not enough. The more the Jew desires to become invisible, the more the Jew's invisibility becomes a sign of difference. We can see this operation in effect once again in the writings of Walter Lippmann, one of the leading American-Jewish intellectuals of the first half of the twentieth century, who commented in the late 1920s that

> the rich and vulgar and pretentious Jews of our big American cities are perhaps the greatest misfortune that has ever befallen the Jewish people. They are the fountain of anti-Semitism. When they rush about in super automobiles, bejeweled and furred and painted and overbarbered, when they build themselves French chateaux and Italian palazzi, they stir up the latent hatred against crude wealth in the hands of shallow people; and that hatred diffuses itself.[78]

The Jew remains a Jew even when disguised. It is in their "painted and overbarbered" essence. One cannot hide—nose job or no nose job—from the lessons of race. And the Jew is the most aware of this. Lippmann creates in his mind's eye the image of his antithesis, the "bad" Jew to his "good" Jew. And this Jew is just as visible as he believes himself to be invisible. Lippmann, in his Wall Street suit and carefully controlled manners and appearance, looks, just like everyone else—or so he hopes. But there is no hiding from the fact of a constructed difference. There is no mask, no operation, no refuge. Indeed, as the plastic surgeon Mark Gorney has recently noted: "Patients seeking rhinoplasty . . . frequently show a guilt-tinged, second generation rejection of their ethnic background masked by excuses, such as not photographing well. Often it is not so much a desire to abandon the ethnic group as it is to be viewed as individuals and to rid themselves of specific physical attributes associated with their particular ethnic group."[79] It is in being visible in "the body that betrays," that the Jew is most uncomfortable. [80] For visibility means being seen not as an individual but as an Other, one of the "ugly" race.

8

THE JEWISH ESSENCE

Anti-Semitism and the
Body in Psychoanalysis

◆

Even though I expect Janet Malcolm to be a controversial commentator on the culture of psychoanalysis, she still startled me when she, in a recent review, focused on the evident anti-Semitism present in Masud Khan's final book, *The Long Wait*. She observe there that "when he writes of throwing off his 'Yiddish shackles' (and complains of the way the 'Judaic-Yiddish-Jewish bias of psychoanalysis . . . cramped my personal ethnic style'), he is chiefly displaying his anti-Semitism . . . ."[1] In contrast to Janet Malcolm, I have come to see Masud Khan's account of his "anti-Semitic" response to his Jewish (and, not unimportantly, as we shall see, gay) patient "Mr. Luis" not as a personal idiosyncrasy, but rather as intimately related to the discourse about the biological nature of the Jew which helped form and frame the structures and rhetoric of psychoanalysis.

I differ in my understanding of the "Jewish" roots of psychoanalysis from both Janet Malcolm and Peter Gay, whom she evokes in the final paragraph of her review. For Gay, Freud's "Jewishness" has nothing to do with the matter of psychoanalysis.[2] And to prove this, he uses religious, ethnic, and political definitions of the Jew and demonstrates Freud's distance or at least his ambivalence to them. Malcolm qualifies Gay's dismissal of the Jewish roots of psychoanalysis (harking back to work done by Bakan in the 1950s[3]) and comments on Masud Khan's personally aggressive style, noting that "Freud may well have drawn on models of rabbinical self-effacement and unpretentiousness" for his understanding of the character of the analyst. Given the fin-de-siècle image of the *Wunderrabbi* especially in the popular acculturated Austro-Jewish literature of the time (such as Karl Emil Franzos's *Der Pojaz* [1905]), this is an incomplete characterization of the image of the "rabbi" in Freud's time at best; at worst, it echoes Gay's image of a worldview in which the "godless Jew" (Freud's juxtaposition of these words is supposed to jar) has been able to discard his Jewishness. But "Jewish" for fin-de-siècle science has, as we have seen, primarily a biological meaning, and according to the "racial" definition of the Jew one can never truly cast off one's Jewishness.

Let us first read Masud Khan: His theme, stated clearly at the conclusion of his introduction is that "the faith one is born to, one can rarely shed. Carl Jung has acknowledged this publicly and professionally, and Professor Doctor Sigmund Freud only in correspondence, privately: 'I . . . would like to take it that if the child turns out to be a boy, he will develop into a stalwart Zionist.' "[4] Khan's initial statement seems to reflect a "religious" definition for the Jew, but his quotation from Freud stresses the biological relationship between "Jewish identity" ("Zionist") and "gender" ("boy"). What Masud Khan evokes is the image of the Jewish male as the marker of Jewish identity. This becomes especially clear if we put the quote in context. It is from a letter of August 28, 1913 from Freud to Sabina Spielrein, C.G. Jung's pregnant former mistress, after Freud's initial break with Jung. Furious with Jung, Freud announced to Spielrein that he was "cured of the last predilection for the Aryan cause . . . He or it must be dark in any case, no more towheads. Let us banish all these will-o'-the-wisps!," and he concludes: "We are and remain Jews. The others will only exploit us and will never understand or appreciate us." In the very next letter, following her announcement that her new born child was a girl Freud comments: "It is far better that the child should be a 'she.' Now we can think again about the blond Siegfried and perhaps smash that idol before his time comes."[5] Freud's discourse about the blond Aryans and their eternal opposition to the "dark" Jews framed his conflict with Jung in terms of the rhetoric of race. It is Khan's replication of the racial definition of the "Jew" (as a category of fin-de-siècle science) and the "male" that underlies his, in Malcolm's word, "aggressiveness."

Khan redefines the idea of the "Jewishness" of psychoanalysis in the course of his case study of Mr. Luis. He stresses its "Yiddish" dimension "because psychoanalysis, for better or worse, is not only Judaic in its inherited traditions, but also Yiddish and Jewish. The three are distinct in my experience." How they are distinct is never defined, but the link between the Eastern Jew and the idea of the Jew is furthered by him through the medium of his analysis of the case which he calls that of "a dismaying homosexual." It is not accidental that the nexus between sexuality and race is to be found in a chapter dealing with "gender confusion." His analysand, whom he calls Mr. Luis, represents for Khan a type of "sexuality" which is neither real nor centered but merely "febrile excitedness, with little true desire or appetite to it. His aggression, or rather aggressivity, expressed itself through wasting others" (100). Mr. Luis is not a valuable patient, a patient who can truly benefit from the interaction of psychoanalysis, for he has little to give the analyst: "You are not ill or sick or neurotic, or my sort of patient. I shall learn little from you. Yourself, you are not a true pervert either. Just a mixed-up Yiddish kid who has started to age suddenly, and is terrified of aging further. I can well believe that you were a beautiful child and a beautiful youth: with your dark gleaming eyes, dark hair, you were, I reckon, smartly sleek of girth and tall-woman height: five foot eight or nine, I guess" (90).

At the center of his counter-transference, Khan sees the body of the Jew as interchangeable with the body of the gay—physically different, exotic, feminine. But the very fact of Mr. Luis's physical (and, therefore, psychological difference) separates his world from that of Masud Khan. It is harder for Masud Khan to deal with this "Yiddish kid" "than for some Yiddish colleagues of mine, here in London" (90). And the reason is made clear by him to the analysand:

"I have little use and less praise for self-made Jews who pretend to be artists, atheists, writers or dancers" (90). (The superficiality of the Jewish parvenu in the realm of culture is a set theme in anti-Semitic discourse within psychoanalysis, as in Jung's comments or those later made by his follower, Joseph Campbell. Jung stressed the differences between a Jewish and an Aryan psychology as early as 1918. He stressed the rootlessness of the Jew, that fact that "he is badly at a loss for that quality in man which roots him to the earth and draws new strength from below."[6] This view of the rootlessness of the Jew made the Jew's creativity, especially in the sphere of psychology, of value only from the Jew: "thus it is a quite unpardonable mistake to accept the conclusions of a Jewish psychology as generally valid."[7]) Khan confronts Mr. Luis quite directly: "Yes, I am anti-Semitic. You know why, Mr. Luis? Because I am an Aryan and had thought all of you Jews had perished when Jesus, from sheer dismay—and he was one of you — had flown up to Heaven, leaving you in the scorching care of Hitler, Himmler and the crematoriums. Don't fret, Mr. Luis; like the rest of your species, you will survive and continue to harass others, and lament, and bewail yourselves. Remarkable how Yiddish/Jewish you are." (92–93)

The analysand's response is quite straightforward: "But please tell me why you won't [help me]? Is it because I am a Jew? Not classy. A mere poof from nowhere. I stink in your nostrils" (90). And Masud Khan's response is just as straightforward: "Let us look at each of us. I am tall, handsome, a good polo and squash player. Fit. Only forty-one. Very rich. Noble born. Delightfully married to a very famous artist. Live in a style of my own making. Am a Muslim from Pakistan. My roots are sunk deep and spread wide across three cultures. . . . I am *different*. And this *difference* matters most for me" (91).

It is the idea of the difference of the Jew, of the Jew as another species, inherently different from the Aryan, which underlies Masud Khan's image of the Jew. And this representation is linked by him to his simulation of gender. Here it is the problem of the biological definition of the Jew—neither religious, ethnic, nor political definitions, though all are evoked in his Trinity of "Jewish-

Yiddish-Zionist." These become labels which disguise the basic racial definition, a definition which draws an absolute boundary between the the "healthy" observer and the pathological object of observation.

This difficulty was already felt by Frantz Fanon, the black Caribbean psychiatrist, when in 1952 he tried to fix questions of black identity formation with the lens of psychoanalysis.[8] His question was one which is not unimportant for the very history of psychoanalysis: How does a political system which sets standards which define humanity deform those who are forced to shape themselves to fit those standards (of decorum, language, psychic organization)? Especially when they are never really permitted to feel that they truly fit. For Fanon, as for Masud Khan, it is the Jew who forms the counter-image to the self: "The Jew and I: Since I was not satisfied to be racialized, by a lucky turn of fate I was humanized. I joined the Jew, my brother, in misery" (122). The Jew and the black are ideological equivalents and yet there is a substantial difference between the idea of the (ungendered) Jew and that of the black (male): "No anti-Semite, for example, would ever conceive of the idea of castrating the Jew. He is killed or sterilized. But the Negro is castrated. The penis, the symbol of manhood, is annihilated, which is to say that it is denied. The difference between the two attitudes is apparent. The Jew is attacked in his religious identity, in his history, in his race, in his relations with his ancestors and with his posterity; when one sterilizes the Jew, one cuts off the source; every time a Jew is persecuted, it is the whole race that is persecuted in his person. But it is in his corporeality that the Negro is attacked. It is as a concrete personality that he is lynched. It is as an actual being that he is a threat" (162–63). The real castration of the black is opposed to the symbolic castration of the Jew. But this is not the lynching of the black in contrast to the social act of circumcision, it is lynching in contrast to the death camps. The Jew becomes a symbolic collective for Fanon; the black—his own body—remains that of an individual.

Fanon's need to "decorporealize" the Jew, to remove the Jewish, male body from the category of the body at risk is a reaction formation against the "corporealizing" of the body of the black, of his own body. The Jew's body can vanish only if it is perceived as the same as the body of the non-Jew. For this to happen, it is the abstract "Jewish body" that Fanon evokes, not the body of the Jewish male. (Even with the male pronoun, it is clear that the Jew evoked is ungendered.) It is the image of the Jew as the equivalent of the Jewish race which is destroyed. Mass murder, then, is not literal castration. (As we have seen, however, it is precisely the increased visibility of the Jewish male which stands at the center of the rhetoric of psychoanalysis.) What Fanon does here is to replace the cultural anxiety about the meaning ascribed to Jewish male sexuality with that ascribed to black male sexuality, thereby causing the Jewish male to vanish. In understanding his masculinity (read: his power to control his body) as castrated, Fanon sees his race as written on his body in a double manner: first, because of his disempowerment by the Western colonial rhetoric of his skin color and second, by his fear of emasculation, the literal destruction of his body by those who fear his repressed anger. This he sets against the image of the Shoah, the mass murder of Jews.

Fanon's denial of the "reality" of the Jewish body must also be measured against his sense of the invisibility of the Jew, the sense that the Jew can pass, can become "white," perhaps even is "white": "All the same, the Jew can be unknown in his Jewishness. He is not wholly what he is. One hopes, one waits. His actions, his behavior are the final determinant. He is a white man, and, apart from some rather debatable characteristics, he can sometimes go unnoticed. . . . Granted, the Jews are harassed—what am I thinking of? They are hunted down, exterminated, cremated. But these are little family quarrels. The Jew is disliked from the moment he is tracked down" (115–16). Here the body of the Jew, his skin, becomes transparent, revealing him as "white" all along. The Shoah—merely a family spat among whites.

Fanon's focus on the lack of difference of the Jew, the sameness of *the Jew's body* and that of his persecutor, places the body of the black as the baseline of difference. Difference, of course, determined and decided in terms of a politics of racial biology. For Fanon's analyses of the nature of the shaping of the black, colonial psyche follow the guidelines of Freudian theory (admittedly in its culturally critical form). He employs the theory of the "Jewish" science of psychoanalysis to "explain" the nature of the black. The black psychiatrist uses Jewish techniques in order to examine his own psychic organization. Central to this self-reflection, which forms the dithyrambic concluding chapter of Fanon's text, is the problem of being both subject and object of a science which is perceived to be foreign to oneself. Psychoanalysis is foreign in the double sense, to Fanon, in that it comes from outside of his own experience and stems from a group labeled as inherently, biologically inferior.

My examples, Masud Khan and Fanon, were selected with an eye to their roles as non-Jewish psychoanalysts, but also as "psychoanalysts of color," individuals labeled as "different" in their culture. While I could have turned to more overtly anti-Semitic, non-Jewish psychoanalysts such as C.G. Jung for my examples of anti-Semitism within self-defined "mainstream" psychoanalysis, Masud Khan writing in the 1980s, and Fanon, writing in the 1950s, seemed to reflect an attitude toward Jews which was not as tightly bound to the political ideology of the moment, as Jung's was and was more a product of the analyst's self-definition as an insider-outsider.[9] Central to both Khan's and Fanon's representation of the Jew is the nature of the Jewish (read: male) body. It is in their need to draw a distinction between their own body and the body of the Jew—all "black" to the colonial eye—that we can seek the meaning of their construction of difference. What I would like to do in this essay is to sketch the parallel views at the turn of the century, views which helped shape the rhetoric and argument of Freud's own project and which continue to be present, not merely within Masud Khan's and Fanon's representation of difference, but also in the difficulty which psychoanalysis has with "cultural" categories such as "race." This difficulty has been acknowledged by some African-American psychologists in their comments that the Freudian therapeutic model is not quite appropriate for their clients.

We can return to the very origins of psychoanalysis in the world of fin-de-siècle Vienna to begin to understand the implications of the biological definition of the Jew for the rhetoric of psychoanalysis. Let us begin, not with Sigmund Freud but with his contemporary Peter Altenberg (1859–1919, the pseudonym for Richard Engländer). Peter Altenberg was one of those self-consciously "marginal" figures in the cultural world of turn-of-the-century Vienna. A highly idiosyncratic essayist who distributed hand-made jewelry in order to receive patronage from a wide range of admirers, Altenberg lived, like other marginal *Luftmenschen*, individuals on his wits and not much else in the middle of Vienna, in the Café Central. For all of his self-styled marginality, in one respect he strove to be a member of the Viennese majority. In 1900 he converted to Roman Catholicism. What conversion meant for Altenberg can be seen in an undated "begging" letter from him which sketches the central dimensions for the self-understanding of the Jew in late nineteenth-century Vienna:

> My dear Dr. Gustav Schönaich:
> Since you have not even acknowledged that you received my gift, I can assume that you have been influenced by the dark, evil soul of that person, an absolute liar, who once called himself my friend and admirer. For you, a Christian, are naive, full of belief and agreeable. He, however, that incarnation of Jewishness, is full of uncontrollable tricks!!! I must suffer for the fact, that nature and fate have made me Christian in my external and internal organization, in my body, my posture, my pronunciation, my nose, my soul, my spirit, while this person attempts unsuccessfully to disguise the sign of Cain of an inferior race through hairsplitting and pseudo-Idealism!!![10]

Altenberg's image of the difference between the Christian and the Jew has to do with "external" (his stress) and "internal" differences: differences in the meaning of the body, of stance, of language, of the mind and of the soul. Altenberg's list moves from the observable to the hidden, from the external to the internal. This is a morphological definition of race rather than a genetic one, yet it also incorporates all those invisible qualities which we later associate with the genetic idea of race. What is created is the genotype of the Jew.[11] Conversion is possible only because Altenberg was created by "nature and fate" as a Christian, i.e., as an Aryan. In Altenberg's letter one can see how traditional religious labels ("Jew" and "Christian") take on the properties of categories of race ("Jew" and "Aryan") or, better said, how categories of religious difference are transformed into categories of racial science.[12] It is the confusion at the turn of the century of these two interlocked but conceptually separate categories of religion and race which can introduce our problem.

Peter Altenberg's categories represent his contemporary European views of Jewishness neither as a religion (Judaism), nor as a political movement (Zionism), nor as an ethnic identity (as a "Austrian or German of the Mosaic Persuasion"), but as a race (the Jews). It is, to quote the German proverb of the time, not religion, but race which defines the Jew: "Was der Jude glaubt ist einerlei / in der Rasse liegt der Schweinerei!" ("The Jew's belief is nothing / it's race that makes him swinish!").[13] Or as the displaced Austrian painter and politician Adolf Hitler rephrased it in *Mein Kampf* (1925): "the whole existence [of the Jews] is based on one single great lie, to wit, that they are a religious community while actually they are a race—and what a race!"[14] Thus the double bind of fin-de-siècle Jewry is the desire to go "beyond Judaism" but the impossibility of undertaking this once "Judaism" is defined racially.[15] And it is in the science of the time that the debate about the racial identity of the Jews was joined.

Freud is quite aware of the implications of the biology of race. He uses its rhetoric often. He can write to Karl Abraham of their common "racial identification" (*Rassenverwandtschaft*)[16] or warn Max Graf against having his son baptized. For this action will change only his religion, it will not change his need to "struggle as a Jew."[17] The Jew as a member of a different race was as distant from the Aryan = Christian as was the Hottentot, the "lowest" rung on the *scala naturae*, the scale of perfection, of eighteenth-century biological science.[18] The categories of race were understood as mutually exclusive. Although the Jew was placed elsewhere on the ladder of development than the Hottentot, the Jew was equally and inherently different from the Aryan (and, by implication, less good). Given the basic philosophy of late nineteenth-century science, this difference was defined in terms of observable phenomena (or phenomena suggested to be observable) by nineteenth-century ethnologists and those they influenced, such as the physicians of the period.[19] The "human" science of the period claimed that Jewish anthropometric difference was an absolute and could be seen and measured. The Jew, as a member of an inherently different race, was "different" from the Aryan in every way. Polygenetic arguments about the nature of the races played a fundamental role anchored in the popular representation of the Jew as well in the "high" science of the fin de siècle. The idea of race was closely linked to the image of the unique construction of the Jewish body and the Jewish psyche.

We can see this representation in a short story about the rebuilding of the Jewish body and psyche at the turn of the century. Written by the German physician-author Oskar Panizza (1853–1921) in 1893, "The Operated Jew," depicts the careful reconstruction of the Jew Itzig Feitel Stern into an "Aryan."[20] The story begins with a detailed description of Stern's physiognomy (his Jewish "antelope's eye," his nose, his eyebrows, his "fleshly and overly creased" lips, his "violet fatty tongue," his "bow-legs," his "curly, thick black locks of hair"). But it is not just his body which marks him as a Jew. His language, whether it is French or high German is "warped" by his "Palatinate-Yiddish" (68). He "meeowed, rattled, bleated and also like to produce sneezing sounds . . ." (64). His speech was a "mixture of Palatinate Semitic babble, French nasal noises and some high German vocal sounds which he had fortuitously overheard and articulated with an open position of the mouth" (65). His body language was equally marked: "When he walked, Itzig always raised both thighs almost to his mid-riff so that he bore some resemblance to a stork. At the same time he lowered his head deeply into his breast-plated tie and stared at the ground. Similar disturbances can be noted in people with spinal diseases. However, Itzig did not have a spinal disease, for he was young and in good condition" (64). His gesticulation was equally "Jewish." Stern goes to Professor Klotz, the famous Heidelberg anatomist, and has his body reshaped. He is forced into molds and retained in order, in his own words, to "become such a fine gentilman just like a goymenera and to geeve up all fizonomie of Jewishness" (68). His "Palatinate-Yiddish" is retrained and formed into a pure high German. But his Jewish soul remains.

Stern desired a "chaste, undefined Germanic soul which shrouded the possessor like an aroma." (The view of at least one distinguished German biologist of the time was that the Jewish soul was marked by a specific smell, a version of the medieval stench, the *foëtor judäicus*, associated with the Jew.[21]) To accomplish this he buys the blood of Christians and has it exchanged for his own. Having been transformed into an Aryan, Stern decides to marry a "blond Germanic lass" (77). Indeed, all of the physical changes which are necessary to make him into the ideal image of the Aryan have taken place—all but one. Feitel Stern remains circumcised. (Panizza never mentions the possibility of uncircumcising Stern even though there are ancient procedures for the reversal of circumcision.[22]) The circumcision of the genitals is the outward sign of the immutability of the Jew within.

On his wedding night, Stern becomes intoxicated and in his drunkenness all of his newly acquired qualities of body, tongue, and mind disintegrate. The *foëtor judäicus* which had been masked by the Christian blood which he had bought reappears and marks his final collapse as he lay "crumpled and quivering, a convoluted Asiatic image in a wedding dress, a counterfeit of human flesh . . ." (79) All of the changes which the Jew acquires are useless. The Jew unravels under the influence of drink, as Immanuel Kant observed in his *Anthropology*: "Women, clergymen, and Jews ordinarily do not become drunk, at least they carefully avoid all appearance of it, because they are weak in civic life and must restrain themselves (for which sobriety is required.)"[23] Jews become their true selves when the constraints of civilization are removed.

All of the changes which the Jew acquires are useless. As we discussed in Chapter 3, the science of the time whether in the writings of the German ethnologist Richard Andree or the British eugenist Francis Galton saw the Jewish body as immutable. Robert Knox, in one of the most widely cited and republished studies on race, expressed this view at mid-century. When " . . . he looked attentively at the Jewish physiognomy on the streets, as he perambulates our pavements, and with a hoarse, unmusical voice, proclaims to you his willingness to purchase cast-off clothes of others; or assuming the air of a person of a different stamp, he saunters about Cornhill in quest of business; or, losing sight of his origin for a moment, he dresses himself up as the flash man about town; but never to be mistaken for a moment—never to be confounded with any other race."[24] It is this biological definition which crystallizes in the representation of the Jew in the fin de siècle. Trained at the University of Munich, where the discussion of the biological difference of the Jew was as powerful as anywhere in Europe, Panizza's own personal life reflected the central problem which appears in the history of psychoanalysis: the identity of the physician as separate or at least separable from the physician. For Panizza was not only a physician but also a syphilitic (at least in his own self-definition).

How radically this view dominates the Jewish response can be seen in an answer to Oskar Panizza's tale called "The Operated Goy," a story published in 1922 by the writer-philosopher Mynona (Salomo Friedlaender [1871–1946]).[25] Mynona's tale represents an assimilated Jew's response to Panizza's message about the immutability of the Jew, a message which still relies on images of the Jewish body and its meaning within fin-de-siècle society. In Mynona's story, the protagonist is the Aryan Count Reschock a noble whose family of anti-Semites can trace its roots back to the destruction of Jerusalem by the Emperor Titus. His body is that of the essential Aryan: "Thin lips, Prussian chin, proud nape of the neck, extraordinary stiff posture; legs, which in their innocence were neither knock-kneed nor bowed; . . . which stood on aristocratic and simultaneously pan-Germanic feet, and walked about as if descending from Mt. Olympus" (280). Through his anti-Semitic demeanor, he captures the interest of the beautiful but very Jewish heiress Rebecka Gold-Isak with her "almond eyes, ebony hair, ivory skin, etc." (282). She presents her father with the ultimatum: she wishes to marry Count Reschock. Her father demands that if such a wedding is to be, the bridegroom must literally become a Jew. Central to his physical transformation is his ritual circumcision. (285–86) His penis must become Jewish if he is to become a Jew. Rebecka manages to "convert" the anti-Semite to a philo-Semite. She manages to persuade him to undertake ritual circumcision by altering his soul through "Jewish" means:

Wasn't his radical hatred of the Jews precisely the most uncanny means of generating the opposite: the most radical shift from one extreme to another? Anti-Semitism is possibly even more Jewish than Judaism. In general, those who hate and discriminate predispose themselves in all secretiveness slowly but surely to the most intimate blood relationship, even to an identification with the object of negation. If she could bring the young count to self-realization, then she could be sure of him. One had to force him to undertake psychoanalysis. She bribed his servant Bör, more with her charm than with money, and sought aid among feudal nobles, who again following her lead, quietly but irresistibly influenced young Reschock until he himself appeared with mysterious psychic inhibitions in the examination room of the famous Freud. This veritable destroyer of fig leaves so anatomically robbed the noble Reschock-ish soul of its protective covering that the Count fell into the arms of his servant, who hurried to him, with a horrendous cry. He pulled himself together and stared into the dark eyes of his fate in the form of the beautiful Jewess, with inherited bravery, yes audacity. At first in his phantasy, then in reality. (286–87)

Mynona, along with Karl Kraus one of the most articulate early critics of psychoanalysis, parodies the use of psychoanalysis as a means of altering the soul.[26] Here it becomes the means of effecting the alteration of the body. This view is echoed by the Czech novelist Ladislaw Klima in 1928, when he has his hero disguise himself as an old Jew "because he already has knock-knees" in order to visit the most famous psychopathologist in all of Germany—who turns out to speak in *Mauschel*.[27]

In order finally to win the Jewess's hand, Reschock must be physically transformed by the famed orthopedist Professor Friedländer into the form of "a Jewish Talmudic scholar." He studies Hebrew. He is finally circumcised and he changes his name to Count Moshe. By the close of the story, he and his beloved have moved to Jerusalem where they raise a family of orthodox children. Professor Friedländer's practice has blossomed. He has become the scourge of all anti-Semites, for he has shown how easily a member of one race can be transformed into another.

The Jewish Essence

The problem with Mynona's retelling of Panizza's story is that the basic ethnographic argument, the biological basis of defining the Jew, persists even in his rebuttal. As Davydd Greenwood has so clearly shown, the fantasy of unchangeable physical forms survives Darwin and the "triumph" of evolutionary theory.[28] It is found especially in theories of racial difference. Unlike in the image of Feitel Stern, whose Aryan image unravels at the conclusion of Panizza's story, Count Reschock-Moshe retains his Jewish image at the conclusion of the tale. This is Mynona's point: the Aryan can become a Jew and live happily ever after. The Aryan can reshape his body and mind into that of a Jew by means of a Jewish science and learning. But is he a *real* Jew, or just a disguised Aryan? The story leaves this point unsettled. Isn't Reschock "passing" after all? There is a powerful belief, even in assimilated Jewish thinkers such as Mynona, of the biological basis of reality, a biology which is mutable but which is real and affects an individual's understanding and response to the world. When the Count first sees his future bride, disguised as an Aryan, his dog immediately "smells" her as a Jew. Mynona elsewhere satirizes the rise of a science of race which has so perfected its biological tools that it is able to raise a generation of "Jew-sniffing" dogs and to breed roses which smell like garlic to Jews (which, as Mynona comments, may actually be an advantage).[29]

What is the reason for Rebecka Isak-Gold's disguise? She had heard of this new arrival in her community, about his anti-Semitic attitude, and had decided to capture him "even if she had to marry him out of vengeance" (282). The hidden nature of the Jew is manifest even in a tale in which the point would seem to be the malleability of the physical and mental. Hidden beneath the "red-blond" wig which Rebecka wears is the "ebony hair" which marks her true difference. Mynona shifts the burden of the science of race as a means of delineating between the "healthy" Aryan and the "sick" Jew on to the science of gender. For it is in the wiles of the feminine that he locates exactly those quality of duplicitousness and manipulation which the fin-de-siècle Viennese-Jewish writer Otto Weininger, in *Sex and Character*, ascribed to the Jew.[30] What the "Jew-sniffing" dog smells is as much the feminine as it is the Jew.

The Jewish Essence

◆

These texts—by Altenberg, Mynona, and Panizza—frame the problem raised by Masud Khan's and Fanon's comments. It is the impact of scientific and popular fantasies of the biological nature of the Jew, the Jew's body, his psyche, his soul, on the development of psychoanalysis. Here is the problem as we have found it in Freud's writing: How can I—Sigmund Freud, racially labeled as a Jew—also be a physician whose object it is to cure exactly those illness for which I am most at risk? Here Khan's claim for the importance of his own "difference" stresses his separateness, not only from the Jew, but from the problem of his own role as psycho-analyst and object of study. For this final volume of studies was written under the impact of Masud Khan's eleven operations for lung and laryngeal cancer. (Khan eventually died of the disease in December 1989.) It was also written at a time when the exoticism of being "Aryan," being a young Muslim prince at Oxford, was replaced with the image of the helpless victim of the skinhead out "Paki-bashing." Both physical and social self-images had altered over the years. Khan had suddenly become both subject and object, the conflicted model of the Jew within fin-de-siècle science. For Fanon, the case is even closer to that of Freud: here we have a Western-trained physician who became aware of his "white mask" and the fact that his object of study must be the impact of this mask upon the black (upon himself). He is, in this remarkable book, both the observing scholar, the critical voice, and the object under study. For Fanon there is no easy out, for the means he choses, the theory of the nature of the psyche, has arisen historically out of the very same conflict.

The conflict between the observer and the observed is also the model for the process of transference and counter-transference. It is the discourse of counter-transference which we hear in both Khan's and Fanon's writings about the Jew. The line between the observer and the observed there is erased and the question of who is "healthy" (and observes) and who is "sick" (and is observed) is drawn into question.

There discourse of masculinity—which as we have seen in previous chapters is Freud's answer to the labeling of himself as racially different—here replaces the discourse of race. (Indeed, it is one of

208

the critiques which has been most strongly lodged against Fanon in recent years.[31]) The image of the masculine—as opposed to the gay or to the feminine—in Khan and Fanon's texts carries through the same rhetorical shift as in Freud's own work. One explanation for this parallel to Freud may be the similar relationships which individuals who perceive of themselves as marginal experience.[32] But the return to the model of the Jew's body has as much to do with the image (not its reality) of psychoanalysis as a "Jewish national concern," as Freud noted himself in a letter to Karl Abraham.[33] Khan and Fanon are using Freud's hidden master narrative about racial difference to define their own sense of difference. It is of little surprise that in looking to understand their own difference, they stumble backwards into the ideas which generated the worldview which they espouse.

9

THE JEWISH DISEASE

Plague in Germany
1939/1989

◆

The question of the national qualities ascribed to an illness has not been widely addressed in the debates about the social construction of the idea of AIDS.[1] Indeed, there has been an assumption—in work as controversial as that of Roy Porter or Susan Sontag, or indeed in my own work—that there is a "Western" (read: Christian or read: medical) tradition which has determined the basic structure of the ideas of disease.[2] My intent with this study is to illustrate some of the discontinuities in such overreaching models or, perhaps more modestly, to show the national variations on such themes. I will be looking at the cultural and social implications of "plague" in German culture under National Socialism and in Germany (both East and West) in the 1980s.

My point of departure will be the cultural representation of disease.[3] I shall use two novels as my artifacts in order to examine the fantasies of contagion and disease within German culture of 1939 and 1989. The first is the best-selling[4] novel by Rudolf Heinrich Daumann, *Patrouille gegen den Tod* (*Patrol against Death*) of 1939 [PLATE 32][5] and the second, the first "AIDS-novel" in German, Peter Zingler's 1989[6] *Die Seuche* (*The Plague*), published half a cen-

PLATE THIRTY-TWO

The dust jacket illustration to Rudolf H. Daumann's science fiction novel of 1939, *Patrol against Death*. The emphasis here is on the technological devices (the electric microscope) which enables the scientist (and us) to "see" the origin of the disease (Source: Private Collection: Ithaca).

tury later **[PLATE 33]**.[7] These two novels reflect a basic set of attitudes present in German culture concerning the relationship between ideas of space and ideas of race, between representations of the body and concepts of difference. These concepts are, of course, "Western"; they make use of the basic paradigms of "race," of "difference," of the "normal" and the "pathological" which are to be found in other "Western" (read: Christian and/or scientific) cultures (not all of them in Europe and North America). But what I would like to stress is the singular construction of ideas of race and ideas of sexuality within the German context.[8]

The texts I have selected bear striking similarities. Both Daumann and Zingler's novels are "science fiction" dystopias/utopias,[9] each set in a designated (but not too distant) future moment which extrapolates certain qualities of a constructed "present" into an image of the future. They are "science fiction" in that they both deal with the "science" of medicine. Both deal with the idea of "plague," indeed, both use the term "plague" (*Seuche*) as their central metaphor. It is therefore important to contextualize the idea of plague as represented in these two books in order to examine the image of the "disease" which is constructed in this context. Let me begin with a cursory reading of the Daumann text, just to sketch the plot and to stress the construction of the representation of ideas of race, space, and disease in utopian novels as distanced in time as 1939 and 1989.

Rudolf Heinrich Daumann's novel begins in a research institute for tropical medicine in Hamburg in 1969—thirty years into the future from the actual publication of the novel. We are introduced to one of the new employees, an out-of-work "Russian" ballerina, Maxie Perussenko, called "Maxie" in the novel. Through one of her female friends she has been appointed as a factotum at the institute and we are shown its daily routine—the counting of lice, the feeding of white mice and lab rats—through her horrified eyes. The head of the institute is the microbiologist Dr. Robert Dobbertin, but the true "hero" of the novel is his assistant Dr. Alfried Kalsten. The laboratory is given the task of identifying the nature of and, of course, finding the cure for an unidentified tropical epidemic which has broken out in a mining camp at Kanda-Kanda in the Belgian

PLATE THIRTY-THREE

The dust jacket illustration to Peter Zingler's AIDS novel, *The Plague*, of 1989. The emphasis here is on the "Wall" which was to control the spread of the disease. It was a visible sign of the discrimination which people with AIDS experienced in German culture (Source: Private Collection: Ithaca).

Congo. Kalsten and Perussenko are sent to Africa to gather tissue samples from the victims of this disease. In Africa the reader learns the true background of the "Russian" assistant. She is really a German ballerina, the daughter of an out-of-work army officer and a German countess, who has adopted a "Russian" identity because of the cachet associated in Germany with Russian dancers such as Pavlova. We also learn that Kalsten had refused a senior academic position because of his desire to work in the field. His banker-father had offered to buy such an appointment for him by funding his own research institute.

In the Belgian Congo our protagonists experience the Africa of the European settlers who understand contagious disease as part of their experience of Africa (108). They meet Alver Reemerzijl, the Flemish physician who is in charge of the health care facilities at the mine. With him they see and marginally interact with a group of cannibalistic and/or marijuana-smoking "natives" whose "hysterical" fear of the disease has made them "revert" to the beliefs and practices of their precolonial past. Later, flying on their way out of the Congo with a box full of infected white mice, they crash in the tropical jungle and are guided through it by a "faithful native" guide. During their escape the protagonists both (unknown to the other) inoculate themselves with one of the strains of the disease so that their research will not be jeopardized by the death of their specimens in the jungle. This altruism causes them to admit their love for each other.[10] They return to Hamburg, bearing the disease within them. At the end of the novel Kalsten, through pure intelligence, uncovers the "cure" for the disease and thus saves them both. A cure for the disease is linked with the "happy end" of their relationship. The lovers find themselves at a hotel in Aswan (Egypt) and are there informed of the successful end of the epidemic but also the death, through overwork, of their Flemish counterpart, Alver Reemerzijl.

The plot for *Patrol against Death* is a standard one for the mass and/or "trivial" literature of the 1930s. These novels are heavily indebted to British models, such as the Tarzan novels of Edgar Rice Burroughs, as well as to the image of Africa in the extraordinarily popular novels of Karl May.[11] (The popularity of both novelists remains high in Germany even today.) Present within this tradition is the image of the diseased nature of "the Black" and the need for the colonial master to serve the cause of "healing" that nature. The "meaning" of this topos shifted radically during the 1930s. Imperial Germany had been stripped of its African (and South Pacific) colonies as a result of the treaty of Versailles. From 1919 on the British became the main villains for the Germans in their struggle for colonial "living space." It was the British who had destroyed the careful work of the Germans in their colonies, specifically in the area of public health. The health of the natives, part of the rationale for colonial rule (a healthy native is a healthy worker) became a touchstone for the image of the failure of colonial policy.[12] In 1919 Hans Poeschel writes of the spread of yellow fever among the black soldiers serving in the British army in Africa during World War I:

> Hundreds of thousands of their fellow-sufferers will never see their villages again. The English neglected the obvious duty of caring for the safe and orderly return of these tremendous armies of carriers, in the most criminal manner. The inevitable consequence was that distempers broke out everywhere—spinal meningitis, dysentery, small-pox, the sleeping sickness—and these wrought terrible havoc among our unhappy natives. The magnificent results attained by the German Administration in the sphere of hygiene may be considered as ruined for generations.[13]

After 1933, under the leadership of General Franz Ritter von Epp, the head of the Office for Colonial Politics of the NSDAP, a conscious political attempt was made to associate the British (and by extension the South African) mandates over the former German colonies with the abdication of this role in maintaining the "hygiene" of the "natives."[14] But after 1933, the ideological context of the term "hygiene" had also taken on a different implication.[15] In the *German Colonial Yearbook* for 1940, entitled "Africa Needs Greater Germany," there is a long essay by Ernst Janisch, a state secretary in the National Biological Institute on the abdication of "racial hygiene," on the need to maintain the pure race of the black inhabitants.[16] The direct accusation was that the other colonial powers,—

including the British and the French—permitted racial mixing thereby weakening the pure racial qualities of the black. This charge was a mainstay of German discussions about the need for the return of the German colonies. H.W. Bauer made the point in his broadside of 1938 that the "Germans had been on the way to creating the *most valuable* type of black on the black continent" through the "cultural and hygienic care of the native population" which time their colonies were taken away from them.[17] All of these commonplaces about "race" and "difference," about "racial mixing" and the "degeneration of pure races" are reflected in Daumann's novel. Thus it is the German pilot, Konrad Steen, in the novel who is disgusted (after the fact) by the suggestion of his Belgian acquaintance to visit a black house of prostitution (174). Indeed, the love story which stands at the center of the book reflects the "pure racial model" for the object of desire reveals herself in the course of the novel to be a "pure" German rather than a mere Slav, and, thus, the relationship can be happily consummated.

The discourse about race and difference, especially in a German reading of 1939, can be more highly contextualized. The "Africa" of German fantasy, with its racial struggle played out within the strict confines of the model of colonialism, also reflects the daily preoccupation of the Germans of the period from 1933 to 1939 with another model of race—a model in which the image of difference was not as visibly written upon the skin, and so had rather to be even more carefully constructed in order to identify the Other. Working within a very specific model of "disease and health," Daumann's novel provided his readers with an ideal image of the future of the Europe as well as its African colonies. What I wish to examine here is the nature of the idea of that disease in *Patrol against Death*, its contemporary implications (i.e., readings), and its relationship to an ideal view of the future.

It is evident that Daumann sees 1969 as an extension of a pre-1932 world. Real Germans, such as Maxie's ex-soldier-father are employed in menial jobs, or, like Maxie herself, have to disguise themselves as foreigners, such as Russians, to have any role in the cultural life of Germany. A strong Germany dominates Europe only because of its role in science. "Science" fiction becomes thus a manner of speaking about the centrality of a German identity rather than a means of escape. But this is a novel published in 1939, not in 1932. It is novel of fulfillment not of longing (two genres which can easily be found within the official NSDAP party literature before and after the Nazi seizure of power).[18] In this rear view mirror image of the future there is an axiom for the construction of ideas of difference and of disease. It is in the immediate events of the past that such images are to be sought, not in an image of the present. For specific images of the past are internalized as part of the discourse of the thought collective about the "origin" of the present. These images are usually representations of trauma—such as the post-World War I image of the collapse of the body politic in Germany—and within the German tradition of 1939 are closely linked to the search for the origin of the collapse of that "healthy" body politic in the defeat at Versailles, in ideas of race and infection.[19]

The quality ascribed to the world of 1969 which is quite missing from the world of 1939 is that the outsiders, the pollutants, are present only "outside"—in Africa, not in Europe. Thus we are confronted with an image of German science which deals with tropical medicine, in other words, that is racially based. This racial construction of the image of the disease starts at the novel's very beginning, when Alfried Kalsten attempts to assuage Maxie's fears of working in the Institute by pointing out to her the ubiquitousness of infection in the "real" world outside the clinic. "Imagine" he says, "that your legs have failed and that you have to work as a bar-girl from eight in the evening to four in the morning. How do you know who is sitting near you in this shady bar? Old travelers with flattened noses, in whom the *Spirochaete palladia*, the white spirochaete, wends its quiet and secret path, transforming human tissue into rubber, destroying the brain and creating the most horrible paralysis" (19). Clearly, syphilis is the novel's model for the idea of disease. Thus the "unknown disease" is described as a "brand-new type of infectious disease" (43), a "plague" (58) which has made "thousands of brown and black people" in the mines unable to work (35). (At the beginning of the novel it seems to have already killed at least 200, and another 6000 are ill [58].) It comes as no surprise that when Alfried looks into his electric microscope the source of this mystery disease in Africa is revealed to be a "tiny, cork-screw shaped virus-like spirochaete" (72). While the form of the disease is not overtly identified as syphilitic—it manifests itself as a liver or a kidney infection—it is continually associated with the "great masquerader," syphilis, throughout the novel. For instance, in explaining the virulence of this new spirochete to two singer-friends of Maxie, who speak in comical Bavarian dialect, Alfried states:

> "And I should be afraid for these snake-lets?" the soprano asked inquisitively, as she placed a bit of eel on her dish.
> The assistant nodded his head strongly, before he supplied her with the necessary amount of dill sauce: "Spirochete are really dangerous, especially the Spirochete palladia, the cause of Lues. Do you know what a Wassermann (=Aquarius) is?"
> "Naturally, a sign of the Zodiac."
> "You have a pure soul! Among us bacteriologists we understand it as a blood sample."
> "Ah so! Parhninger, didn't you once mention a blood sample to me."
> "Keep quiet, Poderl! Mine has been negative for a long while."
> (88)

Syphilis and the "unknown disease" found in Africa are linked through the very use of the word "spirochete." To make this point absolutely clear to his readers, Daumann continues this scene with a discussion of infected specimens of liver brought to Hamburg as tissue samples; they too are "full of unknown spirochete" (90). The disease is thus associated throughout the novel with syphilis and, in the German context, this takes on a specific racial meaning. Moreover, there was a real fear in Germany of the 1920s and 1930s of a substantial increase in the number of cases of syphilis and of the development of a new form of "metalues." Such a fear was also coupled with the sense that such an increase would drastically effect the offspring of the present generation.[20]

But syphilis, as with all stigmatizing diseases, had to be "seen," had to be as evident in its signs and symptoms as the signs of "race," had to be written on the skin. In the realm of German science, as in American medicine during the very same period,[21] syphilis was associated with a racial (as well as a pathognomonic) image of difference. To his readers, it would have been a commonplace to identify syphilis with the shape of the nose—and this is indeed what happens early in Daumann's novel (19).[22] As we saw in previous chapters, in Germany it was the Jewish nose, not that of the African, that was the salient sign of difference. Within the German proverbial tradition the shape and nature of the nose and that of the phallus were inexorably linked. Sexually transmitted disease, especially syphilis, was mythically associated with the Jewish (read: circumcised) penis, the physical aspect ascribed to the Jew (read: Jewish male) which in the German eye defined the Jew as readily as skin color defined the inhabitants of Africa. (This in an age in which more and more German Jews—as defined racially by the Nazis—actually were uncircumcised! Thus the need to construct another "mark" of difference in the concentration camps of the 1930s—the tattoo—an "indelible" mark upon the body which uniformly signified difference.)

In Daumann's novel the Jew seems to be strangely missing. It is Jewishness, this central category of "racial" difference for the German reader and writer of 1939, which has vanished from the world of "1969." The sole exception is the mention of the name of the Jewish bacteriologist August von Wassermann, whose 1906 discovery of the sero-diagnosis of syphilis led to the test which bore his name.[23] While ennobled in 1913, he remained in the anti-Semitic handbooks of the day as well as in public mind as the "Jew" associated with syphilis.[24]

But the Jew can certainly be located in Daumann's novel, if only indirectly. In fin-de-siècle German culture, the offspring of Jews as well as of syphilitics were frequently said to be weak and nervous. Their language was on the verge of collapse. In *Patrol against Death* (as in the general discourse of colonialism) the inability to master language, specifically German is associated with the blacks, as well as with Maxie when she pretends to be Russian. In this novel blacks—Others—speak a mix of German, Flemish and French, all represented in a broken grammar, a language similar in its structure to that affected by Maxie. But unlike the blacks, Maxie cannot help but continually lapse back into "real" German. The blacks' hidden fault manifests itself in the symptom of the degeneration of language; Maxie's "pure" race manifests itself in her inability to maintain this sign.

Like the syphilitic, marked by the collapse of language and discourse and the "hidden language of the Jew," the black bears the mark of pathological difference. Daumann's image of the infected and hysteric blacks has them revert to the primitive religion of their forefathers, to cannibalism and drugs, to a reversion to the older, "pre-Christian" world. For German-language scholars (like the psychiatrist Richard Krafft-Ebing or the anthropologist Wilhelm Schmidt) the primitive stage of European culture was to be found frozen in the world of the Jews. Jews were hysterics at least in part because they were "throwbacks."[25] By the 1930s the myth of the Jewish sacrifice of Christians (as part of a therapy to rid them of specific sexually related pathologies) had reappeared.[26] According to Maxie, the real plague among the "blacks" was their response to the epidemic, for "as bad as or even worse than the illness is the spiritual crisis, the fear, horror, anxiety, and doubt . . . the best example is inner Africa today. An area almost as big as Germany can be seen as plague-ridden (*verseucht*). . . . The quarantine (*Pestkordon*) is a paper fiction" (280). Having learned from her time in the jungle the "truth" about the world in which she now lives, Maxie evokes here two salient images of the syphilitic and of the Jew. First, the Jew's madness, especially apparent in the *Mischling*, and second, the impossibility of creating impermeable barriers to eliminate the presence of the "disease" from society.[27] By 1939 the anti-Jewish laws in Germany had excluded Jews from virtually every sphere of public life, and yet the very isolation of the Jews called forth greater and greater anxiety about the presence in Germany, an anxiety which had had its first major release on *Kristallnacht* in 1938. The Jews could not be kept cordoned off, they could slip through the "jungle of the cities," to use Bertolt Brecht's phrase, and continue to spread infection.

The image of the body politic and the politics of race are inexorably linked in the novel. The presence of "strange blood" in the body causes death, as we learn very early in the novel from Professor Klading's "scientific" excursus about the impossibility of putting "eel's blood" in a test rabbit (45–6). This is associated by him with the need for every race to be literally in its proper place. His "scientific" metaphor is that each race must consume its appropriate kind of protein; thus the primeval German's appropriate diet of swine and fish as grew out of their inhabiting their appropriate place on this planet. What Klading is articulating here is the concept of "Lebensraum" [living space], the basic philosophy which underpins the German rhetoric about their need for African colonies during the late 1930s, but which is also closely related to certain scientific ideas about the absolute location of race. In the work of the nineteenth-century anthropologist Friedrich Ratzel, the founder of the ecological theory of race, the Jews are seen as the one race "out of place." In the Near East they were productive (for example, creating monotheism) but in Europe they can have no real cultural meaning.[28] The association of place and race is linked in the rationale of the German in Africa or the Jew in Europe. They are presented as mirror images, for while the German in Africa "heals," the Jew in Europe "infects." No quarantine is truly successful in controlling the Jew. The image of the "plague" presented in this novel is paralleled to the Black Plague (52–54), which is described as coming from the Middle East and which proceeded to decimate European civilization. This is an image which also appears, as we have seen, in *Mein Kampf*. Again, the subliminal message is that disease comes from outside, from "Byzantium," or from "Kanda-Kanda," and can destroy Europe (55). The traditional association—in Hitler's presentation as well as in the "historical" studies cited in Daumann's novel[29]—is that of the Jews as the "cause" of the Black Plague. These parallels between the medieval plague and a potential future one would not have been lost on the contemporary reader of 1939.

In early 1989 the icon of "plague" in the German context should have been very different. At that time we had two clearly differentiated "Germanies"—the Federal Republic of Germany (FRG) and the German Democratic Republic (GDR)—each of which, in its own manner, repudiated everything about the Nazi period (at least in their official rhetoric). While Westberlin was a space belonging ideologically to the BRD (even though it maintained its status as a four-power city), but it was also a place which was always understood as on the margin between cultures. It was a "dangerous" place, as it was neither truly "west" nor "east." But the public perception of this status was radically altered after November 9, 1989. The special function which Westberlin played in fantasies about disease and its control at least up until then was a reflex of that special status.

Perhaps the best place to begin with an examination of the fantasies about "plague" which haunt the contemporary German idea of AIDS is with the first gay book of belles-lettres officially to appear in the GDR, Ulrich Berkes's 1987 "diary" *Eine schlimme Liebe* (*An Evil Love*), published by the premiere publishing house of the GDR. In this text, part literary manifesto on the nature of the modernism and part autobiographical catalogue of the daily life of a gay poet in the GDR during 1984, there are two passing mentions of AIDS. Dated April 7, 1984 and October 30, 1984, they describe the disease in an American context and in an African one respectively.[30] These fragmentary mentions AIDS are represented as but one of the building blocks in the self-image of the gay in the GDR of 1984. But they also localize the disease as coming from "out there." The disease, which by 1987 had taken a substantial hold on the imagination of German gay as well as straight readers, is seen here on the historical periphery, without any seeming context.[31] Berkes's first mention of AIDS is used to justify the practice of mutual masturbation; his second mention is reported as part of the daily "static" heard through the airwaves which the gay individual assimilates because it relates directly to his sexuality. For Berkes, as it could be argued, by extension, for German culture, the USA and Africa are the "source" of AIDS.[32] (In this context one can mention the parody of the image of the African origin of AIDS in the gay West German filmmaker, Rosa von Praunheim's *A Virus Respects No Morals* [1986].) While the seeking for a specific, localized "source" comes as no surprise—whether in terms of the studies of the genetics of AIDS or of the mock-epidemiological search for "Patient Zero"[33]— it is the implication of this localization for the 1980s in a German context which must be understood. America and Africa are not neutral spaces for the German (especially a German in the GDR) of

1984. Both are part of a web of associations which is not acknowledged within Berkes's text. For that web, we must turn instead to
Peter Zingler's AIDS novel (as well as elsewhere in the discourse
about AIDS in Germany in the past few years). *The Plague* was
written for a "straight" audience from a "straight" point-of-view,
and published by a self-consciously "liberal" press (the Eichborn
Verlag).

If Rudolf Heinrich Daumann's novel of 1939 deals with a "heroic"
image of medicine, with its emphasis on high-tech research (including fantasies of laser-surgery [41]) and cure, Peter Zingler's *The
Plague*, a 1989 science fiction account of AIDS in Germany in 1999
presents the reader with the model of medicine as public health,
with all of its negative associations after the Nazi period. (Over the
course of the novel Zingler seems to be rejecting the Nazi view of
the sick and the healthy, yet, as we shall see, there are disturbing
remnants in his book of the prewar view of deviancy.) The image
of Nazi medicine in Germany—especially during the 1980s—was
inexorably linked with social control and placed into a special
category remote from "good" clinical treatment. This view had
appeared in German as early as 1947 with the publication of Alexander Mitscherlich's studies of the physicians in the concentration
camps.[34] For the German public, "medicine" under National Socialism was tied to the icon of the "concentration camps," to the annihi-
lation of groups labeled by the society of the time as different
and, therefore, diseased (Jews, gays, the mentally ill).[35] Postwar
Germans associated the death and concentration camps with images of social control and mindless, cruel experimentation. Medicine as an agent of control was seen as a negative, destructive
force, and the image of the clinician-as-police was condemned. The
society's sense of collective responsibility was resolved as the acts
of brutality in the camps became (in part) linked to the sterile and
inhumane image of a "science" treating all human beings as if they
were laboratory animals. Science fiction or, at least, the fiction of
futuristic medicine became a nightmare and the day residue in that
nightmare came from the representation of the Nazi past.

Let us turn for the moment to Peter Zingler's AIDS novel and see
how his image of plague is realized. The plot is set on New Year's

Eve of 1999, the beginning of a "new age," and we are confronted
with a scene at a border crossing from Westberlin to the FRG. The
"Hiffies" (HIV-infected) are marching in a column hundreds strong
out of the "AIDS-Ghetto Berlin" (5). In 1992, Zingler explains, the
passage of the "Rules for the Health of the German People" ["Anord-
nungen zum gesundheitlichen Wohl des Deutschen Volkes" (21)]
made Westberlin into the largest German AIDS internment camp
("Intenierungscamp"). At that time all healthy people left the city
and only those labeled as AIDS-carriers or AIDS-infected remained.
["I'm proud to be in Berlin West, in Hiff-Town" (103) sings a street
singer in English.] Only these, the criminals who live off of the
"Hiffies," and the "Turks" who have nowhere else to go except back
to "Istanbul" (50) remain in Westberlin. The "Hiffies" are shipped
to Westberlin once they are found to be "positive." Even the GDR
has begun quietly to expel its "positive" cases into Westberlin (101).
By 1999, 4 million in the FRG are in "camps" with over 400,000
"SSD" police are in place to guard them. Of these, 3 million "Hiffies"
are located in Westberlin. The "SSD" is the "Seuchen-Sicherheits-
dienst," the Plague-Security Force, the "wasps," who are dressed in
clearly identifiable black uniforms with a yellow stripe, and are
armed with "heavy Israeli 44 magnum automatics" (19). The border
guards observe the movement of this column of the "plague-ridden"
and "undertake nothing. The Hiffies can carry their viruses 'back
into the Reich' " (8).

Into this world comes Judith Bahl, daughter of the Minister of
Health, Hans Kaufmann (the most important member of the cabi-
net) and the estranged wife of Harald Bahl, an "AIDS careerist"
(20), the head of Frankfurt's "plague-control-institute" (18). By 1999
everyone in the FRG must carry a recent HIV test result as his/
her identity card and all public facilities are open only with the
presentation of such an identity card. Judith (as the author refers
to her throughout) is tested and is revealed to be "positive." She
is immediately swept off into the machinery which takes her to
Westberlin.

Westberlin is a German fantasy of Alfred Döblin's Berlin of the
1920s—it is the locus of the most extraordinary excesses, drugs of
all types are openly sold on the streets (103) and sex (of all types)

is the rule (173). For the inhabitants of Westberlin are beyond caring about anything except their physical pleasure (173). Westberlin has become a huge concentration camp. Indeed the idea of making Westberlin a camp began in 1992, when the Bavarians reopened Dachau as an AIDS internment camp. "The other states were more discrete" (55). In Westberlin Judith arranges to meet with an escape specialist, Max Isslacker, who for 50,000 Marks has offered to help her escape from the city. Max, whose tattooed body is revealed to us when he and Judith have sex (138), eventually does help her escape. She returns to Frankfurt to retrieve her daughter and flees with her to a asylum, a "Campo de Sida" in Spain. There we learn that she was, in fact, always "negative." Her husband had rigged the test so as to claim their daughter, discredit his father-in-law, and remove his unfaithful wife.

The parallel story to the adventures of Judith is the attempt of an international pharmaceutical concern, KREM, to steal the secret of a Japanese "cure for AIDS." The debate about the nature of the disease reveals the mercenary nature of the drug companies' interest in medication, any type of medication, which can be sold to this huge and ever-growing population. But acquiring AIDS in this novel is not random; it has meaning. It is a disease which is closely linked, in the "scientific" discourse of the novel's physicians and researchers, to those individuals who have already "ruined" their immune system through their "unnatural habits" and their resultant extreme use of medication. The examples cited are "homosexuals, who have to have their syphilis cured every fourteen days" through the use of penicillin and who "eat antibiotics as others eat peppermints" and "whores" who constantly use penicillin to cure their "professional gonorrhea" (26). These social deviants are as "different" from the scientists as are the inhabitants of Africa, who, according to another theory outlined in the novel, "have an immune system quite different than ours and based on their way of life. Then the whites came and introduced diseases that were unknown to them: grippe, colds, syphilis" (26). Here Africa becomes—not the origin of the disease—but its victim. (This reversal is quite different from the popular German view in 1988 that the disease was caused by African black women who had had sex with monkeys.[36] This myth is in line with the postwar German image of the "sexual deviancy" of the black, especially the black out of her own space and in Germany.[37]) But where does AIDS come from in this novel? As in other images of the origins of the disease in contemporary German culture, it is American. It is Rock Hudson "who fifteen years earlier admitted to being gay" (77) who brought the disease into German consciousness. Since then it has been the "American" disease.

One of the scientists, Alfred Droege, has kept the fact that his daughter Manuela has developed AIDS a secret, and is using every means to acquire the drug and treat her. She has developed AIDS through being exposed to her father's research. The research centers are themselves huge concentration camps, with the "Hiffies" serving both as the researchers as well as the subjects for their own research. This is seen as an economically sound manner of using this huge interned labor pool. They are supervised by scientists such as Droege, who lives in a large house with his own laboratory. At the very end of the novel (217) the existence of the daughter is revealed to the "wasps" and the house is stormed. But the daughter has already died of the effects of the drug which has turned her into a hemophiliac. The effect of the drug is to turn everyone into a "bleeder," and the image in German is even stronger: "Alle Menschen werden Bluter" (215), a grotesque pun on the line from Schiller's (and Beethoven's) "Ode to Joy": "Alle Menschen werden Brüder!"—everyone will be brothers. Zingler here reverses the prewar image of victims as guilty—but they are, nonetheless, still "diseased," and, more important, perhaps predestined to be so. This sense, however ironic, of widespread "Otherness" raises disturbing questions.

On the surface, the discourse about difference in this novel is on the surface antithetical to that in Daumann's book. Zingler creates the image of the world as concentration camp, clearly likening Nazi attitudes about health to debates that were taking place in the mid-1980s about the "Bundesseuchengesetze" (the "Law for the Prevention and Control of Infectious Disease in Human Beings"), the German law concerning contagious diseases in the FRG.[38] The parallel is not farfetched. For instance, in 1984 the weekly news magazine *Der Spiegel* writes of "the plague breaking out of the gay-ghetto."[39] In an entry dated August 28, 1987 in his autobiographical account of his struggle with the social stigma of being a person with AIDS, Helmut Zander recounts the publication of an essay which revealed that a number of West German municipal officials had approved the idea for a new "AIDS-camp" based on the plans for the infamous concentration camp at Sachsenhausen.[40] In Fred Breinersdorf's 1989 novel *Quarantäne* (*Quarantine*), also set in "a German metropolis in the near future" the "camp" image haunts the idea of AIDS.[41] There AIDS hospitals are seen as the solution to the "problem of hygiene" ("Hygieneprobleme") and are compared to the concentration camps. (267) Breinersdorf's metaphoric equations were given a "real political" dimension in 1987 when Peter Gauweiler, the Minister of Health of the Bavarian "Republic," suggested the widescale compulsory testing of groups such as foreigners, prostitutes, drug users, and prisoners; he intimated the potential quarantine for those who tested positive.[42] *The Plague* consciously reacts to this eighties debate by drawing upon the format of the vocabulary of disease in the Nazi period. It employs a vocabulary of images which has its origin in a West German understanding of the past. (The phrase "home into the Reich" (8) with which the border guards describe the marching column of "Hiffies," for example, reflects the Nazi rhetoric accompanying the Austrian *Anschluß*. In this novel the rhetoric of political space refers to an Austria of the spirit—Kurt Waldheim's Austria; and the "disease" harbored in Westberlin reflects the "sick" society of the BDR.)

But despite the apparently critical stance Zingler takes towards the Nazi notions of disease, there are disturbing parallels between his novel and Daumann's. A central fact of both works is that the protagonists do not belong in the "place" of the novel. Daumann's scientists "visit" Africa and are infected. But they arrive at a cure from the African disease only when they are back in Hamburg. The disease becomes proof that they really do not belong in "Africa." Similarly, while Judith Bahl belongs to none of the high-risk categories at risk—she is identified as intensely heterosexual—she has had sex with a man outside of her marriage. Thus we could expect her to be "punished" by contracting AIDS (much like the audience expectation in eighteenth-century German tragedy that a single act of coitus must lead to pregnancy, infanticide, and suicide). But she always seems to be "outside" of her status as a "Hiffie." She does not even act in the light of her own knowledge of her status as a "social pollutant." (Indeed, she has sex with a man she knows to be "negative" when she believes herself to be positive without informing him of that fact [66].) Judith is somehow "beyond" the category of disease and, therefore, the revelation that she is truly "safe" comes to reify our sense that her actions are intuitively correct and she has never really belonged in the sick world. She no more belongs in this world of disease than Maxie does in Africa.

The question of why Judith does not belong is important. It is the association of the "normal"—of her roles and identity as created in the novel which "saves" her. Judith becomes the baseline for the healthy in contrast with the society in which she dwells. Her desire to escape from Westberlin is tied to her image as a mother. She is obsessive about returning to rescue her daughter—she is a good mother. And that, within the discourse of difference in the novel, means that she is heterosexual. The sexual contacts described in the novel, both the "good" ones (mutual seductions) and the "bad" ones (unwanted sexual approaches or rapes), are all heterosexual. Indeed, the one overtly lesbian figure described in the novel commits suicide after an attempted rape by exposing herself to freezing weather while she compulsively tries to cleanse herself in a public fountain.

It is through the background given this "deviant" figure that we can begin to tie the structure of representation in Zingler even tighter to Daumann's world. For what is central about Judith is that she is in no way directly tied to the world of the Nazi past. All of the ironization of the vocabulary of difference in the novel, all of the self-conscious evocation of the Nazi past provides a model for difference which is tied to the idea of race. We can begin with that one image of the sexually "deviant" presented in the novel, the "positive" image of the lesbian who befriends Judith when she arrives in Westberlin, but who ends in suicide. Birgit Sattler is in Westberlin because she had acquired AIDS from her gay roommate (130). Her "deviancy" is explained by the factoid that her father had had his health destroyed in a concentration camp and that she had spent her youth on the streets as a result of his early death (132). Her "disease," i.e., her sexual identity is tied to the world of gay men and is explained by her tie to the Nazi past. She is a lesbian because the Nazis destroyed her father, made him into less a man so that he could not serve her as a true parent—and therefore as a model for the ideal male. She becomes the image of the person with AIDS represented in the novel. Gay men are virtually invisible.

Nowhere in this novel do we "see" any ill gay men, any more than we "see" the hoards of the ill blacks in Africa. They form the frame of the novel, but we are "exposed" only to those "deviants" from the diseased norm, who turn out, like Birgit Sattler, to exhibit their "deviance" because of an association with the realities which lay behind the metaphors of the AIDS-Ghetto and the internment camps. Like the blacks, the gay males are the excuse for the novel, not its focus. The "liberal" intent of the novel is to draw the absolute boundary of difference between the "sick" dystopian German society which condemns people with AIDS and a utopian "healthy" German society which would accept them. But in creating these boundaries Zingler reverts to a historically determined model of "health" and "illness." The association of the "normal," i.e., heterosexual, with the "healthy" and the "abnormal," i.e., the gay, with the diseased is presented here within an environmental model. This is, of course, the liberal fantasy which represses the "realities" of disease, realties which in German culture are associated with the oppression of Jews and gays in the Third Reich through the imposition of a medical model, and which stresses the "diseased" nature of those exposed to the forces of evil, such as the camps. Zingler's pseudo-scientific arguments about the theoretical basis of "plague" parallel similar discussions in Daumann's book. The central difference is that they are presented in an ironic mode. But simple reversals of images lead to their structural perpetuation.

The association of the "persecution" of "Hiffies" through a future German response to AIDS is elided with the image of the persecution of the Nazi victims. And for the West German reader the representative victim of the Nazis are the Jews. This is stated quite directly in the novel in both an ironic and an unself-conscious mode.

"All human beings are brothers," but some are more human, less diseased than others. Thus we are given a long monologue by a muckraking newspaperman on the search for a new AIDS scandal. He notes that in the last issue of the newspaper there was a full column about the fact that "circumcised males are especially at risk from the plague" (141). This is ironic—and repeats quite literally the special status of the Jews as especially at risk for sexually transmitted disease which, as we have seen, is part and parcel of the literature of the biological determinism of Jewish pathology. It is clear that this "rumor" is presented in a self-undercutting mode; Zingler is using presenting in this entire monologue the sort of scandal sheet language that one finds in the FRG in the *Bild-Zeitung*. Nevertheless, it is still startling to find this "repressed" image from the past reappearing in the fantasized future. The Jew as diseased has never vanished as an image in German discourse. After the war Jews were accused of having imported the most horrific sexually transmitted diseases into the German-speaking world.[43] In the novel it becomes part of the stereotypical representation of difference which is supposed to characterize the horror and inflexibility of German society toward those suffering from AIDS.

But Zingler also presents an unself-conscious association of the Jew with disease, clearly believing that he is giving a "positive" image of the Jew. In the "Campo de Sida" in Spain we meet the owner of the local bar who speaks in "an accent which lead us to believe that he was a German." (79) But he speaks only in Spanish, as he explains in "clumsy Spanish" (80), because we are "guests, whether welcome or tolerated matters not. But we live here and live free. One should speak the language of the country if just for this reason" (80). He looks "like a vulture . . . his nose looks like a bent saber" (80). It turns out that Alfons is a German Jew, of over seventy, who had been forced to leave Germany first with his parents under the Nazis and then fifty years later again because his lover, with whom he had lived for thirty years, had contracted AIDS. They fled Hamburg and opened the bar in Spain. The lover has died two years before. Since then Alfons has "refused to speak a word of German" (80). Most importantly: "He is not sick" (80). At the very end of the novel we return to the "Campo de Sida" and attend Alfons's funeral: "It is pleasing to be able to accompany some one like Alfons on his last journey, someone who died quite naturally of old age" (215). At the cemetery "only the voice of the Rabbi could be heard" (216). After the burial service, the crowd breaks out in lamentations while one of the participants observes: "It is perverse . . . but I really enjoy crying at the cemetery. Afterwards I feel relaxed and full of life" (216).

Here we have the other side of the argument—circumcised Jews (and male Jews in this myth of the body are by definition circumcised) are immune. They do not get AIDS when they live monogamously together with someone who has an active case. Such Jews are not "perverse," they are "healthy" since they do not bear the stigma of "Jewish hypersexuality." The special discourse of the Jews, the rejection of "German" here for "Spanish" as a sign of the necessary adaptability of the Jew, is contrasted in the novel with the fragments of clumsy German spoken by the Turks in Westberlin. The Turks have to speak German; the Jew adapts out of instinct. The images are precisely those displaced from past. (Indeed, there are even some slight hints of the left anti-Semitism which constantly surfaces in the FRG under the guise of anti-Zionism. The "SSD," an acronym which immediately recalls the Nazi SS, are armed with Israeli weapons [19].) Despite apparent good intentions, Zingler's paralleling of the AIDS victim in effect creates a "positive" reversal of the negative stereotype of the Jew. That is, the novel reflects the image of the Jew as the agent of infection, an image which dominated Hitler's association of Jews and disease, by confusing the "realities" of the person with AIDS or even the person who is HIV positive with the attributes associated with the Jews. The Jew, who is labeled as "sick," is exactly equated with the person with AIDS who is ill.[44] In Zingler's text this association, with all of its power for German readers of the 1980s, most of whose sense of the Nazi past is limited to media clichés, overwhelms any sense of the difference between the Jew and the person with AIDS. The Jew thus acquires a special status in the subtextual structure of this world of images. He is immune as the desired sign of the ultimate reversal of the Nazi stereotype of the Jew as disease carrier or organism, a status which is now attributed to the "Hiffie," a term which comes to replace "kike" in the vocabulary of difference in this text.

One additional argument should be brought up at this point—the fact that AIDS is not seen as a "Jewish" disease in the FRG and the GDR but an "American" one. Here too the association of the intensely negative image of the American and the vicious anti-Americanism present in both Germanies after the Vietnam War is evident. But there is an older association with the image of the pathological representation of the American and its equation with the image of the Jew which should be cited. Nineteenth-century cities were regarded as places of disease and the Jews as the quintessential city dwellers, the Americans of Europe. Just like gays in the 1980s. Thus hidden within the image of the American origins of AIDS is a further association with the Jew, an association made through the image of the city (and for late nineteenth-century Germany Berlin is the exemplary city). Berlin is the biblical Sodom and Gomorra, and, after World War II, the image of Westberlin—as can be seen in Zingler's novel—is closely associated in German fantasy with the image of the American.

But as we have seen, both sides of this issue are present within the medical discourse of the twentieth century concerning the special nature of the Jews' relationship to sexually transmitted diseases. In the dystopia of the world of plague represented in Zingler's novel the simple reversal of images, the ironization and projection of the past, recreates the stereotypical perception of difference. In placing Judith's misdiagnosis, a "mistake"—purposeful and cruel—but a "mistake" at the center of this novel, Zingler undertakes the rescue of the German heterosexual as surely as Daumann rescues his protagonists. It is "science"—in the case of AIDS the now "accurate" AIDS test—which frees the heterosexual woman from the stigma of the disease and permits her to return to her role as mother; in the case of the African plague, it is the heroic activities of the scientist who develops a cure which enables Maxie to undertake the ultimate role in German society, that of the "German" mother "with a little house with a red roof and a green garden, a good husband, and little children who cry 'mama' and suck on their thumbs." (168) Judith's cleanliness is at the novel's end, paralleled to that to her lover Max. Although she had sex with him when she believed she was positive—and he knew he was negative—this is now revealed to have been a non-pathological act. Even though in terms of the law on contagion in force in 1989 this would be understood as inflicting "grievous bodily harm"! And we somehow "knew" that she was not dangerous even during the sex scene. For Max's "tattoo" is not a camp tattoo—it is a tattoo of Mickey Mouse (138). Here the "American"/"Jewish" danger of disease is defused and represented as an icon of childlike innocence. The representation of the "private" sphere in this novel is "safe"; it is only in the "public" sphere that danger, in the form of the mentality of the Nazi past lurks. (At one point of the novel, Max's tattoo is contrasted with the image of a bellicose, pre-World War II Germany in a pub in Frankfurt where Judith waits to meet him. It is called the "Iron Cross" and "naive paintings of tanks, war ships, and fighter planes of the Third Reich" hang on the walls [199].)

The cultural image of "plague" in Germany in 1989 is very different from that of 1939. It tries to be an antithetical presentation of the past in its evocation of a dystopic future. And yet the romanticism of the past, of the Jew as the essential victim, moves the image into the same structure of discourse as is found under the Nazis, a discourse which creates images of the "normal" and the "diseased" with absolute boundaries. Such boundaries are to be expected in any case. But in these German texts they are constructed with an eye toward the German past which is quite unique. In Germany even today it is difficult to evoke a socially stigmatizing disease without also evoking of past metaphors of disease and political persecution. The vocabulary of difference employed in 1989 cannot abandon the imagery of 1939, an imagery empowered by a fantasy of the past and reflecting a basic understanding of the nature of difference expressed within a vocabulary of images taken from that past.

10

CONCLUSION

Too black Jews and too white Blacks

◆

The sum of these essays points toward the continuities of images of the Jews in the West throughout the modern era.[1] The generation of new vocabularies to describe this difference, such as the supposedly neutral language of nineteenth-century science, transmuted many of the assumptions of Jewish difference which had existed in earlier incarnations. It did not abolish them, but merely gave them new life and new form. My approach in these studies is very different from the one first suggested by Robert Merton in 1942.[2] Merton struggled to understand the presence of rampant anti-Semitism, both in terms of practice and theory, within German science. Merton saw this as a process of infiltration, by which the "caste-standards" of the general society were introduced into a "pure" science. This introduction of foreign elements into the world of science not only set the standards for the theory but also provided the rationale for the exclusion of "inferiors" as incapable of doing science.[3] My own view presupposes that inherent in the very definition of the biological and medical sciences of the day, as well as the general culture, are the "caste-standards" which label the Jew as unable to undertake the task of science because of the Jew's inherently pathological nature. It is the very body and mind of the Jew which was placed into question. At the same time, the claims for "universalism" made by the science of the day gave these claims a neutral face. It was as if science spoke in one voice and said: "What I speak is true because it is neutral. And what I say is that you are sick. And my neutrality gives me a special (and powerful) status in this new world now defined by the importance of science." The Jewish physician was forced to deal with this claim if he (and the physicians were primarily men until the beginning of this century) was to share in the social status of the physician, a social status open to him only during the nineteenth century and the rise of civil emancipation.

The science of race secularized many of the prior religious views of the Jews, as well as the unquestioned power associated with the institutions of Christianity. The contemporary political emancipation of the Jews provided greater access to this rhetoric for Jews who could become biological or social scientists or physicians. Unlike the converts to Christianity, these scientists could be "Jews" and "scientists" simultaneously. Their research claimed to represent the difference of the Jews more accurately and was shaped by the scientific rhetoric of their time. In the light of the work of scholars such as Yosef Hayim Yerushalmi, it is clear that the debate about "race" and "racial identity" was fixed in the nineteenth century.[4] It did not originate there.

What I have found is that these themes—the reflection of the body of the Jew—are part of a generalized vocabulary of difference which seems to be part of Western (Christian or secularized) means of representing the Jew. This model of representing the Jew is present in the earliest Christian texts, including, as I discussed in the first chapter, the Gospels. The power of these images enables them to exist, with only shifts in their rhetorical form, through the ages. This sense of difference impacts on the Jew who is caught in the web of power which controls and shapes his or her psyche and body. The assignment of difference to aspects of the body shapes how individuals understand their own essence.[5]

The desire for invisibility, the desire to become "white," lies at the center of the Jew's flight from his or her own body. In certain

societies at certain times, the Jew desires to transform that difference, heard in the very sound of his or her voice, into a positive
sign. For the Jew, whose own invisibility is more possible in some
Western societies than in others, then, the question of visibility is
a central one. Jean-François Lyotard has written on this matter in
his work on Martin Heidegger and the Jews.[6] Lyotard understands
Heidegger's refusal to speak of the Shoah as a refusal to remember,
one which is closely tied to the role which the Jews play in the
cultural world of Christianity as the ultimate object of projection.
The Jew, caught up in such a system of representation, has but
little choice: his essence, which incorporates the horrors projected
on to him and which is embodied (quite literally) in his physical
being, must try, on one level or another, to become invisible. Even
though Lyotard's argument reduces the Jew to an essence, it does
point out one aspect of the complexity of Jewish identity in diaspora. This may well account for the self-imposed invisibility of
Jews as Jews in certain social and politic contexts.[7] For visibility
brings with it true risk. And what was the threat of being seen was
as a Jew? Martin Freud, Sigmund Freud's eldest son, remembers
"walking with [his aunt Dolfi, his father's youngest sister, who
died in the Nazi concentration camp at Theresienstadt] one day in
Vienna when we passed an ordinary kind of man, probably a Gentile, who, as far as I knew, had taken no notice of us. I put it down
to a pathological phobia, of Dolfi's stupidity, when she gripped my
arm in terror and whispered: 'Did you hear what that man said?
He called me a dirty stinking Jewess and said it was time we were
all killed.'"[8] There was good reason to desire invisibility in early
twentieth-century Vienna **[PLATE 34]**. Against this we must pose
the Jew's heightened visibility, and very different history, in early
twentieth-century New York.

This desire to transform one's visibility is the master narrative
in one of the first and most successful representations of the Jew in
Hollywood. Here American culture had one of the truly unique
constellations in early moviemaking: a story about American Jews
written by a Jew becomes a play starring a Jew, is then bought by
a Jewish studio head and is made into a film also starring a Jew.[9]
Warner Brother's *The Jazz Singer* (1927), the first "talking" feature,

Conclusion

PLATE THIRTY-FOUR

The claimed visibility of the Jewish body in the first half of the twentieth century was absolute. It was the difference of the Jew which was to set the Jew apart from the society in which he or she dwelt. Here the difference of the body is the cause of laughter. Walter Hofmann, *Lacht ihn tot! Ein tendenziöses Bilderbuch von Waldl* (Dresden: Nationalsozialistischer Verlag für den Gau Sachsen, n.d.) (Source: Private Collection: Ithaca).

was based on story by Samson Raphaelson in *Everybody's Magazine*, written after he saw Al Jolson perform at the University of Illinois. Dramatized, it opened on Broadway in September 1925 starring George Jessel. When Harry and Jack Warner bought the film rights for $50,000, Jessel was not cast in the title role, which ironically went to its prototype, Al Jolson. Jessel had done a string of Jewish comedies such as *Private Izzy Murphy* and *Ginsberg the Great* and was considered to be "too Jewish" for the role by the Jack Warner, which wanted the film to have a broader, non-ethnic appeal. Warner Brothers wanted to reduce the story to the tale of transgenerational conflict between the older, immigrant generation and their newly acculturated children, a theme of many 1920s films depicting recent American immigrant experience.

The plot of both play and film are quite straightforward. Cantor Rabinowitz, the seventh of his line to be a cantor, assumes his only

237

son Jackie will follow him and continue the religious tradition. But he would rather entertain in nightclubs and transforms himself into an American, becoming Jack Robin. Broken by his son's abandonment, the father is too weak to sing "Kol Nidre" on the holiest of Jewish holidays, Yom Kippur, and asks his son Jack to substitute for him, but Jack's Broadway debut is to be the same night. In the story and the play the Jewish entertainer foresakes his career in show business and takes his father's place in the synagogue. In the play, he sings "Kol Nidre," and abandons the secular life of Broadway; in the movie, he asks that the opening be postponed so that he can both sing "Kol Nidre" and begin his secular career. Then in the well-known epilogue to the film, Al Jolson, on bended knee, sings "Mammy" in black-face for his hugely successful Broadway opening. "You ain't heard nothing yet," is his refrain.

It is Jolson's role as a "Sambo" figure at the close of the movie on which I wish to focus. There was a long vaudeville tradition of "white" performers putting on black-face in order to do those roles which black performers had originated during Reconstruction. Here we have a classic case of it. And yet, to return to the question I raised in my history of the nose job: Are Jews white? Or do they become white when they, like Jack Robin, acculturate into American society, so identifying with the ideals of "American" life, with all of its evocation of race, that they—at least in their own mind's eye—become white? Does black-face make everyone who puts it on white?

But can one be too white? In an extraordinary series of responses to an article by Kathleen Cross in the October, 1990 *Ebony*, readers wrote about their anxieties over "not being Black enough."[10] Cross is an African-American woman with both "black" and "white" parentage. But she is considerably lighter in color than her siblings. Thus she is caught up in a dilemma they do not face. "When I refer to myself as African-American I am often accused of denying my White heritage, being emotionally and socially confused, or referred to by some as a 'Wanna-be.' " Her conflicted sense of identity is labeled by those about her as pathological, as diseased. She feels herself "initially rejected by my own people. This is not an indictment; it is simply a testimonial to the remnants of White racism that have divided, and continue to divide, the descendants of Africa in America. . . . I find myself wanting to apologize again for not being Black enough." The pressure in the African-American community in the 1990s is no longer to "pass," no longer to look white, as Spike Lee illustrated in his recent film *School Daze*. The age of hair-straighteners and skin-lighteners has past. (Though it is evident that among Jews that the age of nose jobs has not.)

One must look like the aesthetic norm and that, in the African-American community, is "Black." "I am an African-American woman of mixed heritage who could pass for White," one reader from Milwaukee, Wisconsin writes. "I was and am rejected by my African-American brothers and sisters because of my pale complexion and light-colored eyes. I have been called everything from 'White girl' to 'wannabe.' It pains me to hear these people talk to me about my appearance, then go around and put weaves in their hair or colored contact lenses in their eyes."[11] The alteration of appearance becomes a touchstone for difference. But it is not just the body which is marked by its difference from the norm. Not only does one change the body to become different, but one acts out this difference. As a reader from Brooklyn, New York commented: ". . . one issue that constantly angers me is what biracial people say to reclaim their African descent: they listen to blues music; they eat ham hocks and sweet potato pie. . . . I wish they would stop mentioning how much neck bones, collard greens and fried chicken they eat to prove that they are still able to hold on to an African heritage." The norm here is blackness, and the assumption is that "biracial people" cannot act "Black" naturally. Their "whiteness" determines their cultural orientation. Kathleen Cross had written about a young man who rejected her as a "white girl": "How could I let him know that I was raised on greens and neckbones and sweet potato pie, that I was a 'mean' domino player from watching my big brothers slam bones across the table on Friday evenings, that my daddy taught me the Phoenician alphabet when I was ten so that I would respect the legacy of ancient Egypt, and that my grandmother still told stories about her mother's life as a slave . . ." This is the cultural context in which Kathleen Cross was raised. Cross's argument is that "biracial" individuals can have an authentic cultural inheritance whether they have been raised within a strictly "black" cultural milieu or both a black and white one—what matters is the character of the upbringing. It is not their biology which determines who they are. It is not the case that they must acquire their cultural practices in spite of or because of their color.

The internal conflict which Jakob Wassermann reported in German-Jews in the early twentieth century who looked too Aryan, reappears in these letters. A letter writer from Indianapolis, Indiana noted that: "I've come to feel like a fraud when I claim I'm Black while I look White. It doesn't seem fair for me to make that claim . . . when I've not had to experience the rage and pain of White racism directed at me. Not that I haven't suffered from both, Blacks and Whites. As a small child, I couldn't play with White children because 'your daddy is colored.' As a young girl, I was chased home from school daily by Black children because of the Whiteness of my skin and my so-called 'good hair.' " The doubts about the nature of the body and its meaning are deep-seated. The pressure to look "Black" presents a normative appearance as positive and "healthy."

What is striking about these two examples—the Jewish-American in black-face singing "Mammy" and light-skinned African-American eating fried chicken and sweet potato pie—is they each reflect the myths of the dominant culture in which they desire to live. Jack Warner sees the Jew entering into American society, becoming "Jack Robin," losing his visibility as a Jew in "white" America. Kathleen Cross and her commentators relate to the new African-American consciousness of the meaning of race. They wish to become invisible within the African-American community. Race remains a potent construction which impacts on the sense of the self. And it is a set of rigid boundaries which give specific meaning to the body. Negative images associated with concepts of race— whether of Jews or African-American—persist strongly into the 1990s and they are also reflected in the internalization of these images within the groups stereotyped.[12] The internalization of doubts about the body are not limited to the fin de siècle.

The internalization of such stereotypes can lead to self-destructive behavior ("self-hatred"), but it can also lead to productive and successful means of resistance. Poets, scientists, critics, philoso-

Conclusion

phers, physicians can take the doubts which are embodied in racial concepts and transform them into constructive actions for the individual, if not for the group.[13] For these projected concerns mirror doubts which all human beings have about their own authenticity: the sense of our own lack of control over destiny, the rigidity which we demand from the world so that we can control our own anxieties, the need to locate where danger lies—these factors are shared by all human beings. But those who are forced to internalize the projections of the dominant culture because of their position of powerlessness (and their desire to achieve the same illusion of control over their lives) suffer under a double burden. This is not to say that this burden prevents people from living productive lives, but they are always lives lived against the sense that one is marked, that one is too visible.

For people caught up under this double burden their understanding of their culture can be controlled by the powerful notions of "racial" biology. As a reader of *Ebony* from Laurel, Maryland commented: "Why are Blacks playing tug-of-war race games with interracial people? Why do you want us to segregate ourselves from our White birthright? It is biologically impossible. Regardless of what some Blacks or Whites say, we are what we were born. Our conception saw to that. Neither race can completely claim us or push us away. There is no reason for interracial people to deny either heritage. Both are our birthright." Biology becomes destiny and the cultural context in which this biology is lived out vanishes.

"Race," as a concept, can be a positive quality—it can provide for a group cohesion or group identity. One need not have only "an over-intense admiration or indeed worship," to evoke Isaiah Berlin's phrase, for the majority culture in which one lives.[14] One can understand oneself as a Jew, or as an African-American, as different. But even in the more contemporary sense of race, not as a biological absolute, but as the aggregate of specific qualities, there has been a continuation of the focused definition of membership in a "race."[15] The success of the idea of alterity which seems now, at the beginning of the 1990s, to provide a positive sense of "racial" identity for individuals in American society, also contains an historical legacy, one which is negative and disturbingly self-renewing.

Conclusion

♦

The concept of "race" is so poisoned in Western society that it is difficult to imagine how it can be resurrected. Once the rhetoric of "race" is evoked, its ideological context is also present. It seems to be impossible to speak of the idea of difference, such as the difference of the Jew, without evoking this sense of the constructed difference of the body.

The Anglo-Jewish writer, Clive Sinclair, reported the following exchange with a leading Bulgarian liberal intellectual:

> "Tell me," he says. "I've often wondered how you know . . . how you recognize one another. I mean, how did you know that Mony was a Jew? Did you give each other signals, or are there secret signs, or what? I mean, what do you do when you are introduced?" This is surely not the voice of Ivailo Ditchev, writer and member of the faculty of Philosophy at the University of Sofia, but that of the old hermit (who surely did not know the difference between a Jew and a freemason) I saw in the pseudo-Byzantine vastness of the Alexander Nevsky cathedral. He had long snowy hair and a flowing beard. He was wearing a brown coat fastened with string. His feet were bound in white cloth. Maybe this is the true reflection of Bulgaria, what Rip Van Winkle himself would see if he glanced in the looking-glass. Perhaps even among these intellectuals a struggle is taking place deep within the psyche, where superstition (the size of a Sumo wrestler) grapples with knowledge (emancipated after its long fast). I raise my trouser leg. "That's what we do," I say, "we show each other our cloven hooves."[16]

The cloven hoof, the sign of the secret meaning of the Jew's body, belongs to the world of myth. But it is part of the powerful myth of race which shapes and alters those who believe in it. But this is 1990, not 1890 or even 1590. How is it that the sense of Jewish visibility is retained? Or indeed, becomes the stuff of legend?

While Clive Sinclair reads the question of the meaning of Jewish identity in terms of the negative understanding of the "common mental construction" of the Jew, Freud and his Jewish contemporaries transform this into a positive quality for themselves. Sinclair's ironic use of the fantasy of the "cloven hoofs" of the Jew stands within the tradition of the disenfranchisement ascribed to

242

the Jew's foot in Western Europe. He places it in a specific, "primitive" context, thereby evoking a sense of the primitive nature of a Christianity which is certainly not that of the Church of England. In effect, he responds by telling a Bulgarian joke. What had startled Sinclair was the contrast between the "liberal," educated Eastern European (coming from the least anti-Semitic nation in the East) and his evident belief in the fantasy about Jewish identity. Sinclair clearly felt himself to be caught up in two different time frames, a rational modernity vs. an irrational antiquity. From his perspective, that of late twentieth-century Anglo-Jewry, the image of the "revolutionary" is associated with the acceptance of the invisibility of the Jew. But, as we have seen, in this he was being naive; the association is clearly not borne out historically.[17]

Shifts in place and time in the evocation of racial stereotypes necessarily occasion different kinds of responses from Jews, depending on their own sense of power in those places and times. Freud could not have expected his colleagues or his culture to treat him invisibly—his very practice was built of the cornerstone of the Jewish mind and body (his own), however much he universalized his research on that body. Sinclair speaks from a perspective that assumes that race, at least amongst the educated, at least concerning Jews, has been already universalized; that, at least concerning himself, it no longer exists as a mark of difference. But bodies have a way of being seen again and again in the past, and identity—whether that of Jews or blacks or Hispanics or women—always has to perform a perilous balancing act between self and Other.

243

NOTES

◆

Preface: The Fall of the Wall

1. Edward Shorter, "Women and Jews in a Private Nervous Clinic in Late Nineteenth-Century Vienna," *Medical History* 33 (1989): 149–83.

2. Deborah Tannen, *Conversational Style* (Norwood, NJ: Ablex, 1984) and *That's Not What I Meant!* (New York: Morrow, 1986).

3. Otto Hauser, *Die Juden und Halbjuden in der deutschen Literatur* (Danzig/Leipzig: Verlag "Der Mensch," 1933), pp. 12–13.

4. Tamar Katriel, *Talking Straight: Dugri Speech in Israeli Sabra Culture* (Cambridge: Cambridge University Press, 1986).

5. Richard Onians, *The Origins of European Thought About the Body, The Mind, The Soul, The World, Time and Fate: New Interpretations of Greek, Roman and Kindred Evidence also of Some Basic Jewish and Christian Beliefs* (Cambridge: Cambridge University Press, 1988).

6. See, for example, the incisive reading by Stephen Greenblatt, "Marx, Marlowe and Anti-Semitism," in his *Learning to Curse: Essays in Early Modern Culture* (New York: Routledge, 1990), pp. 40–58.

7. Maurice Olender, *Les Langues du Paradis: Aryens et Semites—un couple providentiel* (Paris: Gallimard, 1989).

8. Letter from Paul Potts, "Use and Misuse," *Times Literary Supplement* (January 25, 1991), p. 15.

Notes
◆

1.　The Jewish Voice

2. Sander L. Gilman, *Jewish Self-Hatred: Anti-Semitism and the Hidden Language of the Jews* (Baltimore: The Johns Hopkins University Press, 1986; paperback edition, 1990). See also Paul Marcus and Alan Rosenberg, "Another Look at Jewish Self-Hatred," *Journal of Reformed Judaism* 36 (1989): 37–61 and Maria Damon, "Talking Yiddish at the Boundaries," *Cultural Studies* 5 (1991): 14–29.

3. See Rosemary Reuther, *Faith and Fratricide: The Theological Roots of Antisemitism* (New York: Seabury Press, 1974) and John Gager, *The Origins of Anti-Semitism: Attitudes Toward Judaism in Pagan and Christian Antiquity* (New York: Oxford University Press, 1983).

4. Werner H. Kelber, *The Oral and the Written Gospel: The Hermeneutics of Speaking and Writing in the Synoptic Tradition, Mark, Paul, and Q* (Philadelphia: Fortress Press, 1983).

5. Morton Scott Enslin, *Christian Beginnings* (New York: Harper Bros., 1938), p. 421. Compare Sean Freyne, "Vilifying the Other and Defining the Self: Matthew's and John's Anti-Jewish Polemic in Focus," in Jacob Neusner and Ernest S. Frerichs, eds., *"To See Ourselves as Others See Us": Christians, Jews, "Other" in late Antiquity* (Chico, CA.: Scholars Press, 1985), pp. 117–44.

6. St. Augustine, *The First Catechetical Instruction*, trans. Joseph P. Christopher (Westminster, MD: Newman Bookshop, 1946), p. 134.

7. Ann Marie Lipinski and Dean Baquet, "Sawyer Aide's Ethnic Slurs Stir Uproar," *Chicago Tribune* (May 1, 1988), p. 1; Anthony Lewis, "A Dangerous Poison," *New York Times* (July 31, 1988), E25 and Cheryl Deval, "Sawyer Won't Fire Aide over Ethnic Slurs," *Chicago Tribune* (May 5, 1988), p. 1.

8. Cited by Saul Friedländer, *Kurt Gerstein: The Ambiguity of Good*, trans. Charles Fullman (New York: Alfred A. Knopf, 1969), pp. 148–49.

9. Theodor Adorno, *Minima moralia: Reflexionen aus dem beschädigten Leben* (Berlin: Suhrkamp, 1951), p. 200.

10. Theodor Adorno, Else Frenkel-Brunswik, Daniel J. Levinson, R. Nevitt Sanford, *The Authoritarian Personality* (New York: Harper, 1950), p. 643.

Notes
◆

11. Jean-Paul Sartre, *Anti-Semite and Jew*, trans. George J. Becker (New York: Schocken, 1965), pp. 136–37.

12. See my "Jewish Writers and German Letters: Anti-Semitism and the Hidden Language of the Jews," *The Jewish Quarterly Review* 77 (1986–87): 119–48.

13. Henryk M. Broder, "Die unheilbare Liebe deutscher Intellektueller zu toten und todkranken Juden," *Semit* 3 (1989): 29.

14. The term is from Dan Diner, "Negative Symbiose: Deutsche und Juden nach Auschwitz," *Babylon* 1 (1986): 9–10.

15. Compare the passages in Günter Grass, *The Meeting at Telgte*, trans. Ralph Manheim (New York: Harcourt Brace Jovanovich, 1979), p. 35 and Edgar Hilsenrath, *Night*, trans. Michael Roloff (New York: Manor Books, 1974), pp. 278–79.

16. Günter Grass, *Werkausgabe in Zehn Bänden*, ed. Volker Neuhaus: vol 6: *Das Treffen in Telgte*, ed. Christoph Sieger (Frankfurt a. M.: Suhrkamp, 1987), pp. 37–38 and Andreas Graf, " 'ein leises 'dennoch' ": Zum ironischen Wechselbezug von Literatur und Wirklichkeit in Günter Grass' Erzählung *Das Treffen in Telgte*," *Deutsche Vierteljahrsschrift für Literaturwissenschaft und Geistesgeschichte* 63 (1989): 282–94.

17. D. M. Thomas, *The White Hotel* (New York: Penguin Books, 1981). On the "borrowing" see Lady Falls Brown, "*The White Hotel*: D. M. Thomas's considerable debt to Anatoli Kuznetsov and Babi Yar," *South Central Review* 22 (Summer 1985): 60–79; Yevgeny Yevtushenko, "Babi Yar," *The Holocaust Years: Society on Trial*, ed. Roselle Chartock and Jack Spencer (New York: Bantam Books, 1978), pp. 36–45; James E. Young, *Writing and Rewriting The Holocaust: Narrative and the Consequences of Interpretation* (Bloomington, IN: Indiana University Press, 1988); George Levine, "No Reservations: *The White Hotel*," *New York Review of Books* (May 28, 1981): 20–23; Mary F. Robertson, "Hystery, Herstory, History: 'Imagining the Real' in Thomas's *The White Hotel*," *Contemporary Literature* 25 (1984): 452–477; Ellen Y. Siegelman, "*The White Hotel*: Visions and Revisions of the Psyche," *Literature and Psychology* 33 (1987): 69–76. See also D. M. Thomas, "On Literary Celebrity," *New York Times Magazine* (13 June 1982).

18. See the recent special issue of *New German Critique* 46 (Winter 1989) on "Minorities in German Culture" in which the Jew is but one of a growing list of "minorities" which play a role in defining cultural difference in the BRD.

Notes

19. These examples are cited in a letter from Y. M. Bodemann, Berlin, printed in the *SICSA Report* 3 (Winter 1989–90): 3.

20. Geoffrey Wolff, *The Duke of Deception: Memories of My Father* (New York: Random House, 1979).

21. Bernard Wasserstein, *The Secret Lives of Trebitsch Lincoln* (New Haven: Yale University Press, 1988).

22. Howard J. Faulkner and Virginia D. Pruitt, eds., *The Selected Correspondence of Karl A. Menninger, 1919–1945* (New Haven: Yale University Press, 1988), p. 282.

23. Leonard Mosley, *Disney's World* (New York: Stein and Day, 1985), p. 207.

24. Glenn Collins, "Jackie Mason, Top Banana at Last," *New York Times* (July 24, 1988), Section 2: pp. 1, 14.

25. "Highly Touted 'Soup' Goes Down the Drain," *USA Today* (November 8, 1989), pp. 1D–2D.

26. Henry L. Gates, Jr., "TV's Black World Turns—But Stays Unreal," *The New York Times* (November 12, 1989), Section 2: pp. 1, 40.

27. "Highly Touted 'Soup,'" *USA Today*.

28. Cited in the *New York Times* (September 28, 1989), p. B1.

29. Cited in the *New York Times* (October 2, 1989), p. B1.

30. Cited in the *New York Times* (October 14, 1989), p. 28.

31. Richard Merkin, "The Bad and the Beautiful," *GQ* (February 1991), p. 66.

32. Michel Selzer, *The Wineskin and the Wizard: The Problem of Jewish Power in the Context of East European Jewish History* (New York: Macmillan, 1970), p. 18.

33. Paul Brienes, *Tough Jews: Political Fantasies and the Moral Dilemma of American Jewry* (New York: Basic Books, 1990).

34. Daphne Merkin, "Dreaming of Hitler," *Esquire* (August 1989), pp. 75–83.

35. "What Makes New Yorkers Tick," *Time* (September 17, 1990), p. 49.

36. Wendy Wasserstein, *Isn't It Romantic* (New York: Dramatists Play Service, 1984), pp. 56–57.

37. Richard Krafft-Ebing, *Psychopathologia Sexualis: A Medico-Forensic Study*, rev. trans. Harry E. Wedeck (New York: Putnam, 1965), p. 24.

38. Henry James, *The American Scene* (London: Chapman and Hall, 1907), pp. 129–31.

39. Debbie Lukatsky and Sandy Barnett Toback, *Jewish American Princess Handbook* (Arlington Heights, IL: Turnbull and Willoughby, 1982), pp. 142–43.

40. Daniel Landes, "Anti-Semitism Parading as Anti-Zionism," *Tikkun* (May–June, 1989): 85–88.

41. Phillip Lopate, "Resistance to the Holocaust," *Tikkun* (May–June, 1989): 55–65. The debate with Bauer is included in the same issue, pp. 65–70. See the discussion of Lopate (and the others in this debate) in Joseph A. Amato, *Victims and Values: A History and A Theory of Suffering* (New York: Praeger, 1990), pp. 181–85.

42. John B. Beston, "An Interview with Nissim Ezekiel," *World Literature Written in English* 16 (April 1977): 87–94.

43. Nissim Ezekiel, *Collected Poems 1952–1988* (Delhi: Oxford University Press, 1989), p. 236.

44. See Norman Podhoretz, "Vidal's outburst: An Ominous New Stage in Anti-Semitism," *Washington Post* (May 8, 1986); Edwin M. Yoder, "Is Distaste for Israeli Policy Anti-Semitism?," *Los Angeles Times* (May 22, 1986); William Safire, "Vidal, Waldheim, Grant," *New York Times* (May 19, 1986).

45. Sacvan Bercovitch, ed., *Reconstructing American Literary History* (Cambridge, MA.: Harvard University Press, 1986), p. 34.

2.   The Jewish Foot

1. Bernhard Berliner, "On Some Religious Motives of Anti-Semitism," in Ernst Simmel, ed., *Anti-Semitism: A Social Disease* (New York: International Universities Press 1946), pp. 79–84, here p. 83.

2. Joshua Trachtenberg, *The Devil and The Jews: The Medieval Conception of the Jew and Its Relation to Modern Antisemitism* (New Haven: Yale University Press, 1943), pp. 46–48.

3. Robert Burton, *The Anatomy of Melancholy*, ed. Holbrook Jackson (New York: Vintage, 1977): pp. 211–12.

4. Johann Jakob Schudt, *Jüdische Merkwürdigkeiten* (Frankfurt a. M.: S. T. Hocker, 1714–18), 2: 369,

Notes
◆

5. See the discussion in Léon Poliakov, *The History of Anti-Semitism*: vol. 3: From Voltaire to Wagner, trans. Miriam Kochan (London: Routledge and Kegan Paul, 1975), p. 177.

6. See Moritz Lazarus' introduction to Nahida Remy [i.e., Nahida Ruth Lazarus], *Das jüdische Weib* (Leipzig: Gustav Fock, 1891), pp. iii–vi.

7. Joseph Rohrer, *Versuch über die jüdischen Bewohner der österreichischen Monarchie* (Vienna: n.p., 1804), pp. 25–26.

8. On the medical debate in the late nineteenth century about the difference between "weak feet" and "flat feet" see Edgar M. Bick, *Source Book of Orthopaedics* (Baltimore: Williams and Wilkins, 1948), pp. 450–51. See also the general discussion of these historical figures in Stephan Mencke, *Zur Geschichte der Orthopädie* (Munich: Michael Beckstein, 1930), pp. 68–69 and Bruno Valentin, *Geschichte der Orthopädie* (Stuttgart: Georg Thieme, 1961).

9. Theodor Fontane, *Der deutsche Krieg von 1866* (Berlin: Verlag der königlichen geheimen Ober-Hofbuchdruckerei, 1870), Band 1: *Der Feldzug in Böhmen und Mähren*, p. 413. On the Jewish role in the German army see Rolf Vogel, *Ein Stück von uns. Deutsche Juden in deutschen Armeen 1813–1976. Eine Dokumentation* (Mainz: v. Hase und Koehler, 1977) and Werner T. Angress, "Prussia's Army and the Jewish Reserve Officer Controversy Before World War 1," *Leo Baeck Yearbook* 17 (1972): 19–42.

10. Mark Twain, *Concerning the Jews* (Philadelphia: Running Press, 1985), p. 29.

11. Steven Beller, *Vienna and the Jews 1867–1938: A Cultural History* (Cambridge: Cambridge University Press, 1989), p. 189.

12. István Deák, *Jewish Soldiers in Austro-Hungarian Society*. Leo Baeck Lecture 34 (New York: Leo Baeck Institute, 1990), p. 14.

13. Cited by Max Grunwald, *Vienna* (Philadelphia: Jewish Publication Society of America, 1936), p. 408.

14. Cited by Grunwald, *Vienna*, p. 177.

15. H. Naudh [i.e., H. Nordmann], *Israel im Heere* (Leipzig: Hermann Beyer, 1893). On the background see Horst Fischer, *Judentum, Staat und Heer in Preussen im frühen 19. Jahrhundert: Zur Geschichte der staatlichen Judenpolitik* (Tübingen: J.C.B. Mohr, 1968).

16. See Dietz Bering, *Der Name als Stigma: Antisemitismus im deutschen Alltag 1812–1933* (Stuttgart: Klett/Cotta, 1987), p. 211.

Notes

17. Eduard Fuchs, *Die Juden in der Karikatur* (Munich: Langen, 1921), p. 200.

18. Walter Hofmann, *Lacht ihn tot! Ein tendenziöses Bilderbuch von Waldl* (Dresden: Nationalsozialistischer Verlag für den Gau Sachsen, n.d.), p. 23.

19. *Die Juden als Soldaten* (Berlin: Sigfried Cronbach, 1897).

20. See Joachim Petzold, *Die Dolchstosslegende: Eine Geschichtsfälschung im Dienst des deutschen Imperialismus und Militarismus* (Berlin [East]: Akadamie Verlag, 1963) which discusses the statistical arguments.

21. Otto Armin [i.e., Alfred Roth], *Die Juden im Heere, eine statistische Untersuchung nach amtlichen Quellen* (Munich: Deutsche Volks-Verlag, 1919).

22. Jacob Segall, *Die deutschen Juden als Soldaten im Kriege 1914–1918* (Berlin: Philo Verlag, 1922).

23. Franz Oppenheimer, *Die Judenstatistik des preußischen Kriegsministeriums* (München: Verlag für Kulturpolitik, 1922).

24. Elias Auerbach, "Die Militärtauglichkeit der Juden," *Jüdische Rundschau* 50 (December 11, 1908): 491–92.

25. See John Hoberman, *Sport and Political Ideology* (Austin: University of Texas Press, 1984).

26. Heinrich Singer, *Allgemeine und spezielle Krankheitslehre der Juden* (Leipzig: Benno Konegen, 1904), p. 14.

27. Gustav Muskat, "Ist der Plattfuss eine Rasseneigentümlichkeit?," *Im deutschen Reich* (1909): 354–58. Compare J. C. Dagnall, "Feet and the Military System," *British Journal of Chiropody* 45 (1980): 137.

28. In other contexts the atavistic foot is taken to be a sign of insanity. See Charles L. Dana, "On the New Use of Some Older Sciences: A Discourse on Degeneration and its Stigmata," *Transactions of the New York Academy of Medicine* 11 (1894): 471–489, here 484–485. See also my discussion in *Difference and Pathology: Stereotypes of Sexuality, Race, and Madness* (Ithaca, NY: Cornell University Press, 1986), p. 155.

29. George L. Mosse, *Germans and Jews: The Right, the Left, and the Search for a "Third Force" in Pre-Nazi Germany* (Detroit: Wayne State University Press, 1987), pp. 14–15.

30. Moritz Alsberg, *Militäruntauglichkeit und Grossstadt-Einfluss: Hygienisch-volkswirtschaftliche Betrachtungen und Vorschläge* (Leipzig: B. G.

Teubner, 1909), p. 10. Compare the discussion of the rate of military readiness in the various sections of Vienna during this period: Victor Noach, "Militärdiensttauglichkeit und Berufstätigkeit, soziale Stellung und Wohnweise in Österreich-Ungarn, insbesondere in Wien," *Archiv für soziale Hygiene und Demographie* 10 (1915): 77–128

31. See my discussion in *Difference and Pathology* as well as *Disease and Representation: Images of Illness from Madness to AIDS* (Ithaca, NY: Cornell University Press, 1988). Compare to D. B. Larson, et al., "Religious Affiliations in Mental Health Research Samples as Compared with National Samples," *Journal of Nervous and Mental Disease* 177 (1989): 109–11.

32. Gustav Muskat, "Die Kosmetik des Fusses," in Max Joseph, ed., *Handbuch der Kosmetik* (Leipzig: Veit & Co., 1912), pp. 646–64, here, p. 662.

33. Karl Kautsky, *Rasse und Judentum.* 2nd ed. (Stuttgart: Dietz, 1921), p. 62. This was first published in 1914. On the general context of anti-urbanism and its relationship to proto-fascist thought see George L. Mosse, *The Crisis of German Ideology: Intellectual Origins of the Third Reich* (New York: Grosset and Dunlap, 1964).

34. Leopold Boehmer, "Fussschäden und schwingedes Schuhwerk," in *Zivilizationsschäden am Menschen*, ed. Heinz Zeiss and Karl Pintschovius (Munich/Berlin: J. F. Lehmann, 1940), p. 180. Compare J. Swann, "Nineteenth-Century Footwear and Foot Health," *Cliopedic Items* 3 (1988): 1–2.

35. Hoffa is the author of the authoritative study *Die Orthopädie im Dienst der Nervenheilkunde* (Jena: Gustav Fischer, 1900) and the compiler (with August Blencke) of the standard overview of the orthopedic literature of the fin de siècle, *Die orthopädische Literatur* (Stuttgart: Enke, 1905).

36. M. J. Gutmann, *Über den heutigen Stand der Rasse- und Krankheitsfrage der Juden* (Munich: Rudolph Müller & Steinicke, 1920), p. 38.

37. Günther Just, ed., *Handbuch der Erbbiologie des Menschen: I. Erbbiologie und Erbpathologie Körperlicher Zustände und Funktionen: Stützgewebe, Haut, Auge*, 3 vols. (Berlin: Julius Springer, 1939–1940), p. 39.

38. The translation is by Jack Zipes, Oskar Panizza, "The Operated Jew," *New German Critique* 21 (1980): 63–79, here p. 64. See also Jack Zipes, "Oscar Panizza: The Operated German as Operated Jew," *New German Critique* 21 (1980): 47–61 and Michael Bauer, *Oskar Panizza: Ein literarisches Porträt* (Munich: Hanser, 1984).

Notes
39. Erwin Baur, Eugen Fischer, and Fritz Lenz, eds., *Menschliche Erblehre und Rassenhygiene: I: Menschliche Erblehre* (Munich: J. F. Lehmann, 1936), p. 396.

40. Otmar Freiherr von Verschuer, *Erbpathologie: Ein Lehrbuch für Ärtze und Medizinstudierende* (Dresden/Leipzig: Theodor Steinkopff, 1945), p. 87.

41. Benjamin Ward Richardson, *Diseases of Modern Life* (New York: Bermingham and Co., 1882), p. 98.

42. Max Nordau, *Zionistische Schriften* (Cologne: Jüdischer Verlag, 1909), 379–81. This call, articulated at the second Zionist Congress, followed his address on the state of the Jews which key-noted the first Congress. There he spoke on the "physical, spiritual and economic status of the Jews." On Nordau see P.M. Baldwin, "Liberalism, Nationalism, and Degeneration: The Case of Max Nordau," *Central European History* 13 (1980): 99–120 and Hans-Peter Söder, "A Tale of Dr. Jekyll and Mr. Hyde? Max Nordan and the Problem of Degeneracy," in Rudolf Käser and Vera Pohland, eds., *Disease and Medicine in Modern German Cultures* (Ithaca, NY: Western Societies Program, 1990), pp. 56–70.

43. Hermann Jalowicz, "Die körperliche Entartung der Juden, ihre Ursachen und ihre Bekämpfung," *Jüdische Turnzeitung* 2 (1901): 57–65.

44. Isidor Wolff, ed., *Die Verbreitung des Turnens unter den Juden* (Berlin: Verlag der Jüdischen Turnzeitung, 1907).

45. M. Jastrowitz, "Muskeljuden und Nervenjuden," *Jüdische Turnzeitung* 9 (1908): 33–36.

46. I am using the term "Jewish physician" to refer to those physicians who either self-label themselves as Jews or are so labeled in the standard reference works of the time.

47. His first paper on this topic is Jean Martin Charcot, "Sur la claudication intermittente," *Comptes rendus des séances et mémoires de la société de biologie* (Paris) 1858, Mémoire 1859, 2 series, 5: 25–38. While this is not the first description of the syndrome, it is the one which labels this as a separate disease entity. It is first described by Benjamin Collins Brodie, *Lectures illustrative of various subjects in pathology and surgery* (London: Longman, 1846), p. 361. Neither Brodie nor Charcot attempt to provide an etiology for this syndrome. Compare M. S. Rosenbloom, et al., "Risk Factors Affecting the Natural History of Intermittent Claudication," *Archive of Surgery* 123 (1989): 867–70.

Notes
◆

48. The work, dated as early as 1831, is cited in detail by Charcot, "Sur la claudication intermittente," p. 25–26.

49. See my *Difference and Pathology*, p. 155 and Toby Gelfand, "Charcot's Response to Freud's Rebellion," *Journal of the History of Ideas* 50 (1989): 304.

50. Gutmann, *Über den heutigen Stand*, p. 39. Compare Dr. M. Kretzmer, "Über anthropologische, physiologische und pathologische Eigenheiten der Juden," *Die Welt* 5 (1901): 3–5 and Dr. Hugo Hoppe, "Sterblichkeit und Krankheit bei Juden und Nichtjuden," *Ost und West* 3 (1903): 565–68, 631–38, 775–80, 849–52.

51. G. Steiner, "Klinik der Neurosyphilis," in *Handbuch der Haut-und Geschlechtskrankheiten*, ed. Josef Judassohn, et al.: vol. 17, 1, ed. Gustav Alexander (Berlin: Springer, 1929), p. 230.

52. H. Higier, "Zur Klinik der angiosklerotischen paroxysmalen Myasthenie ('claudication intermittente' Charcot's) und der sog. spontanen Gangrän," *Deutsche Zeitschrift für Nervenheilkunde* 19 (1901): 438–67.

53. P. Olivier and A. Halipré, "Claudication intermittente chez un homme hystérique atteint de pouls lent permanent," *La Normandie Médicale* 11 (1896): 21–28.

54. Louis Basile Carré de Montgeron, *La verité des miracles operés par l'intercession de M. de Pâris et autres appellans demontrée contre M. L'archevêque de Sens* ... 3 vols. (Cologne: Chez les libraires de la Campagnie, 1745–47).

55. On the representation of the alteration of gait in the case of Dora see the complex distinction made between the meaning of impaired gait in the syphilitic and the hysteric which Freud documents in Sigmund Freud, *Standard Edition of the Complete Psychological Works of Sigmund Freud*, ed. and trans., J. Strachey, A. Freud, A. Strachey, and A. Tyson, 24 vols.(London: Hogarth, 1955–74), 7: 16–17, n. 2. On the background for Freud's training in neurology see Henri Ellenberger, *The Discovery of the Unconscious: The History and Evolution of Dynamic Psychiatry* (New York: Basic Books, 1970). Compare J. H. Baker and J. R. Silver, "Hysterical Paraplegia," *Journal of Neurology, Neurosurgery and Psychiatry* 50 (1987): 375–82 and J. R. Keane, "Hysterical Gait Disorders: 60 Cases," *Neurology* 39 (1989): 586–89.

56. H. Idelsohn, "Zur Casuistik und Aetiologie des intermittierenden Hinkens," *Deutsche Zeitschrift für Nervenheilkunde* 24 (1903): 285–304.

Notes

◆

57. Idelsohn, "Zur Casuistik," 300.

58. Singer, *Krankheitslehre der Juden*, pp. 124–25.

59. Gustav Muskat, "Über Gangstockung," *Verhandlungen des deutschen Kongresses für innere Medizin* 27 (1910): 45–56.

60. Samuel Goldflam, "Weiteres über das intermittierende Hinken," *Neurologisches Centralblatt* 20 (1901): 197–213. See also his "Über intermittierende Hinken ('claudication intermittente' Charcot's) und Arteritis der Beine," *Deutsche medizinische Wochenschrift* 21 (1901): 587–98. On tobacco misuse as a primary cause of illness see the literature overview by Johannes Bresler, *Tabakologia medizinalis: Literarische Studie über den Tabak in medizinischer Beziehung*, 2 vols. (Halle: Carl Marhold, 1911–13).

61. See Enfemiuse Herman, "Samuel Goldflam (1852–1932)," in Kurt Kolle, ed., *Grosse Nervenärtze*, 3 vols. (Stuttgart: Thieme, 1963), 3: 143–49.

62. Samuel Goldflam, "Zur Ätiologie und Symptomatologie des intermittierenden Hinkens," *Neurologisches Zentralblatt* 22 (1903): 994–96.

63. Toby Cohn, "Nervenkrankheiten bei Juden," *Zeitschrift für Demographie und Statistik der Juden*, New Series 3 (1926): 76–85.

64. Kurt Mendel, "Intermitterendes Hinken," *Zentralblatt für die gesamt Neurologie und Psychiatrie* 27 (1922): 65–95.

65. Wilhelm Erb, "Über das 'intermittirende Hinken' und andere nervöse Störungen in Folge von Gefässerkrankungen," *Deutsche Zeitschrift für Nervenheilkunde* 13 (1898): 1–77.

66. Wilhelm Erb, "Über Disbasia angiosklerotika (intermittierendes Hinken)," *Münchener medizinische Wochenschrift* 51 (1904): 905–8.

67. Compare P.C. Waller, S.A. Solomon and L.E. Ramsay, "The Acute Effects of Cigarette Smoking on Treadmill Exercise Distances in Patients with Stable Intermittent Claudication," *Angiology* 40 (1989): 164–69.

68. Hermann Oppenheim, "Zur Psychopathologie und Nosologie der russisch-jüdischen Bevölkerung," *Journal für Psychologie und Neurologie* 13 (1908): 7.

69 C.E. Brown-Séquard, "On the Hereditary Transmission of Effects of Certain Injuries to the Nervous System," *The Lancet* (January 2, 1875): 7–8.

3.   The Jewish Psyche

1. On the historiography of hysteria see Mark S. Micale, "Hysteria and its Historiography," *History of Science* 27 (1989): 223–61; 319–51. See also

Notes

the work on the early history of hysteria by Helmut-Johannes Lorentz, "Si mulier obticuerit: Ein Hysterierezept des Pseudo-Apuleius," *Sudhoffs Archiv* 38 (1954): 20–28; Ilza Veith, *Hysteria: The History of a Disease* (Chicago and London: University of Chicago Press, 1965); Umberto de Martini, "L'isterismo: da Ippocrate a Charcot," *Pagine di Storia della Medicina* 12.6 (1968): 42–49; Annemarie Leibbrand and Werner Leibbrand "Die 'kopernikanische Wendung' des Hysteriebegriffes bei Paracelsus," *Paracelsus Werk und Wirkung. Festgabe für Kurt Goldammer zum 60. Geburtstag*, ed. Sepp Domandl (Vienna: Verband der Wissenschaftlichen Gesellschaften Österreichs, 1975), pp. 125–33; John R. Wright, "Hysteria and Mechanical Man." *Journal of the History of Ideas* 41 (1980): 233–47; H. Merskey, "Hysteria: The History of an Idea," *Canadian Journal of Psychiatry* 28 (1983): 428–33 as well as his "The Importance of Hysteria," *British Journal of Psychiatry* 149 (1986): 23–28; John Mullan, "Hypochondria and Hysteria: Sensibility and the Physicians." *Eighteenth Century* 25 (1983): 141–73; Monique David-Ménard, *Hysteria from Freud to Lacan: Body and Language in Psychoanalysis*, trans. Catharine Porter (Ithaca, NY: Cornell University Press, 1989); Phillip R. Slavney, *Perspectives on "Hysteria"* (Baltimore: The Johns Hopkins University Press, 1990).

2.   This is the "myth" which Frank J. Sulloway, *Freud: Biologist of the Mind* (New York: Basic Books, 1979), p. 592 wishes to identify as "Myth One," the primal myth, in Freud's falsification of his own history. It is clear that this (and the other "myths") are fascinating insights into Freud's understanding of his own career and provide the material for interpretation, not censure.

3.   Sigmund Freud, *Standard Edition of the Complete Psychological Works of Sigmund Freud*, ed. and trans. J. Strachey, A. Freud, A. Strachey, and A. Tyson, 24 vols. (London: Hogarth, 1955–74), 20: 35. (Hereafter cited as *SE*.) On the background see Henri Ellenberger, *The Discovery of the Unconscious: The History and Evolution of Dynamic Psychiatry* (New York: Basic Books, 1970).

4.   J. M. Charcot, *Lectures on the Disease of the Nervous System delivered at La Salpêtrière*, trans. George Sigerson (London: New Sydenham Society, 1877), p. 264.

5.   Purves Stewart, "Two Lectures On the Diagnosis of Hysteria," *The Practitioner* 72 (1903): 457.

6.   See the review of the first volume of the *Iconographie photographique de la Salpêtrière* in *Progrès médical* 7 (1879): 331. On the general background

of these concepts see Léon Chertok, "Hysteria, Hypnosis, Psychopathology," *Journal of Nervous and Mental Disease* 161 (1975): 367–78; Maurice Dongier, "Briquet and Briquet's Syndrome Viewed from France," *Canadian Journal of Psychiatry* 28 (1983): 422–27; François M. Mai, "Pierre Briquet: 19th Century Savant with 20th Century Ideas," *Canadian Journal of Psychiatry* 28 (1983): 418–21; Jean-Jacques Goblot, "Extase, hystérie, possession: Les théories d'Alexandre Bertrand," *Romantisme* 24 (1979): 53–59; E. Gordon, "The Development of Hysteria as a Psychiatric Concept," *Comprehensive Psychiatry* 25 (1984): 532–37; Leston L. Havens, "Charcot and Hysteria," *Journal of Nervous and Mental Disease* 141 (1965): 505–16.

7.   On the problem of the metaphor of the "germ theory" and its role in the evolution of the depiction of the hysteric see K. Codell Carter, "Germ Theory, Hysteria, and Freud's Early Work in Psychopathology," *Medical History* 24 (1980): 259–74.

8.   Georges Canguilhem, *The Normal and the Pathological*, trans. Carolyn R. Fawcett (New York: Zone, 1989), p. 40.

9.   In this context see John Marshall Townsend, "Stereotypes of Mental Illness: A Comparison with Ethnic Stereotypes," *Culture, Medicine and Psychiatry* 3 (1979): 205–229. See M. J. Gutmann, *Über den heutigen Stand der Rasse- und Krankheitsfrage der Juden* (Munich: Rudolph Müller & Steinicke, 1920) and Heinrich Singer, *Allgemeine und spezielle Krankheitslehre der Juden* (Leipzig: Benno Konegen, 1904). For a more modern analysis of the "myths" and "realities" of the diseases attributed to the Jews see Richard M. Goodman, *Genetic Disorders among the Jewish People* (Baltimore: The Johns Hopkins University Press, 1979).

10.   Maurice Fishberg, *The Jews: A Study of Race and Environment* (New York: Walter Scott, 1911), p. 6 and pp. 324–25 quoting Fulgence Raymond, *L'Étude des Maladies du Système Nerveux en Russie* (Paris: O. Doin, 1889), p. 71.

11.   H. Strauß, "Erkrankungen durch Alkohol und Syphilis bei den Juden," *Zeitschrift für Demographie und Statistik der Juden* 4 (1927): 33–39; chart on p. 35.

12.   Moriz Benedikt, *Die Seelenkunde des Menschen als reine Erfahrungswissenschaft* (Leipzig: O.R. Reisland, 1895), pp. 186–87; 223–26.

13.   Cecil F. Beadles, "The Insane Jew," *Journal of Mental Science* 46 (1900): 736.

14.   Frank G. Hyde, "Notes on the Hebrew Insane," *American Journal of Insanity* 58 (1901–1902): 470.

Notes
◆

15. William Thackeray, *Works*, 10 vols. (New York: International Book Co., n.d.), 10: 16–28, here p. 17.

16. Cited (with photographs) in Joseph Jacobs, *Studies in Jewish Statistics* (London: D. Nutt, 1891), p. xl. These plates were widely reproduced in both scholarly and popular journals. (*The Photographic News* [April 1885] and *The Journal of the Anthropological Institute* [1886]). See Nathan Roth, "Freud and Galton," *Comprehensive Psychiatry* 3 (1962): 77–83; Alan Sekula, "The Body and the Archive," *October* 39 (1986): 40–55; and Joanna Cohan Scherer, ed., *Picturing Cultures: Historical Photographs in Anthropological Inquiry, Visual Anthropology*, (Special Issue) 3 (2–3), 1990.

17. My discussion of the meaning of the gaze is clearly based on the work of Michel Foucault. On this theme in Foucault see Martin Jay, "In the Empire of the Gaze," in David Couzens Hoy, ed., *Foucault: A Critical Reader* (Oxford: Basil Blackwell, 1986), pp. 175–204.

18. Robert Burton, *The Anatomy of Melancholy*, ed. Holbrook Jackson (New York: Vintage, 1977), pp. 211–12

19. Redcliffe N. Salaman, M. D., "Heredity and the Jew," *Eugenics Review* 3 (1912): 190.

20. Jacobs, *Studies in Jewish Statistics*, p. xxxiii.

21. Léon Poliakov, *The Aryan Myth: A History of Racist and Nationalist Ideas in Europe*, trans. Edmund Howard (New York: Basic Books, 1974), pp. 155–82.

22. Arthur de Gobineau, *The Inequality of Human Races*, trans. Adrian Collins (New York: Howard Fertig, 1967), p. 122.

23. Maurice Fishberg and Joseph Jacobs, "Anthropological Types," *The Jewish Encyclopedia* 12 vols. (New York: Funk and Wagnalls, 1904), 12: 291–95, here 294.

24. Gutmann, *Über den heutigen Stand*, p. 17.

25. Leo Goldhammer, "Herzl and Freud," *Theodor Herzl Jahrbuch* (Vienna, 1937): 266–68; reprinted and translated in the *Herzl Year Book* 1 (New York, 1958): 194–96, here, 195.

26. See L. Chertok, "On Objectivity in the History of Psychotherapy: The Dawn of Dynamic Psychology (Sigmund Freud, J. M. Charcot)," *Journal of Nervous and Mental Diseases* 153 (1971): 71–80 as well as Charles Coulston Gillispie, *The Edge of Objectivity: An Essay in the History of Scientific Ideas* (Princeton: Princeton University Press, 1960).

27. George Herbert Mead, *Movements of Thought in the Nineteenth Century* (Chicago: University of Chicago Press, 1936), p. 176.

28. Lou Andreas-Salomé, *The Freud Journal*, trans. Stanley A. Leavy (New York: Basic Books, 1964), p. 74.

29. *SE* 5: 649; 4: 293; 4: 139; 5: 494.

30. Houston Stewart Chamberlain, *Foundations of the Nineteenth Century*, trans. John Lees, 2 vols. (London: John Lane/The Bodley Head, 1913), 1: 359. On Freud's reading of Chamberlain see Sigmund Freud, *Gesammelte Werke*, 19 vols. (Frankfurt a. M.: S. Fischer, 1952–87), Nachtragsband: 787.

31. Henry Meige, *Étude sur certains neuropathes voyageurs: Le juif-errant à la Salpêtrière*. (Paris: L. Battaille et cie., 1893). On Meige and this text see Jan Goldstein, "The Wandering Jew and the Problem of Psychiatric Antisemitism in Fin-de-Siècle France," *Journal of Contemporary History* 20 (1985): 521–52.

32. Meige, *Étude sur certains neuropathes*, p. 17.

33. Meige, *Étude sur certains neuropathes*, p. 25.

34. Meige, *Étude sur certains neuropathes*, p. 29.

35. Richard Andree, *Zur Volkskunde der Juden* (Leipzig: Velhagen & Klasing, 1881), pp. 24–25 cited by Maurice Fishberg, "Materials for the Physical Anthropology of the Eastern European Jew," *Memoires of the American Anthropological Association* 1 (1905–1907): 6–7.

36. Beadles, "The Insane Jew," p. 732.

37. Fishberg, *The Jews*, p. 349.

38. *SE* 1: 17.

39. Toby Gelfand, "'Mon Cher Docteur Freud': Charcot's Unpublished Correspondence to Freud, 1888–1893," *Bulletin of the History of Medicine* 62 (1988): 563–88; here 571.

40. *SE* 26: 29–43. While this paper was published only in 1893 it was conceptualized if not written before Freud left Paris in 1886.

41. Toby Gelfand, "Charcot's Response to Freud's Rebellion," *Journal of the History of Ideas* 50 (1989): 293–307.

42. See for example the collection of images in John Grand-Carteret, *L'affaire Dreyfus et l'image* (Paris: E. Flammarion, 1898).

43. See the discussion in my *Difference and Pathology: Stereotypes of Sexuality, Race, and Madness* (Ithaca, NY: Cornell University Press, 1986),

pp. 150–162. See also Yves Chevalier, "Freud et l'antisémitisme—jalousie," *Amitié judéo-chrétienne de France* 37 (1985): 45–50.

44. Wesley G. Morgan, "Freud's Lithograph of Charcot: A Historical Note," *Bulletin of the History of Medicine* 63 (1989): 268–72.

45. *SE* 1: 98.

46. See, for example George Frederick Drinka, *The Birth of Neurosis: Myth, Malady and The Victorians* (New York: Simon and Schuster, 1984), pp. 108–22. See also Esther Fischer-Homburger, *Die traumatische Neurose: Vom somatischen zum sozialen Leiden* (Bern: Hans Huber, 1975).

47. Sir Clifford Allbutt, "Nervous Disease and Modern Life," *Contemporary Review* 67 (1895): 214–15.

48. C. E. Brown-Séquard, "On the Hereditary Transmission of Effects of Certain Injuries to the Nervous System," *The Lancet* (January 2, 1875): 7–8.

49. As in John Eric Erichsen, *On Concussion of the Spine, Nervous Shock, and Other Obscure Injuries to the Nervous System in their Clinical and Medico-Legal Aspects* (New York: William Wood, 1886), p. 2 or in Hans Schmaus, "Zur Casuistik und pathologischen Anatomie der Rückenmarkserschütterung," *Archiv für klinische Chirurgie* 42 (1891): 112–22 with plates.

50. Compare Otto Binswanger, *Hysterie* (Vienna: Deuticke, 1904), p. 82.

51. See my *Difference and Pathology*, pp. 150–63.

52. Martin Engländer, *Die auffallend häufigen Krankheitserscheinungen der jüdischen Rasse* (Vienna: J.L. Pollak, 1902), p. 12.

53. See my *Difference and Pathology*, pp. 182–84.

54. The discussion of this case is documented in Charles Bernheimer and Claire Kahane, eds., *In Dora's Case: Freud-Hysteria-Feminism* (New York: Columbia University Press, 1985). Hannah Decker, *Freud, Dora and Vienna 1900* (New York: The Free Press, 1991) presents the most detailed and subtle reading of the historical background to the case. See also Dianne Hunter, "Hysteria, Psychoanalysis, and Feminism: The Case of Anna O," *Feminist Studies* 9 (1983): 465–88; Maria Ramas, "Freud's Dora, Dora's Hysteria: The Negation of a Woman's Rebellion," *Feminist Studies* 6 (1980): 472–510; Arnold A. Rogow, "A Further Footnote to Freud's 'Fragment of an Analysis of a Case of Hysteria,'" *Journal of the American Psychoanalytical Association* 26 (1978): 330–56.

55. Catherine Clément and Hélène Cixous, *La jeune née* (Paris: 10/18, 1975), p. 283.

Notes

◆

56. *SE* 2: 134, n. 2 (added in 1924).

57. See the discussion in Robert S. Wistrich, *The Jews of Vienna in the Age of Franz Joseph* (Oxford: Oxford University Press, 1989), pp. 483–85.

58. Bertha Pappenheim (writing as P. Bertold), *Zur Judenfrage in Galizien* (Frankfurt a. M.: Knauer, 1900), p. 23.

59. Jacques Lacan, "Intervention on Transference," reprinted in Bernheimer and Kahane, *In Dora's Case*, pp. 92–105. On the working out of the implications of this theme see the essays by Neil Hertz (pp. 221–42) and Toril Moi (pp. 181–99), reprinted in Bernheimer and Kahane.

60. *SE* 7: 84.

61. *SE* 7: 19.

62. *SE* 7: 19.

63. *SE* 7: 21.

64. See the discussion of the inheritance of disease in the seventeenth chapter of Paolo Mantegazza's study of the hygiene of love, in the German translation, *Die Hygiene der Liebe*, trans. R. Teutscher (Jena: Hermann Costenoble, [1877]), p. 366.

65. *SE* 7: 78.

66. Mantegazza notes this quite literally, stating that diseases such as syphilis, cancer, and madness can merge one into the other through the power of the inherited characteristics, see his *Die Hygiene der Liebe*, p. 369.

67. *SE* 7: 16–17.

68. *SE* 7: 16–17, n. 2.

69. Joseph Babinski, "Sur le réflexe cutané plantaire dans certains affections organiques du système nerveux central," *Comptes rendus hebdomadaires des séances de la Société de biologie* (Paris) 48 (1896): 207–8.

70. On the history of this concept see W. Erb, "Über das 'intermittirende Hinken' und andere nervöse Störungen in Folge von Gefässerkrankungen," *Deutsche Zeitschrift für Nervenheilkunde* 13 (1898): 1–77.

71. P. Olivier and A. Halipré, "Claudication intermittente chez un homme hystérique atteint de pouls lent permanent," *La Normandie Médicale* 11 (1896): 21–28. Plate on p. 23.

72. *SE* 7: 101–2.

73. *SE* 7: 102.

74. Felix Deutsch, "A Footnote to Freud's 'Fragment of an Analysis of a

Notes

◆

Case of Hysteria," reprinted in Bernheimer and Kahane, *In Dora's Case*, p. 41.

75. *SE* 7: 84.

76. *SE* 7: 84.

77. *SE* 7: 84.

78. *SE* 7: 84.

79. *SE* 7: 64.

80. *SE* 7: 90.

81. *SE* 7: 91.

82. I am aware that these two terms have very different etymologies. They become, however, homonyms within German-language urban slang in the latter half of the nineteenth century. A contemporary use of the term "Schmock" in a parallel context to my reading of Freud can be found in the work of the Viennese-Jewish poet Fritz Löhner (1883–1942) whose witty poems on Jewish themes were widely quoted by his Viennese-Jewish contemporaries. In 1909 he published a volume of poems in which he used the term "Schmock" in its perjorative sense, meaning the Jewish (i.e., circumcised) male. See "Beda" [i.e., Fritz Löhner], *Israeliten und andere Antisemiten* (Vienna and Berlin: R. Löwit, 1919), p. 30. (By this edition the volume had sold 15, 000 copies).

83. Sigmund Freud, "Some Early Unpublished Letters," trans. Ilse Scheier, *International Journal of Psychoanalysis* 50 (1969): 420.

84. Martin Freud, "Who was Freud?," in Josef Fraenkel, ed., *The Jews of Austria: Essays on their Life, History and Destruction* (London: Vallentine, Mitchell, 1967), p. 202. See also Franz Kobler, "Die Mutter Sigmund Freuds," *Bulletin des Leo Baeck Instituts* 19 (1962): 149–70.

85. *SE* 7: 51.

86. *SE* 7: 36, n. 1.

87. *SE* 7: 62.

88. On Mantegazza see Giovanni Landucci, *Darwinismo a Firenze: Tra scienza e ideologia (1860–1900)* (Florence: Leo S. Olschki, 1977), pp. 107–28.

89. The authorized German editions of Mantegazza which Freud and Ida Bauer could have read are: *Die Physiologie der Liebe*, trans. Eduard Engel (Jena: Hermann Costenoble, 1877); *Die Hygiene der Liebe*, trans. R. Teutscher (Jena: Hermann Costenoble, [1877]); *Anthropologisch-kulturhist-*

Notes

◆

orische Studien über die Geschlechtsverhältnisse des Menschen (Jena: Hermann Costenoble, [1891]).

90.   Reprinted in Bernheimer and Kahane, *In Dora's Case*, p. 273.

91.   The relevant passages in the German edition, *Anthropologisch-kulturhistorische Studien über die Geschlechtsverhältnisse des Menschen* are on pp. 132–37. All of the quotations from Mantegazza are to the English translation: Paolo Mantegazza, *The Sexual Relations of Mankind*, trans. Samuel Putnam (New York: Eugenics Publishing Co., 1938).

92.   See in this context the most recent and most extensive presentation of this argument: Rosemary Romberg, ed., *Circumcision: The Painful Dilemma* (South Hadley, MASS: Bergin and Garvey Publishers, 1985) which was published in conjunction with INTACT Educational Foundation. In this vein see also Edward Wallerstein, "Circumcision: The Uniquely American Medical Enigma," *The Urologic Clinics of North America* 12 (1985): 123–32 which discusses the debates about infection in the context of an attack on the practice. In this context see E.A. Grossman and N.A. Posner, "The Circumcision Controversy: An Update," *Obstetrics and Gynecological Annual* 13 (1984): 181–95 and E. Grossman and N.A. Posner, "Surgical Circumcision of Neonates: A History of its Development," *Obstetrics and Gynecology* 58 (1981): 241–6; S. J. Waszak, "The Historic Significance of Circumcision," *Obstetrics and Gynecology* 51(1978): 499–501.

The anthropological literature on this topic is often critical and superficial, see Desmond Morris, *Bodywatching* (London: Jonathan Cape, 1985), pp. 218–20. By far the best anthropological discussion of what the difference of the circumcised body means is to be found in the published work of the Princeton anthropologist and cultural critic James Boon, *Other Tribes, Other Scribes* (New York: Cambridge University press, 1982), pp. 162–68; *Affinities and Extremes* (Chicago: University of Chicago Press, 1990), pp. 55–60; but also in an unpublished paper "Circumscribing Circumcision / Uncircumcision" (1990) in which the meaning of the act of circumcision is most intelligently and most sophisticatedly drawn into question. The Jewish context is brilliantly presented by Howard Eilberg-Schwartz, *The Savage in Judaism: An Anthropology of Israelite Religion and Ancient Judaism* (Bloomington: Indiana University Press, 1990).

93.   Armand-Louis-Joseph Béraud, *Étude de Pathologie Comparée: Essai sur la pathologie des sémites* (Bordeaux: Paul Cassignol, 1897), p. 55.

94.   There is no comprehensive study of the German debates on circumcision. See J. Alkvist, "Geschichte der Circumcision," *Janus* 30 (1926): 86–

Notes

104; 152–71. It is very clear that the British view of this practice in the late nineteenth century is very different from the German view. See Ronald Hyam, *Empire and Sexuality: The British Experience* (Manchester: Manchester University Press, 1990), pp. 74–79.

95. See the discussion by Dr. Bamberger, "Die Hygiene der Beschneidung," in Max Grunwald, *Die Hygiene der Juden. Im Anschluß an die internationale Hygiene-Ausstellung* (Dresden: Verlag der historischen Abteilung der internationale Hygiene-Ausstellung, 1911), pp. 103–12 (on the Jewish side) and W. Hammer, "Zur Beschneidungsfrage," *Zeitschrift für Bahnärzte* 1 (1916), 254 (on the non-Jewish side).

96. See for example the discussion by Em. Kohn in the *Mittheilung des Ärtzlichen Vereines in Wien* 3 (1874), 169–72 (on the Jewish side) and Dr. Klein, "Die rituelle Circumcision, eine sanitätspolizeiliche Frage," *Allgemeine Medizinische Central-Zeitung* 22 (1853), 368–69. (on the non-Jewish side).

97. Phyllis Cohen Albert, *The Modernization of French Jewry* (Waltham, MASS: Brandeis University Press, 1977), p. 232.

98. Max Grunwald, *Vienna*. Jewish Communities Series (Philadelphia: The Jewish Publication Society of America, 1936), p. 376.

99. See the letter to Sándor Ferenczi of October 6, 1910 in which Freud wrote: "Since Fliess's case, with the overcoming of which you recently saw me occupied, that need has been extinguished. A part of my homosexual cathexis has been withdrawn and made use of to enlarge my own ego. I have succeeded where the paranoiac fails." Cited in Ernst Jones, *The Life and Work of Sigmund Freud*, 3 vols. (New York: Basic Books, 1955), 2: 83.

100. See the discussion in my *Jewish Self-Hatred: Anti-Semitism and the Hidden Language of the Jews* (Baltimore: The Johns Hopkins University Press, 1986), pp. 293–94.

101. Ludwik Fleck, *Entstehung und Entwicklung einer wissenschaftlichen Tatsache* (1935; Frankfurt a. M.: Suhrkamp, 1980). I am indebted to Fleck's work for the basic conceptual structure presented in this essay.

102. Theodor Fritsch, *Handbuch der Judenfrage* (Leipzig: Hammer, 1935), p. 408.

103. See the first-rate study by Anna Foa, "Il Nuova e il Vecchio: L'Insorgere della Sifilide (1494–1530)," *Quaderni Storici* 55 (1984): 11–34.

104. Cited by Harry Friedenwald, *The Jews and Medicine: Essays*. 2 vols. (Baltimore: The Johns Hopkins University Press, 1944), 2: 531.

Notes

105. Bertha Pappenheim with Sara Rabinowitsch, *Zur Lage der jüdischen Bevölkerung in Galizien: Reise-Eindrücke und Vorschläge zur Besserung der Verhältnisse* (Frankfurt a. M.: Neuer Frankfurter Verlag, 1904), pp. 46–51.

106. Adolf Hitler, *Mein Kampf*, trans. Ralph Manheim (Boston: Houghton Mifflin Company, 1943), p. 247.

107. Compare Edward J. Bristow, *Prostitution and Prejudice: The Jewish Fight against White Slavery, 1870–1939* (Oxford: Clarendon, 1982).

108. N. Balaban and A. Molotschek, "Progressive Paralyse bei den Bevölkerungen der Krim," *Allgemeine Zeitschrift für Psychiatrie* 94 (1931): 373–83.

109. H. Budul, "Beitrag zur vergleichenden Rassenpsychiatrie," *Monatsschrift für Psychiatrie und Neurologie* 37 (1915): 199–204.

110. Max Sichel, "Die Paralyse der Juden in sexuologischer Beleuchtung," *Zeitschrift für Sexualwissenschaft* 7 (1919–20): 98–104.

111. Strauß, "Erkrankungen durch Alkohol und Syphilis bei den Juden."

112. See the discussion by Archer Atkinson, "Clinical Lecture on Rupia Syphilitica," *Virginian Medical Monthly* 12 (1885–86): 333–46 and A. Muron, "Du rupia syphilitique (Gomme de la peau et du tissu cellulaire)," *Gazette médicale de Paris* 27 (1872): 408–10.

113. *The Medical Works of Francisco de Villalobos, The Celebrated Court Physician of Spain*, trans. George Gaskoin (London, Churchill, 1870), p. 94.

114. This is also called the "Juden-Zopff." See the early clinical description by Ambrose Stegmann, "De plica Judaeorum," *Miscellanea curiosa sive Ephemeridum* . . . 7 (1699): p. 57. The best overview of the literature is to be found in E. Hamburger, *Über die Irrlehre von der Plica Polonica* (Berlin: August Hirschwald, 1861), pp. 31–63.

115. A good text for examining the "Jewish" qualities assigned to this disease is Wolf Derblich, *De Plica Polonica* (Diss. Breslau, 1848), pp. 6–9

116. F. L. de La Fontaine, *Chirurgisch-Medicinische Abhandlungen verschiedenen [!] Inhalts Polen betreffend* (Breslau und Leipzig: Wilhelm Gottlieb Korn, 1792), pp. 45–46.

117. Felix von Studzieniecke, *Die Cornification und die Lues Cornificative (Plica Polonica)* (Vienna: Carl Gerold und Sohn, 1854).

118. As late as Singer, *Allgemeine und spezielle Krankheitslehre,*, p. 49 it

was necessary to argue that "Jews show no more significant occurrence of this than other poor inhabitants of Eastern Europe."

119. Saul K. Padover, ed. and trans., *The Letters of Karl Marx* (Englewood Cliffs: Prentice-Hall, 1979), p. 459.

120. S. Wier Mitchell, "Peculiar Form of Rupial Skin Disease in an Hysterical Woman," *The American Journal of the Medical Sciences* n.s. 105 (1893): 244–46.

121. M. Lerche, "Beobachtung deutsch-jüdischer Rassenkreuzung an Berliner Schulen," *Die medizinische Welt* (September 17, 1927): 1222. In long letters-to-the-editor, the Jewish sexologist Max Marcuse strongly dismissed the "anti-Jewish" presuppositions of Lerche's views, while at the same time Professor O. Reche of the University of Leipzig saw in her piece a positive contribution to racial science (*Die medizinische Welt* 1 [October 15, 1927]: 1417–19). Lerche responded to Marcuse's call for a better science of race to approach the question of the *Mischling* with her own claim that her work was at best the tentative approach of a pedagogue. She also disavowed any "anti-Jewish bias" on the part of her study. (*Die medizinische Welt* 1 [November 12, 1927]: 1542).

122. *Wertphilosophie und Ethik: Die Frage nach den Sinn des Lebens als Grundlage einer Wertordnung* (Vienna: W. Braumüller, 1939), p. 29.

4. The Jewish Murderer

1. Cited by Michel Parry, ed., *Jack the Knife: Tales of Jack the Ripper* (London: Mayflower, 1975), p.12.

2. See Dorothy Nelkin and Sander L. Gilman, "Placing the Blame for Devastating Disease," *Social Research* 55 (1988): 361–78.

3. I am here indebted to Lynda Nead, "Seduction, Prostitution, Suicide: *On the Brink* by Alfred Elmore," *Art History* 5 (1982): 309–22. This essay, and other of my essays on the fin de siècle, owe much to the recent work of Elaine Showalter, *Sexual Anarchy: Gender and Culture at the Fin de Siècle* (New York: Viking, 1990). On the general history of prostitution in Great Britain during the nineteenth century see Judith R. Walkowitz, *Prostitution and Victorian Society: Women, Class, and the State* (Cambridge: Cambridge University Press, 1980).

4. W. R. Greg, "Prostitution," *Westminster Review* 53 (1850): 456.

5. *The Language of Flowers* (London: Milner and Co., 1849), pp. 19, 22.

Notes
◆
6. Cited by Nead, "Seduction, Prostitution, Suicide," p. 316.

7. The image of the dead woman is a basic trope within the art and literature of the nineteenth century. See Elisabeth Bronfen, "Die schöne Leiche: Weiblicher Tod als motivischer Konstante von der Mitte des 18. Jahrhunderts bis in die Moderne," in Renate Berger and Inge Stephan, eds., *Weiblichkeit und Tod in der Literatur* (Cologne: Böhlau, 1987), pp. 87– 115. On the general background of the fascination with and representation of death in the West see Philippe Ariès, *The Hour of Our Death*, trans. Helen Weaver (New York: Knopf/Random House, 1981) as well as Mario Praz, *The Romantic Agony*, trans. Angus Davidson (Cleveland: World, 1956), John McManners, *Death and the Enlightenment: Changing Attitudes to Death among Christians and Unbelievers in Eighteenth-century France* (Oxford: Clarendon Press, 1981), and Bram Dijkstra, *Idols of Perversity: Fantasies of Feminine Evil in Fin-de-Siècle Culture* (New York: Oxford University Press, 1986).

8. William W. Sanger, *The History of Prostitution; Its Extent, Causes, and Effects Throughout the World* (New York: The Medical Publishing Company, 1927), p. 322.

9. William Tait, *Magdalenism: An Inquiry into the Extent, Causes, and Consequences of Prostitution in Edinburgh* (Edinburgh: P. Rickard, 1840), p. 96. Compare Margaret Higonnet, "Speaking Silences: Women's Suicide," in Susan Rubin Suleiman, ed., *The Female Body in Western Culture: Contemporary Perspectives* (Cambridge, MASS: Harvard University Press, 1986), pp. 68–83.

10. William Tait, *Magdalenism*, p. 96.

11. See, for example, *Drowned! Drowned!*, reproduced in *The Magdalen's Friend, and Female Homes' Intelligencer* 1 (1860): 71. On the continental background to the image of the female suicide see Aaron Sheon, "Octave Tassert's 'Le Suicide': Early Realism and the Plight of Women," *Arts Magazine* 76 (May 1981): 142–51, as well as Judith Wechsler, *A Human Comedy: Physiognomy and Caricature in Nineteenth-Century Paris* (Chicago: University of Chicago Press, 1982) and Mary Cowling, *The Artist as Anthropologist: The Representation of Type and Character in Victorian Art* (Cambridge: Cambridge University Press, 1989).

12. Thomas Hood, "The Bridge of Sighs," *The Complete Poetical Works of Thomas Hood* (New York: G. P. Putnam, 1869), 1: 27. On the literary image of the prostitute see Martin Seymour-Smith, *Fallen Women: A Skeptical Enquiry into the Treatment of Prostitutes, Their Clients, and Their Pimps, in Literature* (London: Nelson, 1969).

Notes

13. See Sigmund Freud's essay "Medusa's Head," *The Standard Edition of the Complete Psychological Works of Sigmund Freud*, ed. and trans. James Strachey, A. Freud, A. Strachey, and A. Tyson, 24 vols. (London: Hogarth, 1955–74), here 18: 273–74. See Sigrid Weigel, *Die Stimme der Medusa: Schreibweisen in der Gegenwartsliteratur von Frauen* (Dülmen-Hiddengsel: Tende, 1987) and Annemarie Taeger, *Die Kunst, Medusa zu töten: Zum Bild der Frau in der Literatur der Jahrhundertwende* (Bielefeld: Aisthesis, 1988).

14. Gottfried Benn, *Sämtliche Werke* (Stuttgart: Klett-Cotta, 1986), 1: 11. Translation mine.

15. Parry, *Jack the Knife*, p. 14.

16. James G. Kiernan, "Sexual Perversion and the Whitechapel Murders," *The Medical Standard* (Chicago) 4 (1888): 129–30, 170–72, here, p. 172.

17. Alexandre Lacassagne, *Vacher l'éventreur et les crimes sadiques* (Lyons: A. Storck, 1889).

18. Cited in Christopher Frayling, "The House That Jack Built: Some Stereotypes of the Rapist in the History of Popular Culture," in Sylvana Tomaselli and Roy Porter, eds., *Rape* (Oxford: Basil Blackwell, 1986), p. 183. Further citations from "Jack" are taken from Frayling unless otherwise noted.

19. Robert Anderson, "The Lighter Side of My Official Life," *Blackwood's Magazine* 187 (1910): 356–67, here, 356–57.

20. Cited in Alexander Kelley and Colin Wilson, *Jack the Ripper: A Bibliography and Review of the Literature* (London: Association of Assistant Librarians, 1973), p. 14.

21. Frank Wedekind, *Five Tragedies of Sex*, trans. Frances Fawcett and Stephen Spender (New York: Theatre Arts Books, n.d.), p. 298.

22. Cesare Lombroso and Guglielmo Ferrero, *La donna deliquente: La prostituta a la donna normale* (Torino: Roux, 1893), and Alexandre Lacassagne, *L'homme criminel comparé à l'homme primitif* (Lyon: Association typographique, 1882).

23. Peter Pulzer, *The Rise of Political Anti-Semitism in Germany and Austria* (London: Peter Halban, 1988), p. 6.

24. The fantasy of a "Jewish" Jack the Ripper dies very hard. Robin Odell, *Jack the Ripper in Fact and Fiction* (London: George G. Harrap, 1965), proposed again that Jack was a *shochet*, a ritual slaughterer. This theme has reappeared in the recent volume by Martin Fido, *The Crimes*,

Notes
◆

Detection and Death of Jack the Ripper (London: Weidenfeld and Nicolson, 1987), which argues that a Jewish tailor named David Cohen was "Jack."

25. D. Retla, "Judendeutsche Erzählungen aus Südrussland," *Anthropophyteia* 9 (1912): 417–24, here, 417.

26. See the discussion by Alain Corbin, "Commercial Sexuality in Nineteenth-Century France: A System of Images and Regulations," *Representations* 14 (1986): 209–19.

27. Tom Brown, *Amusements Serious and Comical and Other Works*, ed. Arthur L. Hayward (London: George Routledge and Sons, Ltd., 1927), p. 200.

28. *The Bagnio Miscellany Containing the Adventures of Miss Lais Lovecock* . . . (London: Printed for the Bibliopolists, 1892), here pp. 54–55.

29. Frayling, "House That Jack Built," p. 196.

30. Gray Joliffe and Peter Mayle, *Man's Best Friend* (London: Pan Books, 1984).

31. See Mary Wilson Carpenter, " 'A Bit of Her Flesh': Circumcision and 'The Signification of the Phallus' in *Daniel Deronda*," *Genders* 1 (1988): 1–23.

32. See Benjamin Nelson, *The Idea of Usury: From Tribal Brotherhood to Universal Otherhood* (Princeton: Princeton University Press, 1949), and John Thomas Noonan, *The Scholastic Analysis of Usury* (Cambridge, MASS: Harvard University Press, 1957).

33. Joseph Banister, *England under the Jews* (London: [J. Banister], 1907 [3rd edition]), p. 61. For a more detailed account of Banister and the idea of the diseased Jew see Colin Holmes, *Anti-Semitism in British Society, 1876–1939* (New York: Holmes and Meier, 1979), pp. 36–48.

34. The very best presentation of this question (which, however, does not make reference to the medicalization of the Jew) is Albert Sonnenfeld, "Marcel Proust: Anti-Semite?" *French Review* 62 (1988): 25–40, 275–82. See also Gilles Zenou, "Proust et la judéité," *Europe* 705–6 (1988): 157–64.

35. The discussion of the images of the Jew and the homosexual is to be found in "Cities of the Plain," in Marcel Proust, *Remembrance of Things Past*, trans. C.K. Scott Moncrieff and Terence Kilmartin (Harmondsworth: Penguin, 1986), 2: 639.

36. On syphilis and Charcot see Proust, *Remembrance*, 2: 1086.

37. Proust, *Remembrance*, 1: 326.

38.   See the discussion by Galton reprinted in Joseph Jacobs, *Studies in Jewish Statistics, Social, Vital, and Anthropometric* (London: D. Nutt, 1891), p. xl.

39.   See my forthcoming essay "The Indelibility of Circumcision," to appear in *Koroth* (Jerusalem).

40.   Banister, *England under the Jews*, p. 61.

41.   Joseph Jacobs, *Studies in Jewish Statistics*, pp. xxxii-xxxiii.

42.   See Frank J. Sulloway, *Freud: Biologist of the Mind* (New York: Basic Books, 1979), pp. 147–158.

43.   On the tradition of seeing leprosy as a sexually transmitted disease see Saul N. Brody, *The Disease of the Soul: Leprosy in Medieval Literature* (Ithaca, NY: Cornell University Press, 1974).

5.   The Jewish Genius

1.   Werner Sombart, *The Jews and Modern Capitalism*, trans. M. Epstein (Glencoe, IL: The Free Press, 1951), p. 320. On the meaning of the "genius" of the Jew see the detailed exposition by the French historian Anatole Leroy-Beaulieu, *Israel among the Nations: A Study of Jews and Antisemitism*, trans. Frances Hellman (New York: G. P. Putnam's Sons, 1895), pp. 225–62. In refuting the claims about Jewish creativity, he manages to catalogue most of them.

2.   Steven Beller, *Vienna and the Jews 1867–1938: A Cultural History* (Cambridge: Cambridge University Press, 1989), pp. 78–83.

3.   Houston Stewart Chamberlain, *Foundations of the Nineteenth Century*, trans. John Lees. 2 vols. (London: John Lane/The Bodley Head, 1913), 1: 418. On Freud's reading of Chamberlain see Sigmund Freud, *Gesammelte Werke*. 19 vols. (Frankfurt a. M.: S. Fischer, 1952–87), Nachtragsband: 787.

4.   Ludwig Wittgenstein, *Culture and Value*, ed. G. H. von Wright and Heikki Nyman (Oxford: Basil Blackwell, 1980), p. 19

5.   Adolf Hitler, *Mein Kampf*, trans. Ralph Mannheim (Boston: Houghton Mifflin Company, 1943), pp. 302–3.

6.   Arthur Ruppin, "Der Rassenstolz der Juden," *Zeitschrift für Demographie und Statistik der Juden* 6 (1910): 88–92, here 91.

7.   Arthur Ruppin, "Begabungsunterschiede christlicher und jüdischer Kinder," *Zeitschrift für Demographie und Statistik der Juden* 2 (1906): 129–

35. See also Irma Loeb Cohen, *The Intelligence of Jews as Compared with Non-Jews* (Columbus: Ohio State University Press, 1927).

8. See the discussion in Bennett Simon, *Mind and Madness in Ancient Greece* (Ithaca, NY: Cornell University Press, l978), pp. 228–37.

9. Cesare Lombroso, *Genio e follia* (Milan: Chiusi, l864).

10. Cesare Lombroso, *The Man of Genius* (London: Walter Scott, 1901), pp. 136–37. The German translation, which Freud would have known, is Cesare Lombroso, *Der geniale Mensch*, trans. M.O. Fraenkel (Hamburg: Verlagsanstalt und Druckerei Actien-Gesellschaft, 1890).

11. Wilhelm Wundt, *Grundzüge der physiologischen Psychologie*, 4 vols. (Leipzig: Engelmann, 1887), 2: 457.

12. Lombroso, *The Man of Genius*, p. 133.

13. Arthur Schnitzler, *Medizinische Schriften*, ed. Horst Thomé (Vienna: Paul Zsolnay, 1988), pp. 233–39, here, p. 236.

14. Joseph Jacobs, "Distribution of the Comparative Ability of the Jews" (1886), reprinted in his *Studies in Jewish Statistics, Social, Vital, and Anthropometric* (London: D. Nutt, 1891), pp. xlii–lxix.

15. Lombroso, *The Man of Genius*., p. 135.

16. Lombroso, *The Man of Genius*., p. 136.

17. Cesare Lombroso, *Der Antisemitismus und die Juden im Lichte der modernen Wissenschaft*, trans. H. Kurella (Leipzig: Georg H. Wiegand, 1894), pp. 43–50.

18. Lombroso, *The Man of Genius*, p. 152.

19. Schnitzler, *Medizinische Schriften*, p. 236.

20. All quotations are from the English translation, Otto Weininger, *Sex and Character* (London: William Heinemann, 1906). Hereafter represented in the text by page citation.

21. On Weininger see my *Jewish Self-Hatred: Anti-Semitism and the Hidden Language of the Jews* (Baltimore: The Johns Hopkins University Press, 1986), pp. 244–51; Jacques Le Rider, *Der Fall Otto Weininger: Wurzeln des Antifeminismus und Antisemitismus*, trans. Dieter Hornig (Vienna: Löcker Verlag, 1985); Jacques Le Rider and Norbert Leser, eds., *Otto Weininger: Werk und Wirkung* (Vienna: Österreichischer Bundesverlag, 1984); Peter Heller, "A Quarrel over Bisexuality," Gerald Chapple and Hans H. Schulte, eds., *The Turn of the Century: German Literature and Art, 1890–1915* (Bonn: Bouvier, 1978), pp. 87–116; Franco Nicolino, *Indagini su Freud*

e sulla Psicoanalisi (Naples: Liguori Editore, n.d.), pp. 103–10; Jacques Le Rider, *Das Ende der Illusion: Die Wiener Moderne und die Krisen der Identität*, trans. Robert Fleck (Vienna: Österreichischer Bundesverlag, 1990), pp. 229–58 .

22. I am using the term "homosexual" throughout this and other discussions as a reflection of the debates about male and female gay identity within the medical literature of the period. While a number of different terms are used to represent male gay identity (including Homosexual and Uranist), it seemed clearest to reduce these to a single label. See in this context Richard Green, "Homosexuality as a Mental Illness," in Arthur L. Caplan, et al., eds., *Concepts of Health and Disease: Interdisciplinary Perspectives* (London: Addison-Wesley Publishing Company, 1981), pp. 333–51 and G. Hekma, "Sodomites, Platonic Lovers, Contrary Lovers: The Backgrounds of the Modern Homosexual," *Journal of Homosexuality* 16 (1988): 433–55 as well as David F. Greenberg, *The Construction of Homosexuality* (Chicago: University of Chicago Press, 1988).

23. See, for example, the discussion in Carl Dallago, *Otto Weininger und sein Werk* (Innsbruck: Brenner-Verlag, 1912) and Emil Lucka, *Otto Weininger: Sein Werk und seine Persönlichkeit* (Berlin: Schuster & Loeffler, 1921), esp. pp. 37–80.

24. Charlotte Perkins Gilman, "Review of Dr. Weininger's *Sex and Character*," *The Critic* 12 (1906): 414.

25. Jacques Le Rider, "Wittgenstein et Weininger," *Wittgenstein et la Critique du Monde Moderne* (Brussels: La Lettre Volée, 1990), pp. 43–65.

26. Kitâro Nishida, *An Inquiry into the Good*, trans. Masao Abe and Christopher Ives (New Haven: Yale University Press, 1989).

27. *Protokolle der Wiener Psychoanalytischen Vereinigung*, ed. Herman Nunberg and Ernst Federn, 4 vols. (Frankfurt a. M.: Fischer, 1976–81), 2: 351; translation from *Minutes of the Vienna Psychoanalytic Society*, trans. M. Nunberg, 4 vols. (New York: International Universities Press, 1962–75), 2: 387.

28. All references to this hitherto unpublished essay is to the translation by Dennis Klein, published as Appendix C of his *Jewish Origins of the Psychoanalytic Movement* (New York: Praeger, 1981), here, p. 171.

29. See my discussion in my *Difference and Pathology: Stereotypes of Sexuality, Race, and Madness* (Ithaca, NY: Cornell University Press, 1986), pp. 175–191.

Notes

30. On the question of the history of this tradition see John E. Gedo, *Portraits of the Artist: Psychoanalysis of Creativity and its Vicissitudes* (New York: Guilford Press, 1983); Edward Hare, "Creativity and Mental Illness," *British Medical Journal* 295 (1987): 1587–89; John Hope Mason, "The Character of Creativity: Two Traditions," *History of European Ideas* 9 (1988): 697–715; Albert Rothenberg, *Creativity and Madness: New Findings and Old Stereotypes* (Baltimore: The Johns Hopkins University Press, 1990).

31. Sigmund Freud, *Standard Edition of the Complete Psychological Works of Sigmund Freud*, ed. and trans. J. Strachey, A. Freud, A. Strachey, and A. Tyson, 24 vols. (London: Hogarth, 1955–74), 9: 167–176. (Hereafter cited as *SE*.)

32. *SE* 23, 187. In this context see C.M. Hanly, "Psychoanalytic Aesthetics: A Defense and an Elaboration," *Psychoanalytic Quarterly* 55 (1986): 1–22 and D.M. Kaplan, "The Psychoanalysis of Art: Some Ends, Some Means," *Journal of the American Psychoanalytic Association* 36 (1988): 259–93.

33. *SE* 2: 207.

34. *SE* 11: 63.

35. *SE* 9: 143–153.

36. *SE* 9: 143.

37. For a more extensive interpretation see Sarah Kofman, *The Childhood of Art: An Interpretation of Freud's Aesthetics*, trans. Winifred Woodhull (New York: Columbia University Press, 1988).

38. *SE* 9: 144.

39. *SE* 9: 145, Freud's emphasis.

40. See the discussion by Janine Chasseguet-Smirgel, *Creativity and Perversion* (New York: W.W. Norton, 1984) on the relationship between object relations theory and "creativity."

41. *SE* 9: 146.

42. *SE* 9: 147.

43. *SE* 23, 187–188.

44. *SE* 21, 177.

45. *SE* 20, 70

46. Wilhelm Hirsch, *Genie und Entartung: Eine psychologische Studie* (Berlin: Coblentz, 1894).

Notes
---

47. In this context see Maurice Olender, *Les Langues du Paradis: Aryens et Semites—un couple providentiel* (Paris: Gallimard, 1989).

48. See the discussion of Freud's idealization of non-Jewish intellectuals in Peter Homans, *The Ability to Mourn: Disillusionment and the Social Origins of Psychoanalysis* (Chicago: University of Chicago Press, 1989), pp. 88–95. The American-Jewish psychoanalyst Abraham Aron Roback did address this question in an early, popular paper, "The Jews and Genius," *American Hebrew* 40 (1919): 532, 576–78.

49. Joseph Wortis, *Fragments of an Analysis with Freud* (New York: Jason Aronson, 1984), p. 145.

50. SE 23, 292.

51. Beginning with his essay "New Views on the Psychology and Psychopathology of Wit and the Comic," *Psychiatry* 13 (1950): 43–62 to his major study *Creativity: The Magic Synthesis* (New York: Basic Books, 1976), Silvano Arieti's work focused on this question and the, for him related, question of the nature and meaning of schizophrenia.

52. See my discussion of the history and meaning of schizophrenia in *Disease and Representation: Images of Illness from Madness to AIDS* (Ithaca, NY: Cornell University Press, 1988).

53. Silvano Arieti, *New Views of Creativity* (New York: Geigy, 1977), p. 7.

54. Silvano Arieti, *The Parnas* (New York: Basic Books, 1979).

55. Arieti, *Creativity: The Magic Synthesis*, p. 327–28. The slipperiness of this undertaking can be judged by examining Armin Hermann, ed., *Deutsche Nobelpreisträger* (Munich: Heinz Moos, 1978) where the "Jewish" prize winners are suddenly "German" prize winners. The ideology behind both of these categorizations is clear.

56. N.C. Andreasen and I.D. Glick, "Bipolar Affective Disorder and Creativity: Implications and Clinical Management," *Comprehensive Psychiatry* 29 (1988): 207–17.

57. K.R. Jamison, "Mood Disorders and Patterns of Creativity in British Writers and Artists," *Psychiatry* 52 (1988): 125–134.

58. There is a psychoanalytic parallel to these discussions: André Haynal, *Depression and Creativity* (New York: International Universities Press, 1985). On the present state of the discussion of the psychology of "creativity" see Robert J. Sternberg, *The Nature of Creativity: Contemporary Psychological Perspectives* (New York: Cambridge University Press, 1988) and

Notes
◆

Albert Rothenberg, *Creativity and Madness: New Findings and Old Stereotypes* (Baltimore: The Johns Hopkins University Press, 1990).

59.   A.M. Ludwig, "Reflections on Creativity and Madness," *American Journal of Psychotherapy* 43 (1989): 4–14.

6.   The Jewish Reader

1.   All of the Freud references are to Sigmund Freud, *Standard Edition of the Complete Psychological Works of Sigmund Freud*, ed. and trans. J. Strachey, A. Freud, A. Strachey, and A. Tyson, 24 vols.(London: Hogarth, 1955–74), hereafter *SE*, here "Contributions to a Questionnaire on Reading" (1907), 9: 245: "You did not even ask for 'favorite books', among which I should not have forgotten Milton's *Paradise Lost* and Heine's *Lazarus*." For the general context see Ernst A. Ticho, "Der Einfluss der deutschsprachigen Kultur auf Freuds Denken," *Jahrbuch der Psychoanalyse* 19 (1986): 36–53 and Renate Böschenstein, "Mythos als Wasserscheide. Die jüdische Komponente der Psychoanalyse: Beobachtungen zu ihrem Zusammenhang mit der Literatur des Jahrhundertbeginns," in Hans Otto Horch and Horst Denkler, eds., *Conditio Judaica: Judentum, Antisemitismus und deutschsprachige Literatur vom 18. Jahrhundert bis zum Ersten Weltkrieg* (Tübingen: Max Niemeyer, 1989), pp. 287–310.

2.   See Robert Wistrich, *The Jews of Vienna in the Age of Franz Joseph* (Oxford: The Littman Library of Jewish Civilization/Oxford University Press, 1989), p. 181.

3.   On the complexity of reading Freud reading see Avital Ronell, *Dictations: On Haunted Writing* (Bloomington, IN: Indiana University Press, 1985) and on the general parallels which make Freud's reading of Heine more than superficial see the first-rate dissertation by Michael G. Levine, "Writing Between the Lines: Heine, Freud and the Effects of Self-Censorship," Diss. The Johns Hopkins University, 1986.

4.   On the overall history of Heine's reputation in the nineteenth century see Gerhard Höhn, *Heine-Handbuch: Zeit, Person, Werk* (Stuttgart: Metzler, 1987). and on Heine and the anti-Semites see Paul Peters, *Heinrich Heine "Dichterjude"* (Königstein: Anton Hain/Athenäum, 1990).

5.   August Forel, *The Sexual Question*, trans. C. F. Marshall (New York: Medical Art Agency, 1922), p. 494

6.   See my "Karl Kraus's Oscar Wilde: Race, Sex, and Difference," *Austrian Studies* (Cambridge) 1 (1990), 12–28.

Notes

7. Leopold von Sacher-Masoch, "Zwei Ärtze," in his *Jüdisches Leben in Wort und Bild* (Mannheim: J. Bensheimer, 1892), pp. 287–298. On the context see Hans Otto Horch, "Der Aussenseiter als 'Judenraphael,' Zu den Judengeschichten Leopolds von Sacher Masoch," in Horch and Denkler, *Conditio Judaica*, pp. 258–286.

8. See Monika Richarz, *Der Eintritt der Juden in die akademische Berufe* (Tübingen: Mohr, 1974).

9. On the social history of the Jews in this context see George E. Berkley, *Vienna and Its Jews: The Tragedy of Success, 1880–1980s* (Cambridge, MASS: Abt/Madison, 1988); William O. McCagg, Jr., *A History of Habsburg Jews, 1670–1918* (Bloomington, IN: Indiana University Press, 1989); Ivar Oxaal, Michael Pollak, and Gerhard Botz, eds., *Jews, Antisemitism and Culture in Vienna* (London/New York: Routledge & Kegan Paul, 1987); Peter Pulzer, *The Rise of Political Anti-Semitism in Germany and Austria*, rev. ed. (London: Peter Halban, 1988); Steven Beller, *Vienna and the Jews 1867–1938: A Cultural History* (Cambridge: Cambridge University Press, 1989), p. 189.

10. *SE* 22: 113.

11. Ludwig Hirschfeld, *Was nicht im Baedeker steht: Wien und Budapest* (Munich: R. Piper, 1927), p. 56.

12. On the background for this idea of the homologous structure of the genitalia see my *Sexuality: An Illustrated History* (New York: Wiley, 1989).

13. *SE* 25: 212.

14. *SE* 23: 30–31.

15. *SE* 22: 192–93.

16. Heine's own awareness of this problem complicates this question. See Norbert Altenhofer, "Chiffre, Hieroglyphe, Palimpest. Vorformen tiefhermeneutischer und intertextueller Interpretation im Werke Heines," in Ulrich Nassen, ed., *Texthermeneutik: Aktualität, Geschichte, Kritik* (Paderborn: Schöningh, 1979), pp. 149–93.

17. See Manfred Windfuhr, *Heinrich Heine: Revolution und Reflexion* (Stuttgart: Metzler, 1976), p. 109 and Gerhard Höhn, *Heine-Handbuch: Zeit, Person, Werk* (Stuttgart Metzler, 1987), p. 114.

18. Freud presents an image of Heine in the context of Heine's family and relates this to Freud's own family when he writes about the Hirsch-Hyacinth "pun," which will be discussed later in this essay. What he does not note is that his wife's family, the Bernays, were also related to the

Notes
◆

Heines [See David Bakan, *Sigmund Freud and the Jewish Mystical Tradition* (New York: Van Nostrad, 1958), p. 196]. Thus the story about "family" is also a narrative which reflects the medical view that "inbreeding" (read: incest) was the source of madness among the Jews: "I recall a story told by an old aunt of my own, who had married into the Heine family, how one day, when she was an attractive young woman, she found sitting next her at the family dinner-table a person who struck her as uninviting and whom the rest of the company treated contemptuously. She herself felt no reason to be any more affable towards him. It was only many years later that she realized that this negligent and neglected cousin had been the poet Heinrich Heine. There is not a little evidence to show how much Heine suffered both in his youth and later from this rejection by his rich relations. It was from the soil of this subjective emotion that the 'famillionairely' joke sprang." *Jokes and their Relationship to the Unconscious*, SE 8: 141–42.

19. See my *Sexuality: An Illustrated History*, pp. 258–60.

20. See Barbara Spackman, *Decadent Genealogies: The Rhetoric of Sickness from Baudelaire to D'Annunzio* (Ithaca, NY: Cornell University Press, 1989).

21. Georg Brandes, *Das junge Deutschland, Die Literatur des 19. Jahrhunderts in ihren Hauptströmungen*, trans. A.v.d. Linden, 6 vols. (Charlottenburg: A. Barsdorf, 1900), 6: 188–89.

22. Sigismund Rahmer, *Heinrich Heines Krankheit und Leidensgeschichte: Eine kritische Studie* (Berlin: Georg Reimer, 1901), p. 20.

23. Max Kaufmann, *Heines Charakter und die moderne Seele* (Zurich: Albert Müller, 1902), p. 25.

24. Kaufmann, *Heines Charakter*, pp. 21–22.

25. See D. Segal, "Limits in the Therapeutic Effect of the Act of Creation. The Case of the Jewish poet Heinrich Heine," *Confinia Psychiatria* 21 (1978): 183–86; J. Kenez, "H. Heine betegsege. Egy vita, mely a kolt' o halalanak 125. evforduloja utan sem zarult le," *Orvosi Hetilap* 123 (1982): 1246–50; M. Schachter, "Certainties and Doubts concerning the Personality and Disease of the Poet Heinrich Heine (1797–1856)," in Helmut Riese, ed., *Historical Explorations in Medicine and Psychiatry* (New York: Springer, 1978), pp. 99–108.

26. Francis Galton, *Hereditary Genius: An Inquiry into Its Laws and Consequences* (London: Macmillan, 1869), p. 234.

Notes

27. Karl Goedeke, *Grundriss der deutschen Dichtung as den Quellen*, 14 vols. (Dresden: L. Ehrlermann, 1884–), 3: 439.

28. Friedrich Hirth, *Heinrich Heines Briefwechsel*, 3 vols. (Munich/Berlin: G. Müller, 1914–20), 1: 92.

29. Gustav Jung, "Der Erotiker Heinrich Heine," *Zeitschrift für Sexualwissenschaft* 11 (1924): 113–28. This is based on a chapter from his book *Die Darstellung des Weibes in Heinrich Heines Werken* (Leipzig: Ethnologischer Verlag Friedrich S. Krauss, 1920), pp. 41–48.

30. A. Cabanès, "A propos du centième anniversaire de la naissance de H. Heine," *La Chronique médicale* 6 (1899): 769–80, here 771, note 1.

31. Giovanni Papini, "A Visit to Freud," in Hendrick M. Ruitenbeek, ed., *Freud as We Knew Him* (Detroit: Wayne State University Press, 1973), p. 99.

32. *SE* 14: 85.

33. This is clearest in Bartel's programmatic pamphlet on the nature of criticism: *Kritiker und Kritikaster: Pro domo et pro arte, mit einem Anhang: Das Judentum in der deutschen Literatur* (Leipzig: Eduard Avenarius, 1903), see esp. pp. 103–15.

34. *SE* 21: 50

35. See Peter Gay, *A Godless Jew: Freud. Atheism, and the Making of Psychoanalysis* (New Haven: Yale University Press [in Association with Hebrew Union College Press, Cincinnati], 1987), as well as the discussions throughout Peter Gay, *Freud: A Life for Our Time* (New York, Norton, 1988).

36. SE 8: 16.

37. On Freud and humor see Theodor Reik, "Zur Psychoanalyse des jüdischen Witzes," *Imago* 15 (1929): 63–68; Eduard Hitschmann, "Zur Psychologie des jüdischen Witzes," *Psychoanalytische Bewegung* 2 (1930): 580–86; J. Kreppel, ed., *Wie der Jude Lacht: Ein Beitrag zur Psychologie des jüdischen Witzes und zur jüdischen Volkskunde* (Vienna: Verlag "Das Buch," 1933); Theodor Reik, "Freud and Jewish Wit," *Psychoanalysis* 2 (1954): 12–20; Theodor Reik, *Jewish Wit* (New York: Gamut, 1962); G. W. Kelling, "An Empirical Investigation of Freud's Theory of Jokes," *Psychoanalytic Review* 58 (1971): 473–85; Jeffrey Mehlman, "How to Read Freud on Jokes: The Critic as *Schadchen*," *New Literary History* 6 (1975): 439–61; Mary Jacobus, "Is There a Woman in This Text?," *New Literary History* 14 (1982): 117–41; Elliot Oring, "The People of the Joke: On the Conceptualization of a Jewish Humor," *Western Folklore* 42 (1983): 261–71; Elliot Oring, *The Jokes of*

Notes

◆

Sigmund Freud: A Study in Humor and Jewish Identity (Philadelphia: University of Pennsylvania Press, 1984); Michael Neve, "Freud's Theory of Humour, Wit and Jokes," in John Durant and Jonathan Miller, eds., *Laughing Matters, A Serious Look at Humour* (London: Longman Scientific and Technical, 1988): 35–43; Jerry Aline Flieger, *The Purloined Punch Line: Freud's Comic Theory and The Post-Modern Text* (Baltimore: The Johns Hopkins University Press, 1991); on the role of Heine's quotations in Freud's study of humor see Peter Brask, "Rebecca, er det mig so taler?" *Kritik* 36 (1975): 103–26.

38. "Heymans (1896) explains how the effect of a joke comes about through bewilderment being succeeded by illumination. He illustrates his meaning by a brilliant joke of Heine's, who makes one of his characters, Hirsch-Hyacinth, the poor lottery-agent, boast that the great Baron Rothschild had treated him quite as his equal—quite 'famillionairely'. Here the word that is the vehicle of the joke appears at first sight simply to be a wrongly constructed word, something unintelligible, incomprehensible, puzzling. It accordingly bewilders. The comic effect is produced by the solution of this bewilderment, by understanding the word." *Jokes and their Relationship to the Unconscious*, SE 8: 12–13

39. G. Heymans, "Ästhetische Unterschungen in Anschluß an die Lipp'sche Theorie des Komischen," *Zeitschrift für Psychologie und Physiologie der Sinnesorgane* 11 (1896): 31–43; 333–52.

40. On Lipps and Freud see Mark Kanzer, "Freud, Theodor Lipps, and 'Scientific Psychology,'" *Psychoanalytic Quarterly* 50 (1981): 393–410.

41. Theodor Lipps, "Psychologie der Komik," *Philosophische Monatsheft* 25 (1889): 139.

42. Theodor Lipps, *Komik und Humor: Eine psychologisch-ästhetische Untersuchung* (Hamburg/Leipzig: Leopold Voss, 1898), p. 95.

43. *The Complete Letters of Sigmund Freud to Wilhelm Fliess, 1887–1904*, trans. Jeffrey M. Masson (Cambridge, MASS: Harvard University Press, 1985), p. 324.

44. Freud-Fliess, *Letters*, September 27, 1898, p. 329. Compare J.N. Isbister, *Freud: An Introduction to His Life and Work* (London: Polity, 1985), p. 125.

45. See the following passages: *Jokes and their Relationship to the Unconscious*, SE 8: 12–13, 16, 25, 36, 39, 41, 47–48, 50–51, 69, 77, 78–79, 85, 87, 90, 114–15, 141–42, 145, 211, 212.

46. On the function of the idea of Blackness and the body of the black as a marker within German aesthetic theory see my *On Blackness without Blacks: Essays on the Image of the Black in Germany*, Yale Afro-American Studies (Boston: G.K. Hall, 1982).

47. See my *Difference and Pathology: Stereotypes of Sexuality, Race, and Madness* (Ithaca, NY: Cornell University Press, 1985): 29–35.

48. See the commentary with quotations by Mark Kanzer, "Pioneers of Applied Analysis: Vol. III of the *Minutes*," *American Imago* 32 (1975): 59–76, here 66.

49. Jakov Lind, *Counting My Steps: An Autobiography* (London: Macmillan, 1969), p. 55.

50. *SE* 8: 77.

51. *SE* 8: 78–79.

52. See Robert C. Holub, "Heine's Sexual Assaults: Towards a Theory of Total Polemic," *Monatshefte* 73 (1981): 415–28.

53. Freud, "The 'Uncanny,'" *SE* 17: 236. On Freud and Heine see J.M.R. Damasmora, F. A. Jenner, S. E. Eacott, "On Heutoscopy or the Phenomenon of the Double: Case Presentation and Review of the Literature," *British Journal of Medical Psychology* 53 (1980): 75–83.

7. The Jewish Nose

1. *Washingtonian* 26, 4 (January 1991), p. 196.

2. Mary Douglas, *Natural Symbols* (New York: Pantheon Books, 1970), p. 70.

3. Theodosius Dobzhansky, "On Types, Genotypes, and the Genetic Diversity in Populations," in J.N. Spuhler, ed., *Genetic Diversity and Human Behavior* (Chicago: Aldine, 1967), p. 12.

4. See for example, Peter A. Bochnik, *Die mächtigen Diener: Die Medizin und die Entwicklung von Frauenfeindlichkeit und Antisemitismus in der europäischen Geschichte* (Reinbek bei Hamburg: Rowohlt, 1985).

5. Robert Jay Lifton, *The Nazi Doctors: Medical Killing and the Psychology of Genocide* (New York: Basic Books, 1986).

6. See Oliver Ransford, *"Bid the Sickness Cease": Disease in the History of Black Africa* (London: John Murray, 1983).

Notes

◆

7. François-Maximilien Mission, *A New Voyage to Italy*, 2 vols. (London: R. Bonwicke, 1714), 2: 139.

8. Johann Pezzl, *Skizze von Wien: Ein Kultur- und Sittenbild as der joseph-inischen Zeit*, ed. Gustav Gugitz and Anton Schlossar (Graz: Leykam-Verlag, 1923), pp. 107–8.

9. On the meaning of this disease in the medical literature of the period see the following dissertations on the topic: Michael Scheiba, *Dissertatio inauguralis medica, sistens quaedam plicae pathologica: Germ. Juden-Zopff, Polon. Koltun: quam . . . in Academia Albertina pro gradu doctoris . . . subjiciet defensurus Michael Scheiba . . .* (Regiomonti: Litteris Reusnerianis, 1739) and Hieronymus Ludolf, *Dissertatio inauguralis medica de plica, vom Juden-Zopff . . .* (Erfordiae: Typis Groschianis, 1724).

10. Harry Friedenwald, *The Jews and Medicine: Essays.* 2 vols. (Baltimore: The Johns Hopkins University Press, 1944), 2: 531.

11. Joseph Rohrer, *Versuch über die jüdischen Bewohner der österreichischen Monarchie* (Vienna: n.p., 1804), p. 26. The debate about the special tendency of the Jews for skin disease, especially "plica polonica", goes on well into the twentieth century. See Richard Weinberg, "Zur Pathologie der Juden," *Zeitschrift für Demographie und Statistik der Juden* 1 (1905): 10–11.

12. Wolfgang Häusler, *Das galizische Judentum in der Habsburgermonarchie im Lichte der zeitgenössischen Publizistik und Reiseliteratur von 1772–1848* (Vienna: Verlag für Geschichte und Politik, 1979). On the status of the debates about the pathology of the Jews in the East after 1919 see *Voprosy biologii i patologii evreev* (Leningrad: State Publishing House, 1926).

13. Elcan Isaac Wolf, *Von den Krankheiten der Juden* (Mannheim: C.F. Schwan, 1777), p. 12.

14. James Cowles Pritchard, *Researches into the Physical History of Man* (Chicago: The University of Chicago Press, 1973), p. 186.

15. Claudius Buchanan, *Christian Researches in Asia, with Notices of the Translation of the Scriptures into the Oriental Languages* (Boston: Samuel T. Armstrong, 1811), p. 169. On the background to these questions see George W. Stocking, Jr., *Victorian Anthropology* (New York: The Free Press, 1987).

16. Léon Poliakov, *The Aryan Myth: A History of Racist and Nationalist Ideas in Europe*, trans. Edmund Howard (New York: Basic Books, 1974), pp. 155–82.

Notes

◆

17. Sander L. Gilman, *On Blackness without Blacks: Essays on the Image of the Black in Germany*, Yale Afro-American Studies (Boston: G.K. Hall, 1982).

18. See Cheryl Herr, "The Erotics of Irishness," *Critical Inquiry* 17 (1990): 1–34.

19. Houston Stewart Chamberlain, *Foundations of the Nineteenth Century*, trans. John Lees, 2 vols. (London: John Lane/The Bodley Head, 1913), 1: 389.

20. Nathan Birnbaum, "Über Houston Stewart Chamberlain," in his *Ausgewählte Schriften zur jüdischen Frage* (Czernowitz: Verlag der Buchhandlung Dr. Birnbaum & Dr. Kohut, 1910), 2: 201.

21. Robert Knox, *The Races of Men: A Fragment* (Philadelphia: Lea and Blanchard, 1850), p. 134.

22. Knox, *Races of Men*, p. 133.

23. Adam G. de Gurowski, *America and Europe* (New York: D. Appleton, 1857), p. 177.

24. On the question of the definition and meaning of the *Mischling* see Paul Weindling, *Health, Race and German Politics between National Unification and Nazism, 1870–1945* (Cambridge: Cambridge University Press, 1989), pp. 531–32.

25. Chamberlain, *Foundations of the Nineteenth Century*, 1: 332.

26. W.W. Kopp, "Beobachtung an Halbjuden in Berliner Schulen," *Volk und Rasse* 10 (1935): 392.

27. Joseph Jacobs, *Studies in Jewish Statistics, Social, Vital and Anthropometric* (London: D. Nutt, 1891), p. xxiii.

28. Jacob Wassermann, *My Life as German and Jew* (London: George Allen & Unwin, 1933), p. 72.

29. All references are to Sigmund Freud, *Standard Edition of the Complete Psychological Works of Sigmund Freud*, ed. and trans. J. Strachey, A. Freud, A. Strachey, and A. Tyson, 24 vols.(London: Hogarth, 1955–74), 14, 191 (Hereafter cited as *SE*.)

30. *SE* 11: 199; 18:, 101; 21, 114.

31. *SE* 21: 120.

32. Samuel Stanhope Smith, *An Essay on the Causes of the Variety of Complexion and Figure in the Human Species* (Cambridge, MASS: The Belknap Press, 1965), p. 42.

Notes
◆

33. William Lawrence, *Lectures on Physiology, Zoology, and the Natural History of Man* (London: James Smith, 1823), p. 468.

34. Rudolf Virchow, "Gesamtbericht über die Farbe der Haut, der Haare und der Augen der Schulkinder in Deutschland," *Archiv für Anthropologie* 16 (1886): 275–475.

35. George L. Mosse, *Toward the Final Solution: A History of European Racism* (New York: Howard Fertig, 1975), pp. 90–91.

36. Cited from an interview by Neal Gabler, *An Empire of Their Own: How the Jews Invented Hollywood* (New York: Crown, 1988), pp. 242–42.

37. "Types," *The Jewish Encyclopedia*. 12 vols. (New York: Funk and Wagnalls, 1906), 12: 295

38. Wassermann, *My Life*, p. 156.

39. Wassermann, *My Life*, p. 156.

40. On the cultural background for this concept see Jacob Katz, *Out of the Ghetto: The Social Background of Jewish Emancipation 1770–1870* (Cambridge, MASS: Harvard University Press, 1973) and Rainer Erb and Werner Bergmann, *Die Nachtseite der Judenemanzipation: Der Widerstand gegen die Integration der Juden in Deutschland 1780–1860* (Berlin: Metropol, 1989).

41. Moses Hess, *Rom und Jerusalem*. 2nd ed. (Leipzig: M.W. Kaufmann, 1899), Brief IV. Cited in the translation from Paul Lawrence Rose, *Revolutionary Antisemitism in Germany from Kant to Wagner* (Princeton: Princeton University Press, 1990), p. 323.

42. Eden Warwick, *Notes on Noses* (1848; London: Richard Bentley, 1864), p. 11. On the general question of the representation of the physiognomy of the Jew in mid-nineteenth-century culture see Mary Cowling, *The Artist as Anthropologist: The Representation of Type and Character in Victorian Art* (Cambridge: Cambridge University Press, 1989), pp. 118–19, 332–33.

43. Bernhard Blechmann, *Ein Beitrag zur Anthropologie der Juden* (Dorpat: Wilhelm Just, 1882), p. 11.

44. Jacobs, *Studies in Jewish Statistics*, p. xxxii

45. Hans Leicher, *Die Vererbung anatomischer Variationen der Nase, Ihrer Nebenhöhlen und des Gehörorgans* (Munich: J. F. Bergmann, 1928), pp. 80–85.

46. Amos Elon, *Herzl* (New York: Holt, Rinehardt and Winston, 1975), p. 63.

47. Quoted from Konrad H. Jarausch, *Students, Society and Politics in Imperial Germany: The Rise of Academic Illiberalism* (Princeton: Princeton University Press, 1982), p. 350. See also his *Deutsche Studenten 1800–1970* (Frankfurt a. M.: Suhrkamp, 1984), pp. 82–93 as well as Michael Kater, *Studentenschaft und Rechtsradikalismus in Deutschland 1918–1933: Eine sozialgeschichtliche Studie zur Bildungskrise in der Weimarer Republik* (Hamburg: Hoffmann und Campe, 1975), pp. 145–62.

48. W[illiam] O[sler], "Berlin Correspondence," *Canada Medical and Surgical Journal* 2 (1874): 308–15, here, 310.

49. Jarausch, *Students*, p. 272.

50. Quoted by Peter Pulzer, *The Rise of Political Anti-Semitism in Germany and Austria* (London: Peter Halband, 1988), p. 246.

51. Stephan Mencke, *Zur Geschichte der Orthopädie* (Munich: Michael Beckstein, 1930), pp. 68–69.

52. Bruno Valentin, *Geschichte der Orthopädie* (Stuttgart: Georg Thieme, 1961), pp. 101–2.

53. The traditional histories of reconstructive surgery still do not cover cosmetic surgery. See, for example, Joachim Gabka and Ekkehard Vaubel, *Plastic Surgery, Past and Present: Origin and History of Modern Lines of Incision* (Munich: S. Karger, 1983), which mentions Joseph in passing but does not even supply his biography in their biographical appendix. The only comprehensive history of cosmetic surgery discusses his role, without any social context: Mario González-Ulloa, ed., *The Creation of Aesthetic Plastic Surgery* (New York: Springer, 1985), pp. 87–114.

54. "Über die operative Verkleinerung einer Nase (Rhinomiosis)," *Berliner klinische Wochenschrift* 40 (1898): 882–85. Translation from Jacques Joseph, "Operative Reduction of the Size of a Nose (Rhinomiosis)," trans. Gustave Aufricht, *Plastic and Reconstructive Surgery* 46 (1970): 178–81, here, 178; reproduced in Frank McDowell, ed., *The Source Book of Plastic Surgery* (Baltimore: The Williams & Wilkins Company, 1977), pp. 164–67. See also Paul Natvig, *Jacques Joseph: Surgical Sculptor* (Philadelphia: W. B. Saunders, 1982), pp. 23–24. On the general history of rhinoplasty see Blair O. Rogers, "A Chronological History of Cosmetic Surgery," *Bulletin of the New York Academy of Medicine* 47 (1971): 265–302; Blair O. Rogers, "A Brief History of Cosmetic Surgery," *Surgical Clinics of North America* 51 (1971): 265–88; S. Milstein, "Jacques Joseph and the Upper Lateral Nasal Cartilages," *Plastic and Reconstructive Surgery* 78 (1986):424; J.S. Carey,

283

Notes
◆

"Kant and the Cosmetic Surgeon," *Journal of the Florida Medical Association* 76 (1989): 637–43.

55. Joseph, "Operative Reduction," p. 180.

56. John O. Roe, "The Deformity Termed 'Pug Nose' and its Correction, by a Simple Operation," (1887) reprinted in McDowell, *Source Book of Plastic Surgery*, pp. 114–19, here, p. 114.

57. Cowling, *Artist as Anthropologist*, pp. 125–29. The image of the nose reproduced by Cowling from the physiognomic literature of the nineteenth century representing the Irish is identical with those in the "before" images reproduced by Roe.

58. Blair O. Rogers, "John Orlando Roe—Not Jacques Joseph — The Father of Aesthetic Rhinoplasty," *Aesthetic Plastic Surgery* 10 (1986): 63–88.

59. See the papers reproduced in McDowell, *Source Book of Plastic Surgery*, pp.136–64.

60. Jacques Joseph, "Nasenverkleinerungen," *Deutsche medizinische Wochenschrift* 30 (1904): 1095–98, here, 1095; trans. Frank McDowell in McDowell, *Source Book of Plastic Surgery* , pp. 174–76, here, p. 184.

61. Natvig, *Jacques Joseph*, p. 94.

62. Natvig, *Jacques Joseph*, p. 71.

63. See the comments by Eugen Holländer, "Die kosmetische Chirurgie," in Max Joseph, ed., *Handbuch der Kosmetik* (Leipzig: Veit & Comp., 1912), pp. 669–712, here p. 673.

64. Natvig, *Jacques Joseph*, p. 179.

65. Natvig, *Jacques Joseph*, p. 95.

66. See Sander L. Gilman, *Disease and Representation: Images of Illness from Madness to AIDS* (Ithaca, NY: Cornell University Press, 1988), pp. 182–201.

67. Frank J. Sulloway, *Freud, Biologist of the Mind: Beyond the Psychoanalytic Legend* (New York: Basic Books, 1979), pp. 148–50.

68. Wilhelm Fliess, *Die Beziehungen zwischen Nase und weiblichen Geschlechtsorganen. In ihrer biologischen Bedeutung dargetellt* (Leipzig: Franz Deuticke, 1897).

69. Hanns Bächtold-Stäubli, ed., *Handwörterbuch des deutschen Aberglaubens* (Berlin and Leipzig: W. de Gruyter & Co., 1934–35), "Nase," 6:

970–79 and Havelock Ellis, *Studies in the Psychology of Sex: 4. Sexual Selection in Man* (Philadelphia: F.A. Davis, 1905), pp. 67–9.

70. On this principle of reversal and the meaning of the nose as a symbol of the castrated penis see Otto Fenichel, "Die 'lange Nase,'" *Imago* 14 (1928): 502–4.

71. John Grand-Carteret, *L'affaire Dreyfus et l'image* (Paris: E. Flammarion, 1898); Eduard Fuchs, *Die Juden in der Karikatur* (Munich: Langen, 1921) and Judith Vogt, *Historien om et Image: Antisemitisme og Antizionisme i Karikaturer* (Copenhagen: Samieren, 1978).

72. See Dietz Bering, *Der Name als Stigma: Antisemitismus im deutschen Alltag 1812–1933* (Stuttgart: Klett/Cotta, 1987), p. 211.

73. Friedrich Nietzsche, *Beyond Good and Evil*, trans. Marianne Cowan (Chicago: Henry Regnery, 1955), pp. 184–88.

74. Oskar Hovorka, *Die äussere Nase: Eine anatomisch-anthropologische Studie* (Vienna: Alfred Hölder, 1893), pp. 130–40. On the pathological meaning of the nose in German science for the later period see Leicher, *Die Vererbung anatomischer Variationen der Nase*, p. 81.

75. Arthur Landsberger, ed., *Judentaufe* (Munich: Georg Müller, 1912), p. 45.

76. See Sander L. Gilman, *Jewish Self-Hatred: Anti-Semitism and the Hidden Language of the Jews* (Baltimore: The Johns Hopkins University Press, 1986), pp. 193–4.

77. *Protokolle der Wiener Psychoanalytischen Vereinigung*, ed. Herman Nunberg and Ernst Federn, 4 vols. (Frankfurt a. M.: Fischer, 1976–81), 1: 66–67; translation from *Minutes of the Vienna Psychoanalytic Society*, trans. M. Nunberg, 4 vols. (New York: International Universities Press, 1962–75), 2: 60–61.

78. Ronald Steel, *Walter Lippmann and the American Century* (Boston: Little, Brown, 1980), p. 192.

79. Mark Gorney, "Patient Selection and Medicolegal Responsibility for the Rhinoplasty Patient," in Thomas D. Ress, ed., *Rhinoplasty: Problems and Controversies* (St. Louis: C.V. Mosby, 1988), p. 2.

80. Jean-Paul Sartre, *Anti-Semite and Jew*, trans. George J. Becker (New York: Schocken Books, 1965), p. 119.

8.   The Jewish Essence

1. Janet Malcolm, "The Psychoanalyst Plays Polo," *New York Times Book Review* April 9, 1989, p. 25.

2. See Peter Gay, *A Godless Jew: Freud. Atheism, and the Making of Psychoanalysis* (New Haven: Yale University Press [in Association with Hebrew Union College Press, Cincinnati], 1987), as well as the discussions throughout Peter Gay, *Freud: A Life for Our Time* (New York, Norton, 1988).

3. David Bakan, *Sigmund Freud and the Jewish Mystical Tradition* (New York: Van Nostrand, 1958).

4. M. Masud R. Khan, *The Long Wait and Other Psychoanalytic Narratives* (New York: Summit, 1989), here, p. ix. This book was first published in Great Britain under the title *When Spring Comes: Awakenings in Clinical Psychoanalysis* (London: Chatto & Windus, 1988).

5. Aldo Carotenuto, *A Secret Symmetry: Sabina Spielrein between Jung and Freud*, trans. by Arno Pomerans, John Shepley, and Krishna Winston (New York: Pantheon, 1982), pp. 120–21.

6. Carl G. Jung, *Collected Works*, ed. Herbert Read, et al., trans. R.C.F. Hull, 10 vols. (London: Routledge and Kegan Paul, [1966–]), 10: 13.

7. Jung, *Works*, 7: 149, n. 8.

8. Frantz Fanon, *Black Skin, White Masks*, trans. Charles Lam Markmann (London: Pluto Press, 1986). For the context see Irene Gendzier, *Frantz Fanon: A Critical Study* (New York: Grove Press, 1983 [1973]) and Chester J. Fontenot, *Frantz Fanon: Language as the God Gone Astray in the Flesh* (Lincoln: University of Nebraska Press, 1979).

9. See the issue entitled "Jung face au nazisme" of the *Cahiers de psychologie jungienne* 12 (1977) for the facts of Jung's anti-Semitism.

10. Ms. Nationalbibliothek Wien, Altenberg, Beilag zur 290/32–1.

11. On the creation of this concept see G.E. Allen, "Naturalists and Experimentalists: The Genotype and the Phenotype," *Studies in the History of Biology* 3 (1979): 179–209; F.B. Churchill, "William Johannsen and the Genotype Concept," *Journal of the History of Biology* 7(1974): 5–30; J.H. Wanscher, "An Analysis of Wilhelm Johannsen's Genetical Term 'Genotype'," *Hereditas* 79 (1975):1909–26.

12. The shift from the antithesis "Jew/Christian" to "Jew/Aryan" in the German-speaking world takes place in the late 1870s and it is mostly widely disseminated in the works of Wilhelm Marr, who coined the term "anti-Semitism" in 1879. See Paul R. Mendes-Flohr and Jehuda Reinharz, eds., *The Jew in the Modern World: A Documentary History* (New York: Oxford University Press, 1980), pp. 271–73. For the broader, scientific context see Louis Snyder, *Race: A History of Modern Ethnic Theories* (New

Notes

York: Longmans, Green and Co., 1939); Jacques Barzun, *Race: A Study in Superstition* (New York: Harper Torchbooks, 1965); George L. Mosse, *Toward the Final Solution: A History of European Racism* (New York: Howard Fertig, 1975); Léon Poliakov, *The Aryan Myth: A History of Racist and Nationalist Ideas in Europe* trans. Edmund Howard (New York: Basic Books, 1974); James C. King, *The Biology of Race* (Berkeley: University of California Press, 1981); Nancy Stepan, *The Idea of Race in Science: Great Britain, 1800–1960* (Hamden, CN: Archon Books, 1982); Paul Lawrence Rose, *Revolutionary Antisemitism in Germany from Kant to Wagner* (Princeton: Princeton University Press, 1990). Following my initial work in this area I was sent the draft of a dissertation which comprehensively surveys the question of the racial anthropology of the Jews and the Jewish response: John Efron, "Jewish Racial Science: The Self-Perception of the Jewish Scientific Community in Europe, 1882–1933" (Diss.: Columbia University, 1990). I was also the primary reader on a dissertation by Laura Otis, "Organic Memory: Racial Memory in the Works of Emile Zola, Thomas Mann, Sigmund Freud, Miguel de Unamuno, and Thomas Hardy" (Diss.: Cornell University, 1991). I am indebted to both of these scholars.

13.   Quoted in the notes to Raphael and Jennifer Patai, *The Myth of the Jewish Race* (Detroit: Wayne State University Press, 1989), p. 406.

14.   Adolf Hitler, *Mein Kampf*, trans. Ralph Manheim (Boston: Houghton Mifflin, 1943), p. 232.

15.   In George L. Mosse's view the German Jews (and their Austrian contemporaries) of the fin de siècle were attempting to see themselves as members of the cultured middle class (no matter what the strength of their religious identity). This self-identification comes profoundly in conflict with the view of the racialism of the Jew found in science. The scientists are thus Mosse's best examples. See George L. Mosse, *German Jews Beyond Judaism* (Bloomington, IN: Indiana University Press, 1985).

16.   *Sigmund Freud-Karl Abraham, Briefe 1907–1926*, ed. Hilda C. Abraham and Ernst L. Freud (Frankfurt a. M.: S. Fischer, 1980), p. 47.

17.   Max Graf, "Reminiscences of Professor Sigmund Freud," *Psychoanalytic Quarterly* 11 (1942): 473.

18.   The debate about the nature of race is reflected in the very use of the terms "Aryan" and "Jew" which reflect the ideology of the science of race. See Maurice Olender, *Les Langues du Paradis: Aryens et Semites—un couple providentiel* (Paris: Gallimard, 1989).

19.   William F. Bynum, "The Great Chain of Being after Forty Years: An Appraisal," *History of Science* 13 (1975); 1–28.

Notes

20. The translation is by Jack Zipes, Oskar Panizza, "The Operated Jew," *New German Critique* 21 (1980): 63–79. See also Jack Zipes, "Oskar Panizza: The Operated German as Operated Jew," *New German Critique* 21 (1980): 47–61 and Michael Bauer, *Oskar Panizza: Ein literarisches Porträt* (Munich: Hanser, 1984).

21. Gustav Jaeger, *Die Entdeckung der Seele* (Leipzig: Ernst Günther, 1880), pp. 106–9.

22. Jody P. Rubin, "Celsus' Decircumcision Operation: Medical and Historical Implications," *Urology* 16 (1980): 121–24.

23. Immanuel Kant, *Anthropology from a Pragmatic Point of View*, trans. Victor Lyle Dowdell (Carbondale, IL: Southern Illinois University Press, 1978), p. 60.

24. Robert Knox, *The Races of Men: A Fragment* (Philadelphia: Lea & Blanchard, 1850), p. 131.

25. The story is reproduced as an extended footnote to a reprint of Oskar Panizza's tale in Oskar Panizza, *Der Korsettenfritz: Gesammelte Erzählungen* (Munich: Matthes & Seitz, 1981): 279–92. My translation.

26. See his *Das Eisenbahnunglück oder Der Anti-Freud* (Berlin: Elena Gottschalk Verlag, 1925). On Mynona see Peter Cardoff, *Friedlaender (Mynona) zur Einführung* (Hamburg: Ed. SOAK in Junius Verlag, 1988). On Karl Kraus and psychoanalysis see Thomas Szasz, *Karl Kraus and the Soul-Doctors* (Baton Rouge: Louisiana State University Press, 1976); M. H. Sherman, ed., *Psychoanalysis and Old Vienna: Freud, Reik, Schnitzler, Kraus* (New York: Human Sciences Press, 1978); E. Eben, "Karl Kraus und die Psychiatrie. Ein Essay," *Confinia Psychiatrica* 22(1979): 9–18; M.H. Sherman, "Prefatory notes: Arthur Schnitzler and Karl Kraus," *Psychoanalytic Review* 65 (1978): 5–13 and Leo Lensing, " 'Geistige Väter' & 'Das Kindweib': Sigmund Freud, Karl Kraus und Irma Karczewska in der Autobiographie von Fritz Wittels," *Forum* 36 (1989): 62–71.

27. Ladislaw Klima, *Die Leiden des Fürsten Sternenhoch*, trans. Franz Peter Künziel (N.p.: Sirene, 1986), pp. 113–15.

28. Davydd J. Greenwood, *The Taming of Evolution: The Persistence of Nonevolutionary Views in the Study of Humans* (Ithaca, NY: Cornell University Press, 1984).

29. Mynona, *Die Bank der Spötter: Ein Unroman* (Berlin: Kurt Wolff, 1919), pp. 296–98.

30. On Weininger and the idea of the Jew see Jacques Le Rider, *Der Fall*

Weininger, Wurzeln des Antifeminismus und Antisemitismus, trans. Dieter Horning (Vienna: Löckner, 1984).

31.   See the introduction by Homi Bhabha in the reprint of Fanon, *Black Skin, White Masks*, p. xxvi.

32.   See Allan Mazur, "The Accuracy of Classic Types of Ethnic Personalities," *Jewish Social Studies* 34 (1971): 187–211.

33.   *Sigmund Freud-Karl Abraham*, op. cit, p. 47.

9.   The Jewish Disease

1.   See Lynn Payer, *Medicine and Culture: Varieties of Treatment in the United States, England, West Germany, and France* (New York: Henry Holt, 1988).

2.   Roy Porter, "Ever since Eve: The Fear of Contagion, " *Times Literary Supplement* (May 27–June 2, 1988): 582; Susan Sontag, *AIDS and its Metaphors* (New York: Farrar, Straus and Giroux, 1989); Sander L. Gilman, *Disease and Representation: Images of Illness from Madness to AIDS* (Ithaca, NY: Cornell University Press, 1988). On the general background of the image of the person with AIDS see Casper G. Schmidt, "The Group-Fantasy Origins of AIDS," *Journal of Psychohistory* 12 (1984): 37–78; Casper G. Schmidt, "AIDS Jokes, or Schadenfreude around an Epidemic," *Maledicta* 8 (1984–85): 69–75; Dennis Altman, *AIDS in the Mind of America: The Social, Political, and Psychological Impact of a New Epidemic* (New York: Anchor/Doubleday, 1986); David Black, *The Plague Years: A Chronicle of AIDS, the Epidemic of our Times* (New York: Simon and Schuster/London: Picador, 1986); Graham Hancock and Enver Carim, *AIDS: The Deadly Epidemic* (London: Gollanz, 1986); Richard Liebmann-Smith, *The Question of AIDS* (New York: The New York Academy of Sciences, 1985); Eve K. Nicols, *Mobilizing against AIDS: The Unfinished Story of a Virus* (Cambridge, MASS: Harvard University Press, 1986); Lon G. Nungasser, *Epidemic of Courage: Facing AIDS in America* (New York: St. Martin's, 1986); Simon Watney, *Policing Desire: Pornography, AIDS and the Media* (Minneapolis: University of Minnesota Press, 1987); Randy Shilts, *And the Band Played On: Politics, People, and the AIDS Epidemic* (New York: St. Martin's, 1987); Gary Alan Fine, "Welcome to the World of AIDS: Fantasies of Female Revenge," *Western Folklore* 46 (1987): 192–97; Elizabeth Fee and Daniel M. Fox, eds., *AIDS: The Burdens of History* (Berkeley: University of California Press, 1988); Mirko D. Grmek, *Histoire du sida* (Paris: Payot, 1989). See

Notes
◆

George L. Mosse's brilliant study *Nationalism and Sexuality: Respectability and Abnormal Sexuality in Modern Europe* (New York: Howard Fertig, 1985), for a sense of the national context of much of this literature and Stanislav Andreski, *Syphilis, Puritanism, and Witch Hunts: Historical Explanations in the Light of Medicine and Psychoanalysis with a Forecast about AIDS* (Houndsmills, Hampshire: Macmillan, 1989), for a sense of the implications of race and psychoanalysis for an understanding of AIDS.

3. See Douglas Crimp, ed., *AIDS: Cultural Analysis/Cultural Activism* (Cambridge, MA.: MIT Press, 1989).

4. Within the first year of publication (1939), 70,000 copies of the book had been sold.

5. Rudolf Heinrich Daumann, *Patrouille gegen den Tod: Ein utopischer Roman* (Berlin: Schützen-Verlag, 1939).

6. Peter Zingler, *Die Seuche: Roman* (Frankfurt a. M.: Eichborn, 1989).

7. The German literature on AIDS is not as extensive as the Anglo-American. Of importance is the 94th issue of the *Kursbuch* (November 1988) entitled "Die Seuche." One of the first monograph-length studies of AIDS in Germany was Judith Remischovsky, *AIDS: die unheimliche Krankheit* (Freiburg: Rombach, [1984?]). See Reimut Reichem "AIDS im individuellen und kollektiven Unbewussten," *Zeitschrift für Sexualforschung* 1 (1988): 113–22; Karl Heinz Reuband, "Über gesellschaftlichen Wandel, AIDS und die Beurteilung der Homosexualität als moralisches Vergehen," *Zeitschrift für Soziologie* 18 (1989): 65–73.

8. For my earlier work on this topic, see Sander L. Gilman, *On Blackness without Blacks: Essays on the Image of the Black in Germany*, Yale Afro-American Studies (Boston: G.K. Hall, 1982), pp. 119ff. See also Rosemarie K. Lester, *Trivialneger: Das Bild der Schwarzen im west-deutschen Illustrietenroman* (Stuttgart: Heinz, 1982).

9. Bernard Blanc, "Lexique à l'usage des voyageurs en S.F.," *Le Français dans le Monde* 193 (1985): 32–33 and Charles R. Saunders, "Why Blacks Don't Read Science Fiction," Tom Henighan, ed., *Brave New Universe: Testing the Values of Science in Society* (Ottawa: Tecumseh, 1980), pp. 160–168.

10. On the history of self-experimentation and the legends associated with it see Lawrence K. Altman, *Who Goes First?: The Story of Self-Experimentation in Medicine* (New York: Random House, 1987).

11. Everett Franklin Bleiler, "Edgar Rice Burroughs, 1875–1950," in

Notes

Bleiler, ed., *Science Fiction Writers: Critical Studies of the Major Authors from the Early Nineteenth Century to the Present Day* (New York: Scribner's, 1982), pp. 59–64; Dieter Ohlmeier, "Das psychoanalytische Interesse an literarischen Texten," in Jochen Horisch and Georg Christoph Tholen, eds., *Eingebildete Texte: Affairen zwischen Psychoanalyse und Literaturwissenschaft* (Munich: Fink, 1985), pp. 15–25; Gert Ueding, "Die langandauernde Krankheit des Lebens," *Jahrbuch der Karl-May-Gesellschaft* (1986): 50–68.

12. See Oliver Ransford, *"Bid the Sickness Cease": Disease in the History of Black Africa* (London: John Murray, 1983).

13. Hans Poeschel, *The Voice of German East Africa: The English in the Judgment of the Natives* (Berlin: August Scherl, 1919), p. 65.

14. See Prosser Guilford and William Roger Louis, eds., *Britain and Germany in Africa: Imperial Rivalry and Colonial Rule* (New Haven, CN: Yale University Press, 1967) and L. Smythe Barron, ed., *The Nazis in Africa* (Salisbury, NC: Documentary Publications, 1979).

15. See the general discussion and background in Hans-Walter Schmuhl, *Rassenhygiene, Nationalsozialismus, Euthanasie: Von der Verhütung zur Vernichtung lebensunwerten Lebens, 1890–1945* (Göttingen: Vandenhoeck & Ruprecht, 1987); Robert Proctor, *Racial Hygiene: Medicine under the Nazis* (Cambridge, MASS: Harvard University Press, 1988); Peter Weingart, Jürgen Kroll, and Kurt Bayertz, *Rasse, Blut und Gene: Geschichte der Eugenik und Rassenhygiene in Deutschland* (Frankfurt a. M.: Suhrkamp, 1988); Michael H. Kater, *Doctors under Hitler* (Chapel Hill, NC: The University of North Carolina Press, 1989).

16. Ernst Janisch, "Selbstbehauptung und Verpflichtung der weissen Rasse in Afrika," *Afrika braucht Grossdeutschland: Das deutsche koloniale Jahrbuch 1940* (Berlin: Wilhelm Süssrott, [1939]), pp. 60–64.

17. G.W. Bauer, *Deutschlands Kolonialforderung und die Welt: Forderungen der deutschen Raum- und Rohstoffnot* (Leipzig: Richard Bauer, 1938).

18. Helmut Vallery, *Führer, Volk und Charisma: Der nationalsozialistische historische Roman* (Rugenstein: Pahl, 1980).

19. See in this context Klaus Theweleit, *Male Fantasies*, trans. Stephan Conway, 2 vols. (Minneapolis: University of Minnesota Press, 1987).

20. Max Nonne, *Syphilis und Nervensystem* (Berlin: Karger, 1921), p. 6. On the impact on various foreign counties, especially Africa, see p. 679.

21. James H. Jones, *Bad Blood: The Tuskegee Syphilis Experiment—A Tragedy of Race and Medicine* (New York: The Free Press, 1981).

291

Notes
◆

22. On the pathological meaning of the nose in German science of this period see Hans Leicher, *Die Vererbung anatomischer Variationen der Nase, ihre Nebenhöhlen und des Gehörorgans* (Munich: J. F. Bergmann, 1928), p. 81. As important was the general discussion of "types" in medicine spinning off of Ernst Kretschmer's theory of constitution (itself in opposition to ideas of race yet incorporated in these ideas). The brunt of this discussion was that specific types—among them the types normally associated in racial science with the image of the Jew—are particularly at risk for syphilis. See Richard Stern, *Über körperliche Kennzeichen der Disposition zur Tabes* (Leipzig: Franz Deuticke, 1912).

23. Dr. Grob, "Arzt und Judenfrage," *Ziel und Weg* 8 (1933): 186–9. See also Ludwik Fleck, *Entstehung und Entwicklung einer wissenschaftlichen Tatsache* (1935; Frankfurt a. M.: Suhrkamp, 1980).

24. Theodor Fritsch, *Handbuch der Judenfrage* (Leipzig: Hammer, 1935), p. 408.

25. See Jan Goldstein, "The Wandering Jew and the Problem of Psychiatric Anti-semitism in Fin-de-Siècle France," *Journal of Contemporary History* 20 (1985): 521–52.

26. See my *Disease and Representation*, pp.190–91.

27. See the discussion in Sander L. Gilman, *Difference and Pathology: Stereotypes of Sexuality, Race, and Madness* (Ithaca, NY: Cornell University Press, 1986).

28. Friedrich Ratzel, *The History of Mankind*, trans. A. J. Butler, 3 vols (London: Macmillan, 1898), 3: 183 (on the Near East) and 3: 548 (on Europe).

29. Daumann, *Patrouille gegen den Tod*, pp. 53–54 cites Justus Hecker, *Der schwarze Tod im 14. Jahrhundert* (Berlin: Herbig, 1832).

30. Ulrich Berkes, *Eine schlimme Liebe: Tagebuch* (Berlin: Aufbau, 1987), pp. 40–41 and 214. On the background to the question of AIDS in the GDR see Günter Grau, ed., *Und diese Liebe auch: Theologische und sexualwissenschaftliche Einsichten zur Homosexualität* (Berlin: Evangelische Verlagsanstalt, 1989) as well as John Parsons, "East Germany Faces its Past: A New Start for Socialist Sexual Politics," *Outlook* 5 (1989): 43–52.

31. See the extensive coverage in the news magazine *Der Spiegel* during 1987, for example, the cover story of the February 9, 1987 issue, pp. 30–53. Compare James W. Jones, "Conceiving AIDS in West Germany: Some

Notes

Public Discourses," in Rudolf Käser and Vera Pohland, eds., *Disease and Medicine in Modern German Cultures* (Ithaca, NY: Western Societies Program, 1990), pp. 169–83.

32.   For a detailed overview see John Bornemann, "AIDS in the Two Berlins," in Douglas Crimp, ed., *AIDS: Cultural Analysis / Cultural Activism* (Cambridge, MA.: MIT Press, 1989), pp. 223–37.

33.   On this general question see Reneé Sabatier, *Blaming Others: Prejudice, Race and Worldwide AIDS* (London: Panos, 1988). A good response to this search, in terms of Randy Shilts' discussion of "Patient Zero" (see footnote 2) is the recent piece "Scientist Zero," by Charles L. Ortleb in *Christopher Street* 133 (1989): 8–14.

34.   Alexander Mitscherlich and Fred Mielke, *Das Diktat der Menschenverachtung, Ein Dokumentation (Vom Prozess gegen 23 SS-Ärtze und deutsche Wissenschaftler)* (Heidelberg: L. Schneider, 1947); Alexander Mitscherlich and Fred Mielke, *Wissenschaft ohne Menschlichkeit: Medizinische und Eugenische Irrwege unter Diktatur, Burokratie und Krieg* (Heidelberg: L. Schneider, 1949).

35.   On the representation of the treatment of gays in the Third Reich see Richard Plant, *The Pink Triangle: The Nazi War Against Homosexuals* (New York: Henry Holt, 1986) and Hans-Georg Stümke, *Homosexuelle in Deutschland: Eine politische Geschichte* (Munich: Beck, 1989).

36.   See the Berlin *Tageszeitung* (*TAZ*) rebuttal of this on June 6, 1989, p. 13.

37.   Karin Obermeier, "Afro-German Women: Recording their Own History," *New German Critique* 46 (1989): 172–80.

38.   See Wiebke Reuter-Krauss and Christoph Schmidt, *AIDS und Recht von A-Z* (Munich: dtv/Beck,1988).

39.   *Der Spiegel* (November 5, 1984), p. 100.

40.   Helmut Zander, *Der Regenbogen: Tagebuch eines AIDSkranken* (Munich: Knaur, 1988), pp. 235–36.

41.   Fred Breinersdorfer, *Quarantäne* (Stuttgart: Weitbrecht, 1989).

42.   *Der Spiegel* (May 25, 1987), pp. 25–32. See also S. S. Fluss and D. K. Latto, "The Coercive Element in Legislation for the control of AIDS and HIV Infection: Some Recent Developments," *AIDS and Public Policy Journal* 2 (1987): 11–20.

43.   Ruth Beckermann, *Unzugehoerig: Oesterreicher und Juden nach 1945* (Vienna: Lockner, 1989), p. 83.

Notes

◆

44.   This is not to confuse the fact that both Jews and gays can internalize the same sense of social difference in their confrontation with exactly such stereotypical structures. See Paul Parin, " 'The Mark of Oppression': Ethnopsychoanalytische Studie über Juden und Homosexuelle in einer relative permissiven Kultur," *Psyche* 39 (1985): 193–219.

Conclusion

1.   For a more detailed history of the problem in the West and the Middle East see Sander L. Gilman and Steven T. Katz, eds., *Anti-Semitism in Times of Crisis* (New York: New York University Press, 1991).

2.   Robert K. Merton, "The Normative Structure of Science," reprinted in his *The Sociology of Science: Theoretical and Empirical Investigations* (Chicago: University of Chicago Press, 1973), pp. 267–78.

3.   Londa Schiebinger, *The Mind Has No Sex? Women in the Origins of Modern Science* (Cambridge, MASS: Harvard University Press, 1989), pp. 250–56.

4.   Y.H. Yerushalmi, *Assimilation and Racial Anti-Semitism: The Iberian and the German Models* (New York: Leo Baeck Institute, 1982).

5.   Sigmund Diamond, "Sigmund Freud, His Jewishness, and Scientific Method: the Seen and the Unseen as Evidence," *Journal of the History of Ideas* 43 (1982): 613–34.

6.   Jean-François Lyotard, *Heidegger et "les juifs"* (Paris: Galilée, 1988).

7.   Evelyn Torton Beck, "The Politics of Jewish Invisibility," *NWSA Journal* 1 (1988): 93–102.

8.   Martin Freud, *Glory Reflected: Sigmund Freud—Man and Father* (London: Angus and Robertson, 1957), p. 16.

9.   This discussion is based on the material in Neal Gabler, *An Empire of Their Own: How the Jews Invented Hollywood* (New York: Crown, 1988), pp.139–45

10.   Kathleen Cross, "'Trapped in the Body of a White Woman," *Ebony* (October 1990): 70–74.

11.   All of the references are to the materials published in *Ebony* (January 1991): 12–14.

12.   See the summary of the most recent survey of the National Opinion Research Center (University of Chicago) about the image of Jews and

294

Notes

◆

African-Americans (among others) reported in *Newsweek* (January 21, 1991), p. 57. On the history of American understanding of the nature of race see Reginald Horsman, *Race and Manifest Destiny: The Origins of American Racial Anglo-Saxonism* (Cambridge, MASS: Harvard University Press, 1981).

13. See the discussion of the act of transformation in Nancy Stepan and Sander L. Gilman, "Appropriating the Idioms of Science: Some Strategies of Resistance to Biological Determinism," in Dominick La Capra, ed., *The Bounds of Race* (Ithaca, NY: Cornell University Press, 1991), pp. 72–103.

14. Isaiah Berlin, *Against the Current: Essays in the History of Ideas*, ed. Hanry Hardy (New York: Viking Press, 1980), p. 258.

15. W. Petersen, "Jews as a Race," *Midstream* (February 1988): 35–37.

16. Clive Sinclair, "Bulgarian Notes," *Times Literary Supplement* [London], (December 14–20, 1990), p. 1357.

17. See Paul Lawrence Rose, *Revolutionary Antisemitism in Germany from Kant to Wagner* (Princeton: Princeton University Press, 1990).

INDEX

◆

Page numbers in boldface type refer to illustrations.

Index

297

Index

Jew(s): and Aryan, 6, 154–5, 157, 158, 167, 175, 176, 196, 197, 201–2, 207; and Christian, 3, 6, 134, 135–6, 201–2; as different, 2, 11, 13, 172, 176, 183, 197; essence of the, 64–8; feminization of, 63–4, 76, 99, 127, 133–4, 137, 196, 207; in film, 236–8, 241; "good" vs. "bad," 35, 193; as invisible, 21, 22; as label, 5–6; and military service, 40, 42–4, 47–8, 58; as outsiders, 3, 36–7, 119; as victim, 229, 233

Jew(s), Eastern European: diseases linked to, 55, 56; idealized images of, 69, **70**, **71**; as inherently "different," 59, 122, 172; seen as murderer, 113, 115–7, 119; stereotypes of, 12, **16**, 29–30, 34, 172; as unstable, 63, 72–6, 78; vs. Western, 26, 59, 82, 100. *See also* Jews, images of

Jew(s), Western: acculturation of, 32, 99, 176–9, 181; vs. Eastern European, 26, 59, 100; images of **16**, 24–8

Jewish Defense League, 27

Jews, images of: as corrupted or incapacitated by civilization, 49, 51, 63–4, 80; as degenerate, 21, 39, 53, 59, 102; as diseased, 52, 162, 172–3, 179, 223, 230; liberal, 42; as physically weak, 40, 52–3, 54, 76; wandering, 20, 72–5. *See also* disease; stereotypes

Jolson, Al, 237–8

Joseph, Jacques, 181, **182**, 183–8, 191, 192

Jung, C.G., 195, 197, 200

Kant, Immanuel, 162–3; *Anthropology*, 204

Kaufmann, Max, 159

Kautsky, Karl, 49

Khan, Masud, 208; *The Long Wait*, 194–8, 200, 209

Kishon, Ephron, 22

Klima, Ladislaw, 206

Knox, Robert, 174, 204

Koestler, Arthur, 148

Krafft-Ebing, Richard, 31, 90, 220

Kraus, Karl, 135, 151, 206

Krauss, Friedrich Salamo, *Anthropophyteia*, 119–20

Kretschmer, Ernst, 291n22

Kuznetsov, Anatoli, 23

Lacan, Jacques, 83

Lacassagne, Alexandre, *Vacher l'éventreur*, 113, **114**, 117

La Fontaine, F.L. de, 100

Landes, Daniel, 33, 35

Language of Flowers, The, 106

language, Jewish: Christ and, 13, 16, 17; as corrupt and corrupting, 3, **14**, **15**, 20, 34, 64, 68, 102, 203; for Freud, 102–3; and gesture, **14**, **15**, 203; as hidden, 3, 12, 16, 18, 19–20, 25, 26, 29, 30, 31, 32, 35, 87, 220; link to nose, 180; sounding too Jewish, 10–13, 17, 19, 21, 26–32. *See also* Hebrew; *Mauscheln*; Yiddish

Lassalle, Ferdinand, 100

Laube, Heinrich, 159

Lawrence, William, 177

Lee, Spike, *School Daze*, 239

Leonardo da Vinci, 138–9, 161

Lerche, M., 264–5n121

lesbianism, 90–1

Liebermann, Max, 145

Lilien, Ephraim Moses, 69, **71**

Lind, Jakov, 165

Lippmann, Walter, 192–3

Lipps, Theodor, 162–5

Löhner, Fritz, 261n82

Lombroso, Cesare, 89, 90, 117, 144, 159–60; *Genius and Madness*, 131–3, 137–8, 142, 143

London, Victorian: prostitute in, 104, 107; Whitechapel murders in, 111–3, 117–9

Lopate, Phillip, 33–5

Lopez de Villalobos, Francisco, 100

Lubbock, John, 14

Ludwig, A.M., 149

Lukatsky, Debbie, and Sandy Barnett

300

Index

Index
◆

Index

Simonet, Enrique, *Tenía corazón*, 108, **109**
Sinclair, Clive, 242–3
Singer, Heinrich, 48, 58
skin: color, 99–100, 127, 165, 171–2, 176–7; diseases seen on, 99–101, 125, 127, 172–4, 179, 181
Smith, Samuel Stanhope, 177
Sofer, Moses, 93
Spencer, Johann, 92
Spielrein, Sabina, 195
Spinoza, Baruch, 134, 145, 161, 165, 166
Spregnether, Madelon, 90
Steen, Konrad, 216
stereotypes: Christian, of Jews, 3, 12, 17, 18–19, 25, 235–6; literary, 231
Stevenson, Robert Louis, "Dr. Jekyll and Mr. Hyde," 112
Strauß, H, 63, 98
Sulzberger, Arthur, 26
Swift, David, 26
syphilis: and case of "Dora," 81, 83–5; female image of, 108–9, **110**; linked to hysteria, 81, 84, 95; linked to Jews, 55, 79, 86, 93, 96–102, 124–7, 158–60, 173, 219, 291n22; as model, 217–8

Tannen, Deborah, 2
Tausk, Victor, 71, 165
Thackeray, William, *Codlingsby*, 64
Thomas, D.M., *The White Hotel*, 23
Torah, 17, 18
Trillin, Calvin, 30
Twain, Mark, 42

Verschuer, Otmar Freiherr von, 52
Vidal, Gore, 36–7
Vienna: fin-de-siècle, 8; Freud in, 61, 143; Jews in, 32, 97, 138, 172–3, 178–9, 236
Virchow, Rudolf, 51, 177

Wagner, Richard, 134
Waldheim, Kurt, 227
Warner, Harry and Jack, 236, 237, 240
Warwick, Eden. *See* Jabet, George
Wassermann, August von, 219
Wassermann, Jakob, 178–9, 240
Wasserstein, Bernard, 25
Wasserstein, Wendy, *Isn't It Romantic*, 31
Watt, George Frederick, *Found Drowned*, 108
Wedekind, Frank, *Lulu*, 117, 127
Weiniger, Otto, 127, 159–60; *Sex and Character*, 133–7, 143, 144, 145, 147, 207
Weir, Robert, 185
Wittels, Fritz, 135, 191–2
Wittgenstein, Ludwig, 133
Wolf, Elcan Isaac, 173
Wolff, Julius, 183–4
Wundt, Wilhelm, 131

Yerushalmi, Yosef Hayim, 235
Yiddish, 82, 120; accent, 11, 12; as essential language, 20, 34; as hidden, 88

Zander, Helmut, 227
Zingler, Peter, *The Plague*, 210, 212, **213**, 227–33; plot of, 223–6
Zola, Émile, *Nana*, 125

303